The Semantics of English P1

Spatial Scenes, Embodied Meaning and Cognition

Using a cognitive linguistics perspective, this book provides the most comprehensive theoretical analysis of the semantics of English prepositions available. All English prepositions originally coded spatial relations between two physical entities; while retaining their original meaning, prepositions have also developed a rich set of non-spatial meanings. In this innovative study, Tyler and Evans argue that all these meanings are systematically grounded in the nature of human spatio-physical experience. The original 'spatial scenes' provide the foundation for the extension of meaning from the spatial to the more abstract. This analysis introduces a new methodology that distinguishes between a conventional meaning and an interpretation produced for understanding the preposition in context, as well as establishing which of several competing senses should be taken as the primary sense. Together, the methodology and framework are sufficiently articulated to generate testable predictions and allow the analysis to be applied to additional prepositions.

ANDREA TYLER is Associate Professor of Linguistics at Georgetown University. She teaches a range of courses which largely focus on applications of linguistic theory to issues of second language learning and teaching. She has published in numerous journals.

VYVYAN EVANS is Professor of Cognitive Linguistics at the University of Brighton and is author and editor of several books relating to cognitive linguistics. These include: *The Structure of Time; Cognitive Linguistics* (with Melanie Green); *A Glossary of Cognitive Linguistics;* and *The Cognitive Linguistics Reader* (edited with Benjamin Bergen and Joerg Zinken). His research relates to cognitive lexical semantics, meaning-construction, conceptual structure and figurative language.

The Semantics of English Prepositions

Spatial Scenes, Embodied Meaning and Cognition

Andrea Tyler

Linguistics Department
Georgetown University

and

Vyvyan Evans

School of Language, Literature and Communication
University of Brighton

CAMBRIDGE
UNIVERSITY PRESS

CAMBRIDGE UNIVERSITY PRESS
Cambridge, New York, Melbourne, Madrid, Cape Town, Singapore, São Paulo

Cambridge University Press
The Edinburgh Building, Cambridge CB2 8RU, UK

Published in the United States of America by Cambridge University Press, New York

www.cambridge.org
Information on this title: www.cambridge.org/9780521814300

First published 2003
Reprinted 2004 (twice), 2005
This digitally printed version (with corrections) 2007

A catalogue record for this publication is available from the British Library

ISBN 978-0-521-81430-0 hardback
ISBN 978-0-521-04463-9 paperback

This book is dedicated to Lou, Angela and Max

Contents

Preface

Linguists, psychologists and philosophers have long observed the importance of space and spatial experience for both language and thought. In this book, we examine the nature of human spatio-physical experience and how human conceptualization of spatial relations is reflected in the English language. In particular, we are interested in how spatial concepts are systematically extended to provide a wide array of non-spatial meanings. We do so through a study of English spatial particles, an important subset of which are prepositions.

The central notion we explore is that of a *spatial scene*, a conceptualized relation grounded in spatial interaction and experience, involving entities that are related in a particular spatio-configurational way. For instance, in a spatial scene described by: *The cup is on the table*, the cup is in contact with the upper side of the table. A distinct spatio-configuration is described by the following: *The coffee is in the cup*. This scene involves the coffee being located inside (as opposed to outside) the cup. However, spatial scenes do not involve only spatio-physical relations or configurations. It turns out that particular spatial relations have non-trivial consequences that are meaningful to humans. The spatial scene involving *on* also involves a support function between the table and the cup: unless enough of the cup's base is situated on the table, the cup will fall and smash on the floor. Equally, the spatial scene relating to *in* involves a containment function, which encompasses several consequences such as locating and limiting the activities of the contained entity. Being contained in the cup prevents the coffee from spreading out over the table; if we move the cup, the coffee moves with it. These consequences, as well as the spatio-physical configuration between entities, give rise to a range of non-spatial meanings associated with the spatial particles *on* and *in*. For instance, sentences such as: *You can count on my vote* and *She is in graduate school* do not strictly involve spatial relations between physical entities, but rather non-physical concepts associated with the notions of support and containment respectively. Spatial particles offer rich and fascinating evidence of the complex interaction between spatio-physical experience, the human conceptual system and language use. Consequently, they represent an excellent 'laboratory' for investigating the way in which spatial experience grounds many other kinds of non-spatial, non-physical concepts.

Our approach is both cognitive and experientialist. It is cognitive in that we assume that meanings do not match up with a mind-independent objective reality. Rather, 'reality' is determined by the nature of our bodies and our neuro-anatomical architecture, as well as the physical world we inhabit. Hence, the meanings encoded in language relate to and reflect our conceptual system, which constitutes our 'representation' of reality. Our approach is experientialist as we acknowledge that our representation of reality is contingent upon a world out there, which in turn is meaningful, precisely because it, and our interactions with it, have non-trivial consequences for our survival.

Spatial experience provides a substantial portion of the conceptual bedrock for the human conceptual system, that is, for the nature of meaning. Hence, this book, through a detailed analysis of the range of meanings associated with English spatial particles, argues for the foundational role of experience in the development of meaning in general, and word meaning in particular.

Acknowledgements

The idea for this work has its origins in discussions and research undertaken by the Metaphor Research Group at Georgetown University whose members were united by a common interest in cognitive linguistics and conceptual metaphor. We are indebted to the members of that research group, and would particularly like to thank Elizabeth Lemmon, Suzanne Matula, Chikako Mori, Mari Takada and Viphavee Vongpumivitch. We would like to acknowledge the members of the Georgetown Cognitive Linguistics Research Group (Akiko Fujii, YiYoung Kim, Dainora Kupcinskas, Olga Liamkina, David MacGregor, Kristin Mulrooney, Mari Takada and Paula Winke) whose ongoing project is to conduct experiments aimed at testing the claims made in the present work. Vyvyan Evans has benefited from discussions with a number of people involved in the Sussex Meaning and Grammar Group (SMAGG). In particular he would like to thank the participants of the seminar series on Polysemy during Summer 2002. We are grateful to a number of scholars for their support and comments related to this research project, particularly Mark Aronoff, Steven Cushing, René Dirven, Bev Hartford and Mark Turner. We are particularly indebted to Joseph Grady who provided extensive comments on large portions of the manuscript and whose work has so influenced our analysis. His generous support and incisive comments have been invaluable. We owe a special thanks to Dominiek Sandra whose numerous comments and queries pushed us to think and rethink many points of our analysis. Pieces of this work have been presented at various conferences; the questions and comments of members of those audiences have contributed to our thinking in important ways. We want to acknowledge particularly Carol Moder, Sally Rice and Eve Sweetser. We thank Angela Evans for assistance with the diagrams in chapter 4. Finally, we wish to express our gratitude to a number of organizations and people for their support and assistance, without which we could not have completed this project. For financial support for indexing we thank the School of Cognitive and Computing Sciences (COGS) at the University of Sussex. We are particularly grateful to the Dean of the School, Professor Richard Coates. We also gratefully acknowledge financial support from the Georgetown University Department of Linguistics and the Georgetown University Graduate School. For first persuading us to approach

Cambridge University Press with our manuscript and for support early on in the project we owe an important debt to Christine Bartels. We would also like to thank our editor at Cambridge, Andrew Winnard. For compiling the index we are grateful to Sue Lightfoot. For gracious and astute copy-editing we owe an immense debt to Jacqueline French without whom this work would have been much poorer. We would like to thank the several anonymous reviewers whose questions and comments resulted in a much deeper, more complete analysis.

1   The nature of meaning

> My grandmother was a great one for mixing historical lessons in with child
> rearing. A favorite, regularly used when one of the grandchildren was being
> rebuked for failing to satisfactorily complete some minor task and was, con-
> sequently, being required to do it over$_A$, involved pointing to the needle-point
> text hanging over$_B$ the sofa which read, 'We won't come back 'til it's over$_C$,
> over$_D$ there.' This was inevitably followed by the question, 'Where would the
> world be if they hadn't done their jobs properly?'

This text might strike contemporary readers as a little unusual. References to
lines from old war songs and needle-pointed mottoes hanging on the wall belong
to a bygone era and anecdotes relying on them are likely to be somewhat vague.
However, what is even more striking about the text is exactly what typical native
speakers of English are likely to find unremarkable, namely the numerous, very
different interpretations assigned to the single word, *over*. In this short text, *over*
has four distinct interpretations – *over*$_A$ can be paraphrased by 'again', *over*$_B$
by 'above', *over*$_C$ by 'finished' and *over*$_D$ by 'in some other place'. For us,
the fundamental question that texts such as the one above raise is whether the
various meanings regularly associated with a single word are simply accidental
(the fact that *over* has four very different meanings might, after all, be a bizarre
accident), or systematically related.

Linguists have often assumed that words constitute lexical forms that are
conventionally paired with meanings, and that these form-meaning pairings are
stored in a mental dictionary or lexicon. Traditional approaches to the mental
lexicon have tended either to ignore the issue of whether distinct meanings
associated with a single form are related or to assume that the relationships are
arbitrary, which is to say, the forms are unrelated. However, the linguist Bernd
Heine (1997) has observed that finding a satisfactory solution to the problem
of how to represent the multiple meanings associated with a single linguistic
form is both a central and a controversial issue for linguistic theory. The position
taken on this question affects not only how we model the semantics of individual
lexical items and the architecture of the mental lexicon, but also the rest of one's
model of language.

The lexicon represents a pivotal interface between syntax, semantics and pragmatics; the representation of the semantic component of lexical items has crucial implications not only for a theory of word meaning but also for a theory of sentence-level meaning construction. At stake are issues concerning the source of the information that is necessary in the interpretation of an utterance and the appropriate location of the productive (rule-governed) elements of the linguistic system. Such issues bear on the interaction between words and the human conceptual system. In addition, establishing the semantic content of the lexical representations directly impinges on the distinction between conventionalized linguistic knowledge and encyclopedic, general world knowledge in the process of meaning construction, which is to say, the traditional distinction between pragmatics and semantics.

In this book we take up the challenge of how best to represent the distinct meanings or senses associated with a single lexical form. We do so through an examination of the semantics of a range of English spatial particles, such as *over, up, down, in* and *out*, etc. There are a number of reasons for choosing spatial particles. Perhaps most importantly the variety and complexity of the numerous different meanings associated with even a single spatial particle represents a significant descriptive challenge. Hence, insights gleaned from such an analysis promise to have considerable applicability to other classes of words.[1] But also important is the relatively transparent experiential basis of spatial morphemes. The meanings of this set of words are clearly grounded at some level in our spatio-physical interaction with the world. Hence, investigating the meanings associated with spatial particles will offer fundamental insights into the relation between language, mental representation and human experience.

Our investigation leads us to the conclusion that the various meanings associated with spatial particles are related in systematic and highly motivated ways. In other words, we advance a polysemy approach to word meaning (our polysemy commitment), arguing that the multiple, distinct meanings associated with the same lexical form are often related.[2] We suggest that the distinct but related senses associated with a single spatial particle constitute a semantic

---

[1] Evans (2000) has successfully extended the same model to an examination of the conceptualization of time.

[2] It is important to emphasize that we do not claim that all representations of a form in semantic memory are part of that form's semantic network. We adhere to the basic tenet of cognitive linguistics that language is usage based and, as a result, likely to be more redundant than traditional accounts. As such, collocations and longer phrases involving context may become established in semantic memory. Thus, phrases such as *over the bridge* or perhaps constructions (Goldberg, 1995) such as 'Motion Verb + *over the bridge*', which appear largely decomposable, may be part of permanent semantic memory. The construction itself, then, may take on additional meaning. For the most part, it is beyond the scope of this book to examine the many longer phrases and possible constructions in which English spatial particles regularly participate.

network organized with respect to a primary sense. In chapter 3, where we advance the model upon which the analysis in this book will be based, we explore in detail what constitutes a primary sense, and in what way other senses might be diachronically and perhaps developmentally related to this sense. Each distinct sense is potentially subject to a number of inferencing strategies which account for additional or on-line interpretations. Consequently, in the course of developing a theory of word meaning and mental representation, we advance a concomitant theory of meaning construction or conceptual integration. Our findings reveal the largely non-idiosyncratic and systematic organization of the mental lexicon and the highly creative nature of the human conceptual system.

A number of basic assumptions underlie our approach:

- Language (lexical items and the syntactic arrangements in which they occur) radically underdetermines the rich interpretations regularly assigned to naturally occurring utterances. A consequence of this is the assumption that lexical entries, albeit crucial, act merely as prompts for meaning construction, and that meaning construction is largely a conceptual process, involving elaboration and integration of linguistic and non-linguistic information in a highly creative way (Fauconnier, 1994, 1997; Fauconnier and Turner, 1998, 2002; Turner, 1991, 1996). This is discussed later in this chapter and in chapter 3.[3]

- The representation of meaning is fundamentally conceptual in nature. Language does not refer directly to the 'real world'. Rather, language refers to what is represented in the human conceptual system. The conceptual system contains conceptual structure (i.e., concepts, schemas, scripts, etc.) which indirectly reflects and interprets the world as mediated by human experience and perception (Fauconnier, 1997; Jackendoff, 1983, 1987, 1990, 1992; Langacker, 1987, 1991b). This is discussed in detail later in this chapter.

- Conceptual structure is a product of how we as human beings experience and interact with the spatio-physical world we inhabit. The world 'out there' provides much of the raw sense-perceptual substrate for the conceptual system. However, how and what we experience is crucially mediated by the precise nature of our bodies and our unique neuro-anatomical architecture. In other words, experience is embodied (Johnson, 1987; Lakoff, 1987; Lakoff and Johnson, 1999; Mandler, 1992, 1996; Sweetser, 1990; Varela, Thompson and Rosch, 1991). This is the subject of chapter 2.

- Language is a continually evolving, organic system. Hence, to study the synchronic 'slice' of a language will reveal only one point in a continuum of change (Bybee *et al.*, 1994; Hopper and Traugott, 1993). Synchronic studies,

---

[3] We specifically attempt to build this assumption into our model through the inferencing strategy of real-world force dynamics.

such as the present one, must be mindful that lexical structure of even a single form (its semantic network) will exhibit the co-existing 'layers' of its past.[4]

- The development and extension of lexical meaning result from pragmatic inferencing (i.e., situated implicatures). This leads to conceptual reanalysis and concomitant conventionalization of the inference as a new meaning component associated with the linguistic form. This results in the development of a semantic network. Borrowing terminology from Traugott (e.g., 1989), we refer to this context-based process of lexical meaning extension as *pragmatic strengthening*. Hence, meaning extension is usage based and pragmatic in nature. This is discussed in chapter 3.[5]

Approaches to the representation of distinct meanings associated with a single form

The question of how best to model the distinct meanings associated with a single lexical form has been approached from three perspectives. These are homonymy, monosemy and polysemy. We turn now to a consideration of these three approaches.

In the text that began this chapter, the form *over* is associated with four different meanings. We paraphrased these four meanings as 'again', 'above', 'finished' and 'in some other place' respectively. In attempting to account for these different meanings, one could assume that they are unrelated. That is, one could argue that as speakers of English we have simply memorized several

---

[4] We attempt to build this assumption into our model through our choice of the primary sense associated with each spatial particle, which reflects both the diachronic and ontogenetic nature of the semantic network. The choice of the appropriate primary sense for a spatial particle has been a controversial one in discussions of the semantic networks of spatial particles (e.g., Dewell, 1994; Kreitzer, 1997; Lakoff, 1987). Some scholars in the field have openly appealed to intuition concerning the most primary meaning of a spatial particle (Dewell, 1994). However, intuitions on 'the' primary sense of many spatial particles vary widely. Others (e.g., Lakoff) have argued for a primary sense that best fits a particular analysis of a particular preposition. Our goal is to begin to work out a principled framework that accounts for the development of the polysemy networks for all English spatial particles. Working out principles and criteria which apply to the entire system of particles places substantial constraints on the nature of the primary sense which are not apparent when one focuses on the analysis of a single spatial particle in isolation. Our study of twenty spatial particles has led us to conclude that positing a proto-spatial scene (which includes both a configurational component and a functional component, to be outlined in detail in chapter 3) for the primary sense (the proto-scene) allows us to develop a consistent, principled analysis which calls for a minimal amount of theoretical machinery. Consultation of the OED has also revealed that the proto-scenes for each spatial particle also tend to represent the diachronically earliest uses of the lexical form. Moreover, in attempting to explain the relationships among senses associated with a single form, we found ourselves explaining how attested uses plausibly developed from prior uses. Again, we have attempted to constrain these arguments for a plausible path of development to a minimal number of theoretical constructs which would apply to all spatial particles.

[5] We attempt to build this assumption into our model through the notion of pragmatic strengthening (see chapter 3).

distinct meanings which are coded by the form *over*. This might be viewed as being parallel to our learning that the form *bank* is arbitrarily associated with both 'the sides of a river' and 'a certain type of financial institution'. Accordingly, it would be claimed that there are several distinct form-meaning pairings for *over* which language users represent in their mental lexicons. This position would thus posit that each of the form-meaning lexical entries are homonyms, which is to say that they are unrelated. The fact that the different senses are coded by the same linguistic form is presumably just an accident. This is essentially the position taken by traditional representations of the lexicon. Starting as early as Bloomfield (1933) and rearticulated as recently as Chomsky (1995), influential linguistic theories have asserted that the lexicon is the repository for the arbitrary and the idiosyncratic. Such analyses hold that all creativity and systematicity is in the morpho-syntactic component.

The homonymy approach suffers from a number of weaknesses when we attempt to account for words such as *over*. First, it ignores any systematic relationships among the distinct meanings associated with a single linguistic form. This stands in sharp contrast to a growing body of work (e.g., Brugman and Lakoff, 1988; Jackendoff, 1997; Lakoff, 1987; Langacker, 1987, 1991b; Levin, 1993; Lindner, 1981; Pustejovsky, 1998) which demonstrates that systematic, rule governed relationships do exist in the lexicon.

Second, the homonymy position takes a narrow synchronic view. That is, it fails to represent language as an evolving system whose changes over time are largely constrained in a motivated, principled manner. The synchronic semantic network associated with a lexical item is a historical product. In assuming that distinct meanings within a semantic network are arbitrarily related, the homonymy approach makes the implicit claim that the process of meaning extension itself is arbitrary, leading to the unsatisfactory conclusion that language change is ad hoc, lacking motivation. This contradicts the view that language evolution is a systematic process, as revealed by the voluminous grammaticalization literature (e.g., Bybee *et al.*, 1994; Heine *et al.*, 1991; Hopper and Traugott, 1993, for overviews, summaries and references).

Moreover, it is reasonable to assume that at an earlier stage in the language, a form such as *over* had fewer distinct, conventionalized meanings associated with it;[6] thus, many of the uses now conventionally associated with the form at one point represented novel uses. The homonymy approach begs the question of why it should be the case that a speaker would choose to use a particular established form in a novel way, rather than coining a new phonological string altogether.

It is perhaps self-evident that an important function of language is communication. Moreover, communication is fundamentally purposeful (Gumperz,

---

[6] This point is also made by Sweetser (1990).

1982). This fact places certain non-trivial constraints on the use of lexical items. It is obvious that a speaker intending to communicate, and hence achieve the desired purpose, would not use a lexical form with one established meaning to indicate something else, unless the speaker assumed the listener could readily work out the novel usage. In order for a novel use to be readily interpretable by the hearer, meaning extension must be somehow constrained and systematic. This strongly suggests that when a speaker uses a form with an established meaning to indicate something other than the conventional meaning, the choice of which lexical item to select is motivated. If this were otherwise, the speaker could not assume that the listener had a reasonable chance of interpreting the novel use. This line of reasoning suggests that there must be something about the conventional meaning associated with the lexical item that led the speaker to choose that lexical form rather than some other.

Finally, the homonymy approach fails to explain the ubiquity of the phenomenon. Every spatial particle of English demonstrates multiple senses. Moreover, careful examination of spatial particles as a word class reveals regular patterns of meanings across the individual members of the class. For instance, all spatial particles whose primary senses have a distinct goal sense share a clearly defined set of properties. The homonymy approach argues that this too is accidental. While we readily acknowledge that the 'accidents' of history have resulted in instances of homonymy, the failure to account for the considerable systematicity that does exist misses important generalizations. As the homonymy approach fails to recognize that distinct meanings may be motivated and, hence, at some level systematically related, we are forced to conclude that it is inadequate.

An alternative approach, monosemy, has been advocated by Charles Ruhl (1989). Ruhl argues in detail that forms are paired with a single highly abstract meaning. This abstract meaning can be filled in by contextual knowledge, such that all the distinct meanings associated with a lexeme are derived. This position is termed monosemy, as it holds that the multiple meanings associated with a particular form are merely contextually derived variants of a single monosemous meaning.

Monosemy, like homonymy, has a number of problems associated with it. Perhaps most serious is that while it may well be that the distinct meanings associated with a particular form are related to a primary, abstract meaning, some meanings are demonstrably context independent. That is, although important, pragmatic knowledge alone is insufficient in predicting all of the distinct meanings associated with a particular form. For instance, in our examples for *over* it is difficult to see what kind of contextual knowledge would allow us to derive the spatial meaning of 'above', the non-spatial meaning of 'again' and the non-spatial meaning 'finished', all from a single, abstract meaning associated with *over*.

A second, and equally fatal, problem is that the primary meaning would need to be so abstract to be able to derive a set of such distinct meanings that it is difficult to see how the meanings associated with other spatial particles, such as *above* or *on*, could be mutually distinguished. Clearly, while accepting the insight that real-world pragmatic and contextual knowledge plays a significant role in the process of meaning construction, the linguistic evidence points to the conclusion that language users do store some distinct form-meaning pairings in long-term semantic memory. Hence, although the nature of meaning construction is a dynamic and highly creative process, not all meaning can be the result of situated (i.e., contextual) interpretation. Some of the interpretations associated with a particular form must be due to distinct meanings paired with the words themselves.

The position we advocate is that of polysemy. A polysemy approach suggests that the meanings associated with a spatial particle such as *over* are related in some fashion. We briefly preview our model below. The specifics are developed in chapter 3, and illustrated in detail by the analyses of English spatial particles throughout the course of this book. Our account of polysemy holds that a linguistic form is paired at the conceptual level, not with a single meaning, but rather with a network of distinct but related meanings. Hence, the meanings associated with a particular form constitute a semantic network. However, it is important to note that not all usages are contained within the semantic network. While some of the variation in uses of a word must be instantiated in long-term memory, and hence persist in the semantic network, some uses are created on-line in the course of regular interpretation of utterances. For instance, when we consider the semantic network for *over* in chapter 4, we will show in detail that the various senses in the text with which we began this chapter are instantiated in the semantic network, and hence are stored in long-term memory, whereas the meaning of moving from one side of an obstacle to the other in sentences of the following kind: *The cat jumped over the wall*, is a situated on-line interpretation, constructed for the purpose of local understanding in context.

We take the primary tasks for a model of the polysemy exhibited by spatial particles to constitute the following: (1) to establish what information is most appropriately included in the representation of the individual lexical entry and what information is appropriately represented as arising from cognitive processing and general world knowledge; (2) to model the systematic processes through which on-line contextually determined interpretations of spatial particles arise; (3) to model the systematic processes through which meaning is extended and through which the distinct senses – represented in long-term memory – become part of a lexical item's semantic network.

A major challenge for any theory of word meaning, and one we explore in detail in chapter 3, is to establish when a usage constitutes a distinct meaning component, which is legitimately instantiated in the semantic network, and when a usage is simply a contextually derived interpretation constructed on-line. This is a methodological issue, but one which, as will be demonstrated, is tractable, in the light of linguistic evidence. As already intimated, another significant challenge is to establish what constitutes the primary sense for a particular semantic network. Again this is a methodological issue, and as we will see in chapter 3, we will rely on both linguistic and empirical evidence.

Interpretation of the utterance and the underspecification of meaning

A cognitive approach to meaning construction holds that the interpretation of language is integrative, elaborative and inherently conceptual in nature. On this view, interpretation, which is to say meaning construction, is not simply the result of compositionally adding linguistic items. Rather utterances – lexical items and the syntactic configurations in which they occur – provide only min-imal prompts for meaning construction. Language vastly underdetermines the rich interpretations normally assigned to even simple, de-contextualized sen-tences; sentential interpretation results from the integration and elaboration of these minimal linguistic cues at the conceptual level.

While the importance of pragmatic inferencing (e.g., implicature) and back-ground knowledge in meaning construction is generally acknowledged, pre-vious approaches to word meaning, both in the generative tradition (e.g., Pustejovsky, 1998) and in the cognitive linguistic tradition (e.g., Brugman and Lakoff, 1988; Lakoff, 1987), have failed to adequately take account of the largely non-linguistic nature of meaning construction, or what is more appro-priately termed conceptual integration (Fauconnier and Turner, 1998, 2002). This has led previous scholars to fail to distinguish appropriately between information coded by the lexical item and information recruited from context, background knowledge and cognitive processing. As a result, these accounts have included a considerable amount of information in their representations of individual lexical entries, which is more appropriately understood as deriving from background and world knowledge, and human cognitive processing abil-ities (Kreitzer, 1997; Sandra, 1998; Sandra and Rice, 1995; Tyler and Evans, 2001b; Vandeloise, 1990). Sandra and Rice (1995), based on psycholinguis-tic experiments, have argued that such a degree of granularity is unwarranted, a view echoed forthrightly by Vandeloise (1990). As Kreitzer (1997) points out, the fine-grained distinction between instances of *over* as argued for in Lakoff (1987) provides a semantic network which is methodologically so un-constrained that 'the model ... [allows] ... *across, through* and *above* all to be related to the polysemy network of *over*' (1987: 292).

To fail to recognize that the source of much of the information which is necessary to establish an interpretation is not conventionalized information associated with a lexical item poses a significant problem. After all, if a theorist

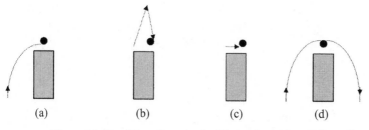

Figure 1.1 Possible trajectories for *The cat jumped over the wall*

believes that meaning is largely determined by language, then it follows that the theorist will attempt to explain meaning construction as deriving from the composition of lexical entries. But in order to produce the highly elaborate and complex interpretations that we regularly and ordinarily construct, the lexical entries would need to be spectacularly complex, as the next section will demonstrate. As we will see, assuming that lexical items are fully specified, that is, to assume that meaning is largely linguistic in nature, rather than conceptual, runs into immense difficulties, even in accounting for the correct interpretation of the most straightforward of sentences.

A 'simple' example: the cat jumped over the wall

The following discussion demonstrates some of the problems encountered with an approach to sentence interpretation that relies on highly specified lexical entries. Consider the following sentence:

(1.1)   The cat jumped over the wall.

In all probability, the reader will find this sentence unambiguous and readily understandable. Figure 1.1 presents four diagrams labelled (a) through (d). Before reading on, we ask that the reader select the diagram which best represents the event described by the sentence in (1.1).

We anticipate that the reader selected the fourth diagram (d). After all, the conventional reading of the sentence is that the cat begins a jump on one side of the wall, moves through an arc-like trajectory, and lands on the other side of the wall. Diagram (d) in figure 1.1 best schematizes this interpretation. On first inspection, this exercise seems straightforward, with no need for puzzlement or explanation. However, modelling how speakers of English consistently construct just the right interpretation, that is, (d), presents several complications. In the following, we will focus on how we know that the trajectory is the arc-shaped one, and not any of the others. In essence, where do we get this information from?

Even though the sentence in (1.1) is typically interpreted as unambiguous, it contains lexical items that have a range of interpretations. The behaviour

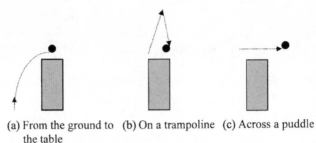

(a) From the ground to   (b) On a trampoline   (c) Across a puddle
the table

Figure 1.2   Trajectory paths potentially coded by *jump*

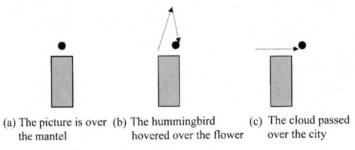

(a) The picture is over   (b) The hummingbird   (c) The cloud passed
the mantel   hovered over the flower   over the city

Figure 1.3   Trajectory paths potentially coded by *over*

described by *jump* has the potential to involve a variety of trajectory shapes, as in figure 1.2, some of which match the diagrams just rejected.

Similarly, figure 1.3 shows that *over* can be associated with several potential spatial configurations holding between the object in focus (i.e., *picture, hummingbird* and *cloud*) and the locating, backgrounded object (i.e., *mantel, flower* and *city*). Notice that these trajectory shapes also match some of the rejected diagrams from figure 1.1.

Thus, we face a seeming contradiction. The sentence in (1.1) which contains apparently ambiguous lexical items is consistently interpreted as unambiguous. The flip side of this contradiction is that, in spite of the range of different potential interpretations for *jump* and *over*, speakers of English consistently pick out just the right ones to assign interpretation (d) in figure 1.1 to the sentence *The cat jumped over the wall.*

Consider a further complication. Diagram (d) in figure 1.1 crucially represents the cat's motion ending at a point on the opposite side of the wall relative to the starting position of the jump. Yet, no element in the sentence explicitly provides us with this information.[7]

---

[7] Dewell (1994) argues that the primary mental representation associated with *over* involves the arced trajectory. He justifies this choice of primary meaning component in the following manner:

This exercise points to two fundamental and interrelated questions for an investigation of the role of lexical items in meaning construction. First, what is the source of information that is involved in the normal interpretation of sentences? And second, what constraints on interpretation must be posited in order to account for the native speaker's ability to choose consistently between competing interpretations of individual, polysemous items?

Many previous approaches to meaning construction have tended to assume what Jackendoff (1997) terms the strong version of the 'simple compositional' approach. This asserts that 'all elements of content in the meaning of a sentence' (1997: 48) are provided by the lexical items and the syntactic configuration in which they occur. In consequence, 'no aspects of a sentence's interpretation can arise from outside of the sentence itself' (1997: 41). Following this approach, let us consider just what kind of information it would be necessary to include in the lexical entries for *over, jump* and *cat* in order to obtain the interpretation diagrammed in (d) of figure 1.1.

First, we will consider *over*. Most previous studies of the polysemy exhibited by *over* assume that it codes the trajectory followed, as represented in a sentence like (1.1) (e.g., Brugman and Lakoff, 1988; Dewell, 1994; Kreitzer, 1997;

'If we ... simply imagine best examples of *over*, it seems that the "semicircular path" sense of over is the typical sense ... It seems intuitively more accurate to posit a central schema that looks like [figure n.1]' (1994: 353).

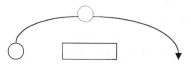

Figure n.1 After Dewell, 1994: 353

While we agree with much of the spirit of Dewell's analysis, in which information about the shape of the landmark (LM) – the entity which serves to locate the motile trajector (TR) in figure n.1 – and contact between the LM and the TR are eliminated, we are not convinced by his appeal to intuition. Our intuitions about the primary sense of *over* differ from Dewell's, as they do from Lakoff's and Brugman's. Clearly, intuitions concerning the primary sense of a spatial particle vary among analysts. Thus, Dewell's analysis fails to establish any criteria for determining the primary sense of spatial particles generally. Moreover, we find his primary mental representation problematic in that it actually contains two TRs – one at the beginning of the trajectory and one at the apex, as well as a LM. No explanation is offered for this dual TR representation. It seems that he is forced to this dual trajector representation in order to capture a static Higher-than Sense commonly associated with *over*, as well as a dynamic Above–across Sense. Finally, while adjusting the primary representation of the trajectory for *over* from Lakoff's flat above-and-across trajectory to a semicircular trajectory allows improvements in the analysis of a subset of senses associated with the particular particle *over*, including a trajectory as part of the primary sense of a particle is problematic when applied to many other uses of *over*, as well as to many other spatial particles. This will become clearer as we analyse various spatial particles in later chapters. Our goal is to develop a more general, principled framework which can be applied to all English spatial particles. We feel that the tendency to focus on analysis of only one or two particles has led to explanations which might work with a particular item, but which tend to be ad hoc and not generalizable.

Lakoff, 1987). One reason why this may have been assumed is that a change of the spatial particle involved often results in a change in the interpretation of the trajectory, as attested in (1.2):

(1.2)   a. Jane marched up the stairs.
         b. Jane marched down the stairs.

In sentences such as these, information provided by the spatial particle clearly affects the interpretation of the trajectory. Theorists who assume that meaning must (predominantly) come from the sentential elements (i.e., from language) must also assume that it is the spatial particle which codes the trajectory, as with *over* in the example in (1.1). Hence, all permissible usages of *over* that exhibit configurational differences with respect to the shape of the trajectory and the landmark element (e.g., *the wall*) must be stored in memory as distinct senses. In such an approach, there is seemingly no room for non-linguistic information. To make this more concrete, let us consider some examples. Following Langacker (1987), we will refer to the focal element which follows the trajectory (e.g., *the cat*) as the trajector or TR and the backgrounded element as the landmark or LM. In one scenario, *over* can code a spatial relation in which the TR is located statically higher than the LM (as in *The picture is over the mantel*); in a second scenario, the TR is positioned higher than the LM while being in continuous motion (as in *The hummingbird hovered over the flower*); in a third, the TR moves on a trajectory which is above and across the LM (as in *The plane flew over the city*); in a fourth, in which there is contact between the TR and the LM, the trajectory is crucially shaped by the LM itself (as in *Sam crawled over the wall*), etc. However, such explanations run into difficulty, as they are unable to specify the shape of the trajectory in situations in which there is no contact between the TR and the LM (as is the case in sentence (1.1)).

Lakoff's (1987) fully specified account of *over*, for instance, assumed that the 'above-and-across' trajectory, as in sentences such as: *The plane flew over the city*, represented the primary sense of *over*. He argued that extensions of this 'above-and-across' trajectory should include information about the physical (i.e., metric) attributes and dimensions of the LM. Thus, different senses are suggested if the LM is vertical (e.g., a wall), extended (e.g., an ocean), vertical and extended (e.g., a city with high buildings), etc. Importantly, there is no claim that the trajectory shape is necessarily affected by the changes in the dimensions of the LM if there is no contact between the TR and the LM.

In a situation in which there is contact between the TR and LM, as in a sentence such as *Sam crawled over the wall*, the specifically mentioned LM provides the overall shape as well as the beginning and end points for the motion labelled as *crawling*. In order to specify an arc trajectory for 'above and across', when there is no contact between the TR and LM, additional semantic features (beyond those provided by the LM) which code where the movement started and ended seem to be required. If such specification is necessary for one trajectory in which there is no contact, we might conclude that it should be included in the representation of all trajectories in which there is no contact. However, in the sentence *The plane flew over the city* the normal interpretation does not include information concerning where the motion associated with flying started and ended. If not all non-contact trajectories are coded by the spatial particle for beginning and end points, one might well wonder what criteria could be used in order to determine, in a non-arbitrary fashion, which uses of a spatial particle would need to have starting and end points of the trajectory specified. Even the most fully specified models of polysemy have shied away from this conundrum.

It might be possible to argue that the verb also carries information concerning trajectory shape. Previous accounts have been hesitant to do this. One reason for this is presumably because requiring the verb to code trajectory information would greatly expand the number of lexical listings or senses associated with each verb. In the case of *jump*, we have already seen three possible trajectories (as diagrammed in figure 1.2) and one can readily construct several more. In addition, there are instances in which the spatial particle crucially provides information about the direction of the trajectory (as in sentences (1.2a) and (1.2b)). Thus, placing information about the shape of the trajectory in the lexical entry for the verb would involve a good deal of redundancy, something most theories shy away from (Jackendoff, 1997).

Even if we set aside these difficulties and assume one could offer a principled account of *over* and *jump* which resulted in fully specifying all potential trajectory shapes, one is still faced with the question of how to account for selection of the correct sense within a particular sentence. A model which assumes the strong simple compositionality position might be able to account for the interpretation represented by (d) in figure 1.1 by somehow 'coercing' the appropriate choice given the other lexical items in the sentence.

One hypothesis for accomplishing this involves including information about the agent's goals in the lexical entries for nouns (Pustejovsky, 1998). In the sentence in (1.1), beyond the basic four-legged-mammal-says-meow-type information, the entry for *cat* would need to include information about possible kinds of motion a cat could engage in. One subcategory of motion would include certain kinds of jumping. Since cats regularly engage in jumping, which entails varying trajectory shapes, information concerning the particular kind of jumping would have to be detailed. For instance, we might posit a putative taxonomy of the kinds of jumping and trajectories cats engage in. Consider some examples: Trajectory1: when the goal is to move from a lower position to a higher position (as from the floor to the table, say, as in diagram (a) in figure 1.2), the cat jumps in a roughly diagonal motion; Trajectory2: when there is no goal of forward motion (perhaps when startled), a cat can jump roughly straight up in the air (as in diagram (b) in figure 1.2); Trajectory3:

when the goal is to pass higher than and beyond a vertical impediment, the cat can jump with an arc trajectory (as in (d) in figure 1.1).

Nonetheless, even this amount of detail does not ultimately solve the problem because without knowing the cat's goal (which is not overtly signalled in the sentence in (1.1)), there is no way to rule out selecting the jump diagrammed in (b) in figure 1.1, for instance, in which the cat's trajectory begins on the wall, moves to a point relatively straight up and hence higher than the wall, and returns to the wall. That is, we would still be unable to predict that (d) in figure 1.1 is the normal interpretation assigned to the sentence in (1.1), namely *The cat jumped over the wall*.

A second attempt to coerce the correct selections might involve some kind of feature matching between *jump* and *over*. However, this solution runs into similar problems, as a match between *jump* in diagram (b) figure 1.2 and *over* in diagram (b) figure 1.3 cannot be excluded. Thus, we arrive at the inevitable conclusion that the information supplied by the syntactic configuration and individual lexical items, even when highly specified, cannot account for the interpretation normally assigned to this seemingly most straightforward of sentences.

The role of background knowledge

Related problems in interpreting sentences in context led Grice (1975, 1978), Reddy (1979) and others to suggest that much of the normal interpretation of utterances does not derive from information coded by the utterance per se. Rather, they concluded that interpretation of ordinary sentences crucially involves humans drawing rational inferences based not only on what is uttered (the linguistic production), but additionally on the surrounding context, knowledge of speakers' intentions and knowledge of speakers' beliefs, including beliefs about how the world works (see especially, Reddy, 1979). As Green (1989) notes, virtually all natural language utterances are vague and ambiguous. Speakers must always add information to the linguistic elements present in an utterance in order to establish an appropriate interpretation. Grice has articulated this general approach to natural language interpretation in terms of the Cooperative Principle and the maxims which he saw as particular instances of the Cooperative Principle. More recently, Sperber and Wilson (1986) have argued that Grice's insights are more appropriately framed in terms of the single principle of relevance. (See Green, 1989 and Sperber and Wilson, 1986 for a full discussion.)

A simple compositional approach to meaning construction and lexical items advocates including in the lexical entry all information a speaker would require in order to establish the appropriate interpretation of any sentence in which the lexical item occurs. This position forces inclusion of vast amounts of information in the mental lexicon. Setting aside the cumbersome nature of such a model, even then, the listener would still be required to make inferences about the speaker's intentions and beliefs, and the relevance or probability of a particular interpretation within the exact context in which the utterance is issued.

As we have just seen, even normal interpretation of simple, de-contextualized sentences in which spatial particles occur seems to involve information that is not explicitly provided by the individual lexical items. Although our work departs from the theorists cited above (e.g., Grice and those who accept his position that pragmatics supplements a truth-conditional semantic component) in many important ways, we take their conclusion that linguistic utterances radically underdetermine the meaning involved in normal interpretation of utterances as both foundational and fundamental.

Some of the strongest support for this general position has come from the field of experimental psychology. Starting in the early 1970s a number of experimental psychologists such as Frank and Bransford (1973), Rummelhart (1975), and Wilson and Anderson (1986) demonstrated the importance of background knowledge and expectation in interpreting connected text. For instance, numerous experiments established that otherwise vague text could readily be assigned a reasonable interpretation if the reader were provided with a relevant title, such as 'Doing the Laundry'. Lacking this background frame, readers with comparable reading skills found the same text confusing and difficult to interpret. In other experiments, readers with background knowledge relating to a text were consistently shown to remember more information and make more appropriate inferences than readers with comparable reading skills who lacked the appropriate background knowledge. Many researchers have come to the conclusion that the interpretation of text represents a synthesis of knowledge in the reader's/speaker's mind and the information provided by the linguistic code.

We hypothesize that, for a sentence such as *The cat jumped over the wall*, the nature of the normal interpretation constitutes meaning construction conducted at the conceptual level. Moreover, we will argue that the processes which mediate and facilitate such a conceptualization – we equate meaning with conceptualization – are conceptual (rather than linguistic) in nature.

This position stands in sharp contrast to theories which argue that interpretation of sentences relies primarily on the cumulative information supplied by the individual lexical items and the syntactic configurations in which they occur (compositional semantics). We will argue that the linguistic utterance acts as a minimal prompt for conceptual construction which is far richer than the combined information provided by the lexical items.

Normal interpretation of even a simple sentence, such as *The cat jumped over the wall*, is crucially tied to basic, recurring experiences with the world. A major part of this experience involves understanding force dynamics, such as gravity, and how these dynamics affect physical objects, such as cats (Talmy, 1988a, 2000). Given our recurring experiences with gravity and how objects move, we know that the action we label as *jump* involves pushing off from a surface, momentarily leaving the surface, and eventually returning to a stable surface. A fundamental component of the semantics of *jump* is that the TR is physically displaced, that is, motion is involved, and hence a trajectory is projected. The linguistic prompt *over* in sentence (1.1) provides the specific, key information that, at some point in the trajectory, the cat is higher than the wall. Our knowledge of gravity and cats tells us that a cat, unlike a hummingbird, cannot suspend itself in midair for long periods of time. The process of conceptual integration of the information prompted for by *over* with our knowledge of objects and force dynamics results in the conceptualization represented by our diagram (d) in figure 1.1. Thus, we argue that none of the individual lexical items explicitly provides information concerning the shape of the trajectory. Rather, we will argue that this information, and indeed a good deal of the information needed to establish normal interpretation of most sentences, comes from cognitive processes, conceptual structure and background knowledge rather than the individual lexical items. We will return to *The cat jumped over the wall* in chapter 4.

Throughout this book, we will argue that attempting to list detailed information in the basic lexical representation of spatial particles fails to account for everyday meaning construction. In contrast, we posit lexical representations which are more abstract in nature. Our analysis models detailed knowledge of the spatio-physical world which forms part of the normal interpretation of utterances via application of a set of inferencing strategies and ways of construing (i.e., seeing) *spatial scenes*. Spatial scenes, such as the scene prompted for by a sentence like: *The cat jumped over the wall*, involve conceptualizing a spatio-configurational relation between entities we encounter in the world around us and with which we interact. Hence, a spatial scene is a conceptualization grounded in spatio-physical experience. This analysis allows us to avoid the problems encountered with a more fully specified lexical representation while revealing the systematic semantic relations among the many meanings of individual English spatial particles.

Nevertheless, we must emphasize that we are not so much relegating the role of lexical items in meaning construction to an unimportant place, as assigning them their appropriate place. To say that lexical items act as prompts for meaning construction is not to say that lexical forms do not crucially contribute to the meaning-construction process. Clearly, lexical items, in general, and spatial particles, in particular, do contribute meaning. For instance, *The cat jumped over the wall* is regularly assigned a different interpretation from *The cat jumped beside the wall*. However, we must also be aware that what they contribute is a prompt for a complex conceptual elaboration.

Dictionaries versus encyclopedias

The distinction between treating lexical items as fully specified versus seeing them as merely prompts for complex conceptual elaboration has been framed by some scholars in terms of a distinction between a dictionary versus an encyclopedic view of word meaning (cf. Haiman, 1980; Langacker, 1987; Wierzbicka, 1988). On this view, linguists who subscribe to the dictionary view of word meaning attempt to identify a restricted and finite set of specifications that constitute the linguistic knowledge properly associated with the lexical entry for a particular lexical item. However, as both Haiman (1980) and Langacker (1987) observe, attempts to restrict and, hence, determine which specifications should be included in a particular lexical entry and which should be excluded is impossible on practical grounds. Moreover, as the foregoing discussion has highlighted, such attempts will inevitably fail to account for the variety and range of distinct interpretations ordinarily associated with a particular lexical item.

The mistake in adopting a dictionary view of lexical items has been to view words as 'containing' meaning, a naïve view of communication, which Reddy (1979) argued was to fall prey to what he termed the conduit metaphor. We suggest not that words contain meaning, but rather, in the spirit of scholars such as Fauconnier (1997), Langacker (1987) and Turner (1991), that words *prompt for* highly complex conceptualizations. As Langacker has felicitously put it: 'linguistic expressions are not meaningful in and of themselves, but only through the access they afford to different stores of knowledge that allow us to make sense of them' (1987: 155). This view, which might be termed the encyclopedic view of word meaning, treats lexical items as *points of access* (in Langacker's terms) to the totality of our knowledge regarding a particular conceptual entity. This reflects what we know about how a particular linguistic expression is used and our knowledge of that aspect of the conceptualized world which the entity it prompts for inhabits. Moreover, such knowledge is accessed in conjunction with various inferencing strategies which allow us to build elaborate conceptualizations in ways maximally coherent with, and contingent upon, our experiences of the world.

One way in which we will attempt to capture the encyclopedic knowledge prompted for by a particular spatial particle is to model the meaning component associated with a form such as *over*, for instance, in terms of a semantic network (we will develop the notion of a semantic network in detail in chapter 2). That is, a lexical item should be thought of as prompting for a range of meanings, the particular meaning selected being determined by conceptual integration in context. Moreover, in chapter 3 we will argue that within a semantic network not all of the meanings associated with a particular spatial particle have equal status. For instance, we will suggest that some meanings can be determined as being what we will term more *primary* than others (the notion of *primariness* will be taken up in chapter 3).

In essence, then, in normal communication lexical items do not occur in isolation. In point of fact, when humans use lexical items, the lexical items always occur in context and their precise interpretation changes with each use. Hence, a typical dictionary definition inevitably fails to provide for the infinite amount of variation and detail that arises when a lexical item is interpreted in context. Put another way, a lexical item prompts for a highly specified conceptualization. Crucially, however, this rich specification emerges at the conceptual level, due to integration of prompts in context, and is vastly more complex than anything which can be derived or predicted from the individual lexical items integrated in compositional fashion. Accordingly, it is to the notion of conceptualization which we now turn.

The conceptual nature of meaning

Within the study of linguistic semantics, both in the philosophical and linguistic traditions, it has been widely assumed that meaning derives from the fact that language refers directly to the world. The means whereby language 'matches up' with the world has relied on the notion of truth. Yet, two fundamental problems fatally undermine this approach. In terms of the study of meaning, some scholars have suggested that so-called truth-conditional or model-theoretic approaches to semantics are concerned with what has been termed informational significance rather than cognitive significance, and hence do not represent the study of meaning, properly conceived. As Wierzbicka (1996) puts it, 'truth-conditional' semantics 'doesn't seek to reveal and describe the meanings encoded in natural language, or to compare meanings across languages and cultures. Rather, it sees its goal as that of translating certain carefully selected types of sentences into a logical calculus. It is interested not in meaning (in the sense of conceptual structures encoded in language) but in the logical properties of sentences such as entailment, contradiction, or logical equivalence' (1996: 8).

A second problem is that a truth-conditional approach assumes that much of language directly reflects and refers to the world. As the cognitive scientist Gilles Fauconnier observes: 'When language expressions reflect objective events and situations, as they often do (and often do not), they do not reflect them directly, but rather through elaborate human cognitive constructions and construals' (1997: 8). This point has been elaborated in detail by Ray Jackendoff (1983, 1990, 1992). Jackendoff has pointed out that one of the most important insights to emerge from the work on perception is that our perceptions of the world are determined largely by conceptual organization being imposed on sense-perceptory input. That is, what we directly experience is not an objectively real world. Rather, what we experience as everyday reality is mediated and shaped

Figure 1.4

by human conceptual organization to which we necessarily and unconsciously subject sense-perceptory input (cf. Dennett, 1991; Putnam, 1981).[8]

In essence, the patterns and organization we perceive as reality do not in fact exist independently in the world itself, but are largely the result of our cognitive processing. For instance, in figure 1.4, the reader might see either a vase or alternatively two faces. Yet, the particular image seen is not dependent upon the raw input, which presumably remains unchanged. What changes is the organization of our perceptions, by mental operations to which we do not have conscious access. These present us with two alternating and conflicting interpretations of experience. It would be erroneous to claim that the vase interpretation is true and the two-face interpretation is false, or vice versa. It is also contradictory to say both exist simultaneously; by fixating on the figure what is seen will alternate between the two perceptions, but we cannot perceive both simultaneously. Clearly, figure 1.4 is not a drawing of something that exists in the world. It is we who perceive it to be of something. This is instructive as it demonstrates that although there is a world of sense-perceptory information out there, what we in fact perceive is determined by how we unconsciously organize and hence make sense of the input.

---

[8] In other words, as humans we only have access to our conceptual system. Words (linguistic elements) reference concepts. Concepts are not, however, unrelated to the 'world out there'. We believe that concepts are best understood as arising from redescribed percepts. Many percepts arise from sensorimotor experiences derived from the world. Because of humans' particular physical and neurological architecture, we perceive objects and actions in particular ways. Percepts can also arise from internal states, such as an emotional state.

These percepts are the raw data which, when reanalysed, form the concepts to which we have direct access. When we 'refer' to some object or event which we have perceived in the 'world out there', we are 'referring' to a mediated percept (i.e., one which has been filtered through our particular human neurological apparatus) which has, in turn, been redescribed into a format accessible to our conceptual system. It is only once the raw stimulus from the 'outside world' has been so mediated and redescribed that it can be assigned a linguistic label, such as *dog*, for instance.

This insight has profound consequences for a theory of meaning and language. If our world of experience is not the real world itself, but the real world as mediated by our cognitive faculties, then the world to which we have direct and conscious access is the mental world of experience, which is to say the conceptual system. Jackendoff terms this our projected world. When we use language, then, we are referring to concepts in our projected world, which indirectly reflects the real world. Jackendoff has felicitously summarized this position as follows:

[W]e must take issue with the naïve [truth-conditional] position that the information conveyed by language is about the real world. We have conscious access only to the projected world – the world as unconsciously organized by the mind; and we can talk about things only insofar as they have achieved mental representation through these processes of organization. Hence the information conveyed by language must be about the projected world. We must explain the naïve position as a consequence of our being constituted to treat the projected world as reality. (Jackendoff, 1997: 29)

If language cannot refer to an objective world, precisely because we have no direct access to such, then language prompts for concepts. Moreover, linguistic elements, as we have noted, consist of form-meaning pairings (where the meaning component constitutes a semantic network). That is, words (and constructions more generally) are symbolic assemblies consisting of a phonological pole and a semantic pole (Langacker, 1987, 1991b).[9] In line with the assumptions set forth at the beginning of the chapter, the semantic pole derives from conceptual structure. We conclude from this that the semantic value of a lexical item can be equated with a particular concept. This conclusion has now been reached by an increasing number of scholars who have recognized the fundamentally conceptual nature of language and conceptual representation (e.g., Heine, 1997; Fauconnier, 1997; Jackendoff, 1983, 1990; Langacker, 1987, 1991b; Lakoff, 1987; Talmy, 2000). The cognitive linguist Ronald Langacker (1991a) has summarized the position as follows: 'Semantic structures [meanings] are conceptual structures established by linguistic convention – the form which thoughts must assume for purposes of ready linguistic symbolization. Thus, semantic structure is conventionalized conceptual structure' (1991: 108–9). In other words, lexical items prompt for conventionalized concepts.

In order to make the claim that words prompt for concepts more concrete, let us consider an example. Consider the word *bird*. The concept which corresponds to this linguistic form is but a sketch. The details of shape, size, vocalization ability, even ability to fly are filled in by contextual and real-world

---

[9] Langacker argues that not only words but any kind of complex expression, such as certain grammatical constructions, are symbolic assemblies. By saying that words are symbolic assemblies consisting of a phonological pole and a semantic pole, we are not claiming that they are the only such symbolic assemblies.

knowledge. Semantic representation (word meaning) provides only a skeletal prompt, which subsumes little more than the scaffolding for the construction of meaning. Lexical items prompt for conceptualization, the process whereby rich and elaborate meanings are constructed.

The assumption that semantic representation prompts for a conceptually mediated representation of the world also provides powerful insights into, and accounts for, many uses of spatial particles which have previously been labelled as arbitrary. If one assumes that language directly reflects the real world, then one assumes that the objectively metric properties and principles of Euclidean geometry which appear to hold for the spatio-physical world 'out there' will form the basis of linguistic descriptions of spatial scenes and uses of spatial particles. Talmy (1988b, 2000) has argued persuasively that conceptualized space as reflected in language is not Euclidean in nature, that is, it is not held to notions of fixed distance, amount, size, contour, angle, etc. He argues that conceptualized space is topological in nature, that is, conceptualized space 'involves relativistic relationships rather than absolutely fixed quantities' (1988b: 170). Assuming that language refers to conceptual structure provides the insight that the relationships between objects are subjective and largely influenced by the interpretation imposed by the conceptual system.

A further benefit of assuming that language is conceptual in nature is that we now have a means of distinguishing between mundane, yet ubiquitous sentences such as: *Jane stood in the flower-bed*, versus: *Jane stood on the flower-bed*. If we assume that there is a direct relation between the real world and language, as in truth-conditional approaches, there is no explanation for why English speakers can describe the event of a person standing such that her feet are in contact with the piece of ground designated as the flower-bed, using either *on* or *in*. Traditional approaches have assumed that examples such as these are semantically equivalent. However, we are now able to see that each sentence represents a distinct conceptualization (or construal in the sense of Langacker, e.g., 1987) of an objectively identical scenario. This is analogous to the way in which in figure 1.4 we were able to see either the vase or the faces. What we see is mediated by the conceptual system, which has a number of ways to represent the same scene. These issues will be pursued further in chapter 3.

Conclusion

We began this chapter by demonstrating that spatial particles typically have numerous meanings associated with them. We claimed that a subset of interpretations represent those meanings which must be stored in memory, and hence are permanently available. These meanings we termed senses. We also suggested that some meanings associated with words must be due to pragmatic inferencing, context and background knowledge. These meanings, we suggested, are constructed on-line in the moment of speaking and listening. In attempting to distinguish between the meaning contributed by language and the meaning due to world knowledge and cognitive processing, we saw, as with our illustration of *The cat jumped over the wall*, that many previous accounts have vastly underestimated the amount of information which is not accounted for by the conventionalized meaning of lexical items and the grammatical construction in which the lexical items occur. This led us to the general conclusion that meaning construction must be inherently conceptual in nature. This also points to a finding which is coherent with studies which are broadly 'cognitive' in the sense adduced – namely that meaning is fundamentally mental in nature, referencing conceptual structures rather than directly referencing entities inhering in an objectively verifiable and mind-independent world. Language refers to conceptual structure, which indirectly reflects the world. (See Evans, 2000: chapter 2; Jackendoff, 1992: chapter 12.) These general findings have profound consequences for a theory of word meaning, a theory of meaning construction, and perhaps most crucially, for an understanding of the relationship between language, thought and the nature of reality.

2   Embodied meaning and spatial experience

In the previous chapter we argued that our knowledge of the world is indirect because it is constrained by how we experience it. This follows as our experience of the world is always mediated via our uniquely human perceptual system, physiology and neural architecture. A hummingbird's understanding of gravity as a force which can be overcome for extended periods of time, albeit with effort, would be significantly different from a human's. Thus, a hummingbird no doubt experiences and represents the same world to itself in quite different ways from how human beings do; both versions of the world, while presumably very different, are equally 'real'. As pointed out by the philosopher Hilary Putnam (1981), to claim that we can have direct access to and conscious knowledge of an objective reality (i.e., an objective god's-eye view of the world) is wrongheaded.

Nonetheless, we are not claiming that there is not a world 'out there' nor that our experience of it is unimportant. To say that our experience with and perceptions of the world are mediated by our conceptual system, and are fundamentally conceptual in nature, is not to say that the real world and its properties do not largely constitute the nature of our experience. On the contrary, it is the real world which provides the raw substrate for our sensory perceptions and the conceptualizations which arise from them. Accordingly, the spatio-physical properties of the world of humanly perceived experience are fundamental to human cognition. To take this tack, then, is to suggest that lived human experience is ultimately constrained and determined by the nature of the bodies we have (including both physiology and neurological apparatus). This entails the notion of the embodiment of experience.

Embodied experience constitutes the notion that human experience of the world is mediated by the kinds of bodies we have, and hence is in large measure determined by the nature of the bodies which mediate how we experience the world. Moreover, many cognitive scientists are increasingly suggesting that it is this embodied experience that gives rise to conceptual structure. It does so, it has been suggested, because our perception of the world is meaningful in various ways to us as human beings. In other words, our world, as mediated by our perceptual apparatus (our physiology and neural architecture, in short, our bodies), gives rise to conceptual structure, that is, to thought and concepts. Hence, our claim, one supported by an impressive and growing body of research, is that meaning itself is embodied (e.g., Evans, 2000; Grady, 1997a; Heine, 1997; Jackendoff, 1983, 1990, 1992; Johnson, 1987; Lakoff, 1987; Lakoff and Johnson, 1980, 1999; Langacker, 1987; Sweetser, 1990; Svorou, 1994; Talmy, 2000; Turner, 1991, 1996; Varela *et al.*, 1991).

What does it mean to say that embodied experience is meaningful? Quite simply, the nature of our experience has non-trivial consequences for survival. Hence, the nature of human behaviour, in terms of both evolutionary change and how we react to ongoing experience in the here and now, has profound consequences for our ecological viability as a species. In a very obvious way, the presence of a hungry lion, for instance, is meaningful because whether we stay put or run has important consequences in terms of the survival of the individual and ultimately the species. How a particular organism responds to its environment, in terms of both ongoing behaviour (e.g., knowing whether an approaching lion constitutes a potential threat or not) and phylogenetic behaviour (i.e., the way in which it evolves in response to its ecological niche), has non-trivial consequences for its survival and hence its ecological viability. The meaningful nature of experience (and experience is necessarily embodied as we have no access to a disembodied, i.e., god's-eye, view of the world) is apparent at all levels of interaction between humans and their environment. For instance, our experience of gravity has certain consequences: a larger object such as a table will prevent a smaller object such as a cup from falling to the ground. That is, the spatial relation involving contact between two such objects is meaningful. It is meaningful precisely because this spatial configuration has important consequences. After all, if we let go of a cup without placing it on a larger object, then it will fall to the floor potentially smashing and hence becoming functionally useless.

In chapter 1, we argued that the semantic representation coded by language reflects conceptual structure. If the embodiment of experience indeed gives rise to meaning, which is to say, conceptual structure, then the concepts expressed by language should largely derive from our perception of spatio-physical experience. That is, the argument we are making predicts that spatio-physical experience provides much of the fundamental semantic (or conceptual) structure from which other concepts are constructed.[1] This book analyses spatial

---

[1] Within cognitive linguistics it has been common to assume that all concepts, both concrete and abstract, are grounded in terms of spatio-physical experience. More recently scholars are beginning to realize that there is a bifurcation in the conceptual system between what Grady (1997a) terms image concepts and response concepts (see also Evans, 2000). That is, while image concepts, such as the spatially-based concepts that we will be analysing in this book derive from redescriptions of sensorimotor, i.e., external, experience, other concepts, traditionally termed abstract, such as time, in fact derive from internal experience. While such concepts may

scenes and the English spatial particles which prompt for them. Time and again we have found, as will be seen, that without understanding the foundational nature of spatio-physical experience, we would fail to understand why it is that speakers of English consistently use spatial particles (e.g., *over, in*, etc.) as they do.

Spatial relations and meaning

To illustrate our claim, consider the trajector (TR)-landmark (LM) configuration in which the TR is surrounded by the LM. Typically, being in such a TR–LM configuration has consequences for both the TR and the LM. For instance, the surrounding LM will often offer physical protection from outside forces and hide the TR from outside view (Deane, 1992; Johnson, 1987). Thus, the spatial configuration is not conceived as neutral, but as meaningful and consequential; we understand this TR–LM configuration in terms of, and hence giving rise to, the concept of containment. We encounter numerous spatio-physical examples of containers and containment on a daily basis. For instance, when we wake up, we find ourselves surrounded by walls, floor, and ceiling – we are contained within a room. We move from one room to another and we have moved from one container to another. We open a cupboard in the kitchen and we've opened a large container. We pull out a box of cereal and we pour the contents (the TR) out of the box-container into a bowl, another container. As we eat the cereal, we are transferring the contents from the bowl into our bodies – which are themselves containers.

Basic human understanding of containers and containment is apparently established very early. In psychological experiments, infants of less than six months show surprise when containers without bottoms hold objects (Mandler, 1992); this suggests that these infants have already formed a theory of containment and support. By nine months infants have a concept of containers as places where things disappear and reappear (Lloyd, Sinha and Freeman, 1981).[2]

---

be at some level responses to external experience, it may be too strong to claim that they directly derive from a redescription of sensorimotor experience. (See Evans, 2000 for an analysis of time concepts.)

[2] The fact that infants appear to universally develop a general notion of containment does not entail the claim that the general spatial scene with its particular spatial configuration and functions will be divided up and lexicalized in precisely the same way in all languages. Work by Choi and Bowerman (1992) shows that young children learning Korean and English are sensitive to language-specific patterns in the way they express particular LM–TR configurations. For instance, while English uses the spatial particle *in* to express a relation of containment, Korean has several lexical items such as *kkita* 'fit tightly' (for instance, when putting earplugs in an ear) and *nehta* 'put in loosely' (for instance, said when putting toys in a large container). Thus, it seems clear that different languages can attend to various aspects of a particular spatial scene and that children learning the language are sensitive to these differences.

English speakers regularly use the spatial particle *in* to code the concept of containment linguistically.[3] Thus, English speakers say:

(2.1)   I awoke in my bedroom
(2.2)   I went to the cupboard in the kitchen
(2.3)   I found the box of cereal in the cupboard

All these sentences express clear spatio-physical relations between physical TRs and physical containers (LM).[4] English speakers also use *in* to express non-spatio-physical containment:

(2.4)   I read it in the newspaper
(2.5)   Anne Frank lived in perilous times
(2.6)   Will is in love

We will offer more detailed accounts of the extension of spatio-physical particles to the description of non-spatio-physical situations throughout the book. What is important to note here is that in the examples in (2.4) through (2.6) the spatial particle *in* is being used to convey respectively the relation between an idea and a text, a person and a temporally delimited event-sequence, and a person and a particular emotional state. When an entity is in a particular spatial configuration with another entity, there are usually important consequences for the participating entities. A spatial configuration resulting in containment involves meaningful consequences for the TR, such as the container constraining and delimiting the environment experienced by the TR.[5] Being surrounded by a physical container ensures that the TR to some extent is constrained and hence influenced in a fundamental way by the LM. In the sentences in (2.4) and (2.5), the TR in each case is not physically 'surrounded' by the LM: it is questionable whether a TR can be physically 'surrounded' by an entity such as *perilous times* at all. However, as being contained by a particular LM is meaningful in terms of the LM representing a pervasive influence on the TR, English speakers

---

[3]   In the analysis which we develop in later chapters, we will argue that the primary sense of a spatial particle involves what we call a proto-scene. Each proto-scene involves two aspects – a spatial configuration between two entities and a functional element. In the case of *in*, the configurational aspect is a TR enclosed by a LM; the functional aspect involves the concept of containment.

[4]   Again we note that while we believe all humans perceive relations between objects in the same way and establish the same primitive theories of relations such as support and containment, these percepts and primitive concepts are subject to reanalysis which results in more complex concepts. Some aspects of reanalysis are apparently guided by the language to which the child is exposed. Languages can and do divide up and label various elements within a spatial scene in different ways. Choi and Bowerman have established this for Korean and English; Tyler and Evans (1999) discuss this in regard to French and English.

[5]   We represent the meaningful consequences of the particular spatial configurations coded by each spatial particle through what we term the functional element (Herskovits, 1986; Vandeloise, 1991). A functional element is part of the basic representation or lexical entry of each spatial particle.

readily extend *in* from its use to express TR–LM relations involving physical containment to express relations involving concepts which are conceptualized as exerting a pervasive influence such as *perilous times*. Equally, a containment relation serves to restrict a particular TR – if you move your coffee cup, the coffee moves with it. Accordingly, containers serve to locate TRs. As we invariably experience particular states in a given location, we can say that states and location co-occur or correlate. This pattern is evidenced by our ability to employ spatial particles such as *in* to mediate a relation between *Will* in (2.6) and states such as love. This example illustrates that the functional nature of spatial scenes gives rise to correlated non-spatial consequences and inferences. These, in turn, can lead to the development of non-spatial meanings becoming associated with a particular spatial particle (see chapter 7 for a detailed discussion of *in*).

Such usage is not limited to English. In language after language, spatio-relational morphemes are regularly exploited to describe non-spatial relations and domains. In fact, spatial particles provide some of the clearest, most intriguing evidence of the complex interaction between human physical experience of the world, thought and language. Thus, these linguistic elements not only code the relational architecture of physical space but also embed that rich spatial understanding into the very fabric of language and grammar. Their use and ubiquity are testimony to the far-reaching influence of the human experience of spatio-relational configurations on more complex conceptualization.

Spatial scenes

Our basic assumption is, then, that as humans, we segment our perceptions of the world and the way in which we experience it into spatial scenes. We believe these spatial scenes result from entities in the world – which exist independently of human beings – being perceived, then analysed and understood in ways which are wholly dependent upon the kind of neural architecture of the human brain, the particularities of the human body and the way these bodies interact with the world. Hence, a spatial scene coded linguistically by the phrase *the cup is on the table* is constructed conceptually when a cup and a table are understood as sharing a particular spatial relation in which there is direct contact between the cup and the table, and functionally the table supports the cup.[6] The conceptualization of this spatial scene (which involves a primitive theory of the support relationship and its consequences) derives from basic human understanding of gravity, knowledge that certain surfaces can prevent

---

[6] We are assuming a broad definition of support which potentially includes the notion of attachment. This allows for *on* to be used in sentences such as: *The fly is on the ceiling* or *He always wore a ring on his index finger*.

an item such as a cup from falling to the ground, and an understanding of the physical properties of the entities involved (e.g., cups tend to be smaller than tables, cups tend to be made of relatively lightweight material so that they can be easily lifted by humans, tables tend to be made of materials which can support objects like cups, etc). Spatial scenes, then, and our conceptualization of spatial scenes involve entities in the world being related to each other in certain recurring ways. The conceptualized relation is dependent upon our uniquely human understanding and experience of the physical world (we will discuss the nature of spatial scenes in greater detail in the next chapter).

Once a spatial scene, in which two entities are conceptualized as being related in particular ways, has been constructed, this conceptualization is meaningful, providing concepts such as support and containment. A concept such as support, which derives from spatio-physical experience, in turn, can be systematically extended to non-physical domains, as was seen with containment in examples (2.4) through (2.6). Sentences such as the following:

(2.7)   Can I count on your vote?
(2.8)   You can rely on me

utilize the notion of support associated with the spatial particle *on*, without being related to gravity or spatio-physical experience in any way. In short, humans regularly extend their understanding of physical-spatial relations and entities to non-physical domains; these extended conceptualizations are regularly reflected in the linguistic system.

Perceptual analysis and the embodiment of meaning

Some of the earliest formative experiences humans undergo involve battling with gravity to remain upright, attempts to achieve balance and discovery of force dynamics (e.g., that we can cause something to move away from us when we push it and towards us when we pull it; that large, solid objects, such as doors, can act as impenetrable barriers to forward motion). Work in developmental psychology indicates that the understanding and organization assigned to experiences with the spatio-physical world form the conceptual basis for much of language (e.g., Baillargeon, 1993, 1995; Baillargeon, Needham and DeVos, 1991; Bertenthal, 1993; Eimas and Quinn, 1994; Jones and Smith, 1993; Legerstee, 1992; Leslie, 1984; Lloyd, Sinha and Freeman, 1981; Mandler, 1988, 1992, 1996; Quinn, Eimas and Rosenkrantz, 1993; Quinn and Eimas, 1997; Spelke, 1988).

The developmental psychologist Jean Mandler (1988, 1992, 1996) notes that starting at a very early age (certainly by two months) infants attend to objects, spatial displays and movement in their environment. She argues that this close attending gives rise to a level of analysis which constitutes a new,

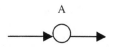

A

Figure 2.1 Diagram of the redescription for caused motion (after Mandler, 1992: 595)

Figure 2.2 Diagram of the redescription for containment (after Mandler, 1992)

constructed representation of objects and spatial structure. Mandler discusses this constructed level of analysis as a redescription of sense-perceptory (i.e., spatio-physical) information that is derived from what she terms *perceptual analysis*. The product of perceptual analysis is a kind of information which is distinct from unanalysed perceptual information (note that even unanalysed perceptual information is mediated by conceptual apparatus and is at least minimally conceptual). Mandler observes that these redescriptions[7] differ from any spatial displays infants have actually seen in the real world. Much of the perceptual information that would give rise to a redescription is not represented in human memory. Rather a redescription is 'a piece of perceptual information which is recoded into a non-perceptual form that represents meaning' (1992: 589). In the process of redescribing or recoding, new information is created and much of the original perceptual information is lost.

Mandler argues that redescriptions constitute the infant's first fundamental abstractions. These early redescriptions capture essential notions of movement and spatial relations. As she puts it '[O]ne of the foundations of the conceptualizing capacity is the image-schema [i.e., the redescription], in which spatial structure is mapped into conceptual structure' (Mandler, 1992: 591). Basic conceptual abstractions (i.e., redescriptions) are in turn used to construct more complex concepts, such as animacy, and spatial relations, such as support and containment. Figure 2.1 represents Mandler's attempt to represent the fundamental notion of caused motion (which, she argues, is basic to distinguishing between animacy and inanimacy; Bertenthal (1993) has shown that three-month-old infants are sensitive to such a distinction).

In figure 2.1, the object labelled A is caused to move by an entity which moves into contact with it. Figure 2.2 is an attempt to represent the fundamental spatial

---

[7] Mandler terms these redescriptions *image-schemas*. It should be noted that the term *image*, as used in psychology, does not mean a mental image, but rather information recruited from any sense-perception, e.g., haptic, visual, auditory, etc. Because the term *image-schema* has been interpreted in a variety of ways, and because the term *image* may connote only the visual modality for some readers, we have decided not to use this term in an attempt to avoid confusion.

relationship of containment. Mandler concludes that redescriptions are a crucial part of human mental architecture and that they begin developing at an early age. For instance, Baillargeon, Needham and DeVos (1991) have shown that infants as young as three months express surprise when support relations are violated. Kolstad (1991, cited in Mandler 1992) found that infants of five and a half months showed surprise when containers without bottoms appeared to hold things. Some basic theory of containment and containers as places where things appear and disappear seems to explain five-month-old infants' better performance on object-hiding tasks when the occluding object consists of an upright container rather than a screen or an inverted container (Lloyd, Sinha and Freeman, 1981). As Mandler puts it: 'Basic, recurrent experiences with the world form the bedrock of the child's semantic architecture, which is already established well before the child begins producing language' (Mandler, 1992: 597). This experientially based semantic architecture is in turn recruited for the conceptualization and articulation of more abstract concepts and relations. Redescriptions 'are not only used to create meanings but also to help form the specific ... [conceptual representations] ... that instantiate them and to understand the words that refer to them. In summary, perceptual analysis operates on perceptual information, leading to ... [redescriptions] ..., which in turn form the foundation of the conceptual system, a system that is accessible first via imagery and later via language as well' (Mandler, 1992: 592).

The nature of lexical representation

A basic tenet of our approach (and the cognitive linguistic enterprise more generally) is that the meaning associated with an individual lexeme is conceptual in nature. That is, the meanings associated with words are instantiated in semantic memory not in terms of linguistic or semantic features, nor as abstract propositions, but rather meaning prompted for by symbols such as words, morphemes and grammatical constructions (in the sense of Goldberg, 1995) constitutes a redescription of perceptual information, at some level related to external sensorimotor experience. One attempt to model such conceptual representations has been termed an *image-schema* (cf. Lakoff, 1987; Johnson, 1987; Mandler, 1992). Image-schemas constitute an attempt to understand conceptual structure or concepts not in terms of propositional information, but as redescriptions of spatio-physical, that is, external experience. While we agree that a significant portion of conceptual structure is external in origin, there is a body of evidence which suggests that a portion of conceptual structure represents a redescription not of external perceptory experience, but rather of internal perceptory experience (Evans, 2000; Grady, 1997a). Evans (2000) argues that concepts for time, for instance, do not ultimately originate in redescriptions of external sensorimotor experience, although they are elaborated, in part, by redescribed external content. As we feel it is unsafe to claim that all conceptual structure can be accurately modelled in terms of image-schemas, as envisaged by scholars such as Lakoff and Johnson, we will refrain from employing this term, and refer to mental representations as redescriptions (i.e., perceptual information, which could be external or internal in origin, see Evans, 2000; Tyler and Evans, 2001a).

Nevertheless, whatever stance is taken regarding the nature of conceptual representations, we concur with previous scholars working within cognitive linguistics that the nature of such representations necessarily reflects embodiment. That is, as meaning is itself embodied (determined by the nature of our bodies), then the conceptual redescriptions will reflect this fact at the conceptual level. This fundamental assumption stands in sharp contrast to other approaches towards the nature and organization of the mental lexicon, which represent lexical items as bundles of semantic, syntactic and morphological features. Ungerer and Schmid (1996) refer to such approaches to lexical semantics as positing 'linguistic' representations.

An analysis of the lexicon that relies on linguistic representation argues for a strict categorical definition of lexical items, in which a category is defined by a limited set of necessary and sufficient conditions. These conditions stipulate that meanings should be represented as discrete, listable features. Not surprisingly, cognitive linguistics also takes a substantially different perspective on lexemes as discrete categories and the mental lexicon as a list of these discrete categories. Instead, the lexicon is seen as constituting a highly complex and elaborate network of form-meaning associations in which each form is paired with a semantic network or continuum (see Brisard, 1997; Evans, 2000; Sandra and Rice, 1995; Tyler and Evans, 2001b). Under such an analysis, the relations within the lexicon are much more motivated and far less arbitrary than has traditionally been assumed (see Dirven, 1993; Lakoff, 1987).

Cognitive semanticists have argued that polysemous lexemes, such as English spatial particles, form semantic polysemy networks. Such analyses have traditionally attempted to model the lexicon in terms of a radiating lattice structure, reflecting the working assumption adopted by cognitive semanticists which views the lexicon as a 'mental coordinate system' (Rice, 1993: 206). Within a semantic polysemy network, a lexical item has been treated as a conceptual category, which subsumes a variety of distinct but related (i.e., polysemous) meanings or senses. Each sense is treated within the network as a node. Such networks are typically diagrammed with one sense being central from which other senses are derived in radial fashion. While we agree with many of the general assumptions underlying the semantic polysemy network approach, we will refine the notion of a semantic polysemy network in the next chapter.

We assume that polysemy networks form as a result of speakers perceiving communicatively useful connections between a non-primary use and the primary sense (to be explicated in chapter 3). Returning to the multiple senses of *over* with which we began chapter 1, we assume that these distinct senses did not just accidentally arise because, for instance, speakers could not think of another phonological string with which to label the distinct concept. Rather, speakers must have found something in the basic spatio-physical configuration of *over* which connected – in a way which was also discernible to the listener – to the concept of, say, 'completion' (e.g., *The movie is over* [= complete]). In other words, we assume that non-arbitrary, motivated connections exist between the primary sense and the distinct senses within a semantic polysemy network. This constitutes our polysemy commitment. The central issues facing a principled theory of polysemy networks, then, are to model (1) the appropriate representation of the primary sense and (2) the relationships among the elements in the network. In terms of the second issue, an adequate model of polysemy should be able to offer clear criteria for distinguishing between interpretations that are constructed on-line and distinct senses which have come to be instantiated in memory.[8] In the next chapter, we will briefly review how previous models have handled these issues.

Experiential correlation

We have been concerned in this chapter with the notion of embodied meaning, which, as has been seen, concerns the way in which the physical world of spatial experience is meaningful to us as human beings. One of the clearest examples of experience giving rise to meaning is the notion of experiential correlation, which has been explored in detail by Joseph Grady (1997a, 1999a, 1999b, in preparation). Grady notes that a consequence of the nature of interaction between humans and their environment is that certain kinds of experiences are frequently correlated. A common, recurring experience in the world is the correlation between the vertical elevation of a physical entity and an increase in the quantity of the entity, which is to say when there is an increase in vertical elevation, there is a correlative increase to the original amount of the entity.[9]

---

[8] We also acknowledge that a third type of representation of spatial particles in semantic memory is likely to exist. Spatial particles are likely to be represented as elements within conventionalized constructions. Within a construction, the spatial relation mediated by particular TRs and LMs in the context of particular types of verbs may involve additional inferences, and hence additional spatial-physical meaning, beyond that prompted for by the spatial particle in similar contexts in which the particular attributes of the TR and/or LM are different. Presumably constructions, with their specialized meaning, become instantiated in memory through recurrent usage.

[9] In earlier accounts, e.g., Lakoff (1987), Lakoff and Johnson (1980), experiential correlation and what Grady (1997a, 1999a) terms perceptual resemblance were not distinguished, and the two distinct phenomena were analysed as metaphor. More recently, Panther and Radden (1999),

By way of illustration, if there are two boxes stacked one on top of the other and a delivery person adds another two boxes to the stack, the height of the stack increases. Hence, height (vertical elevation) and number of boxes (quantity) are correlated in our experience. Similarly, if there is a certain amount of liquid in a container, and more liquid is added, the level of the liquid rises. So, humans frequently experience greater quantity in terms of an increase in vertical elevation.

The notion of two distinct experiences being correlated is an important one, as it leads to two distinct concepts becoming linked at the conceptual level. Because an increase in vertical elevation is typically a consequence of an increase in quantity, and this correlation is pervasive in human experience, we come to conceptualize greater quantity in terms of increased vertical elevation, as attested by the following examples:

(2.9)   Prices have gone up recently
(2.10)   The stock market is rising
(2.11)   She's just got her highest test score of the semester
(2.12)   The population size is on the way up

Consider (2.9). This sentence has a conventional interpretation in which prices have increased. Yet, this interpretation is achieved by utilizing the linguistic prompt *gone up*, which has a conventional meaning denoting vertical elevation. The point is that English (and many other languages) systematically utilizes expressions that conventionally denote vertical elevation to provide an interpretation of greater quantity. Moreover, assuming that language reflects thought, then the linguistic correlation between vertical elevation and quantity reflects the conventional association or link between these two concepts at the conceptual level. We hold that sentences such as (2.9) through (2.12) are not merely linguistic in nature but also reflect how English speakers experience and consequently think about the world.

Let us now consider another example of experiential correlation – the experiences of knowing and seeing. Typically, sight is one of the most reliable sources of information which humans have. On a daily basis, we confirm the perceived verity of the existence of objects and relationships in the world through seeing them. This is reflected in phrases such as, *I saw it with my own eyes*; *seeing is believing*; and *eye-witness accounts* (Sweetser, 1990). The centuries-old appeal of magic and illusion is that such phenomena confound our everyday reliance on our visual perceptions to provide information that we can reliably take as

among others, have argued that many of the cases which we analyse as experiential correlation give rise to metonymy. Under such an analysis, the reason for more and up becoming conceptually linked is that one aspect of an increase in quantity, i.e., an increase in vertical elevation, can come to stand for an increase in quantity, as an increase in quantity is entailed by an increase in vertical elevation.

reality. Having confirmed something to be the case through vision, we generally assume that we know that it is the case. That is, knowing is necessarily and unavoidably correlated with seeing in our experience. Accordingly, we conceptualize knowing and knowledge in terms of seeing and sight,[10] as illustrated by the following:

(2.13)   I see what you mean
(2.14)   I see what you're trying to say
(2.15)   Now I see! [= understand]
(2.16)   Your vision is just what our company needs

In each of these examples, seeing, sight and vision are conventionally interpreted as representing knowledge and understanding.

What is fascinating is that two concepts which are clearly distinguishable and in many ways dissimilar – quantity and vertical elevation or seeing and knowing – can become conceptually linked and, in turn, provide such conventionally accepted linguistic readings. Without pausing to think about this issue, we might otherwise miss the fact that when we say *I see what you mean* we are not literally talking and thinking in terms of seeing, but rather in terms of the experiential correlate of seeing – knowing and understanding. Grady has suggested (personal communication) that there may be in the order of hundreds of sets of concepts which come to be linked conceptually via experiential correlation. He has also provided a tentative taxonomy of many of these (cf. Grady, 1997a).

The kinds of experiences that are correlated in our experience are an unavoidable consequence of the nature of our experience, which is to say, the objective world 'out there' and our bodies. That is, while we unconsciously organize our experience, we are being crucially influenced by the very spatio-physical experience that we organize. Hence, our experience of space and physical forces are among the most primitive (in the sense of earliest and most foundational) and are those upon which our conceptual system is based. This point has been powerfully made by a number of cognitive scientists, philosophers and linguists such as Herbert Clark (1973), Bernd Heine (1997), Ray Jackendoff (1983), Mark Johnson (1987), George Lakoff (1987), Ronald Langacker (1987), Soteria Svorou (1994), Leonard Talmy (2000), Mark Turner (1991, 1996), and Francisco Varela, Evan Thompson and Eleanor Rosch (1991).

Given the nature of our experience, it is an unavoidable consequence that knowing and seeing come to be correlated at the conceptual level. Hence, experiential correlation provides a means for the instantiation in long-term memory

---

[10] Other sensory experiences, such as hearing, also provide important means of gaining information and hence can be associated with knowing. In English it is possible to say, 'I hear you' and mean something like 'I understand you'. Apparently a few Australian languages exploit the experiential correlation between hearing and knowing more fully. See Grady (1999b) for a cross-linguistic survey of experiential correlations.

of unavoidable conceptual links or associations. We would therefore expect associations between concepts such as knowing and seeing, quantity and vertical elevation, importance and size (e.g., *Tomorrow is the big* [= important] *day*), etc., to manifest themselves in a variety of languages and cultures. This is the very finding that work by Grady and others is beginning to uncover (cf. Grady, 1999b).

Perceptual resemblance

The process of experiential correlation provides a powerful mechanism for the associations between concepts strongly linked in human experience to be conventionalized in the conceptual system. A second process, which is less reliant on the nature of experience itself, also exists. This is the process of perceptual resemblance. However, unlike experiential correlation, perceptual resemblance establishes links between concepts based not on experiential givens (such as correlation), but rather as a result of conceptual organization and perception. That is, two concepts which are perceived as resembling each other in some way (e.g., perceived physical resemblance, or the perception of shared abstract qualities or characteristics) come to be associated at the conceptual level. Consider some examples:

(2.17)   She's just a twig
(2.18)   The new boss is a real pussy-cat

In (2.17) the perceived resemblance between the physical appearance of a person and a twig (presumably that in both cases there is no excess flesh to conceal the rigid structural material of the entity) causes the speaker to conceptualize the person in terms of a twig. Similarly in (2.18), the perception of shared characteristics between the new boss and pussy-cats (e.g., that they are typically friendly, domesticated, and relatively non-threatening to humans, at least, and in relation to other felines, such as tigers) allows the speaker of (2.18) to conceptualize the boss in terms of a pussy-cat. Perceptual resemblance differs from experiential correlation in that it is not experience per se which gives rise to the resemblance, but rather our perception of shared characteristics. Hence, perceptual resemblance provides us with a means of comparing and in turn perceiving (or creating) similarity and dissimilarity between distinct entities.

Many previous analyses have subsumed both experiential correlation and perceptual resemblance under the rubric of conceptual metaphor. In an attempt to develop a more refined understanding of how association and linking of concepts develops, we will not use the term conceptual metaphor, but rather use the more specific terms of experiential correlation and perceptual resemblance. We distinguish between these two processes in order to remind ourselves that perceptual resemblance is a process which relies on conscious human perceptual organization, and hence we are conceptualizing one kind of entity in terms of another. Crucially, experiential correlation leads to necessary and unavoidable associations between concepts that would not ordinarily be construed as similar.

A growing body of research by both developmental psychologists and language acquisition scholars suggests that both experiential correlation and perceptual resemblance are important in the development of conceptual structure in young infants. Christopher Johnson (1999) has been conducting research into what he terms the conflation hypothesis. This research, based on corpus studies of first-language acquisition, suggests that children originally begin with a single concept, for example seeing, which subsumes both seeing and knowing. During a process of separation or deconflation, the child begins to distinguish two aspects of the developmentally earlier single concept. These two aspects emerge as two distinct, albeit related, concepts. The notion of conflation provides a tentative hypothesis for understanding how the phenomenon of experiential correlation produces meaning from experience.

Similarly, a good deal of developmental psychological research with infants supports the conclusion that infants not only actively attend to sensory input from their physical environment, but also actively compare various sensory experiences to one another. Piaget (1951) documented that nine-month-old infants who were trying to learn to imitate acts they could not see themselves perform, such as blinking, often engaged in opening and closing actions of other parts of their bodies – such as opening and closing their mouths or their hands. Mandler was clearly struck by the 'perceptual analysis in which the infants were engaging and their analogical understanding of the structure of the behavior they were trying to reproduce' (Mandler, 1992: 598). This appears to be an early example of the process of perceiving resemblances in which the infants are comparing the opening and closing of their eyes to the motion involved when other things open and close.

Conclusion

In this chapter we have argued that meaning ultimately derives from the complex interaction between real-world experience and conceptual processes which create and organize this experience in meaningful ways. It is in this sense that meaning is embodied, as it can ultimately be traced back both to how we actually experience our world and to the nature of our bodies and neural architecture, which in part constrain and delimit the nature of the world for us. In the next chapter we will begin to weave the notion of embodied meaning developed in this chapter, and the view of contextual knowledge and word meaning developed in chapter 1, into a theory of conceptual representation, language and meaning construction.

3 Towards a model of principled polysemy: spatial scenes and conceptualization

In chapter 1 we saw that a spatial particle such as *over* has a number of distinct meanings or senses associated with it. We reviewed two positions that have been proposed to account for the relationship between such distinct meanings. The first, homonymy, holds that the meanings associated with a particular form are simply stored in the mental lexicon, as unique entries. While this position may sometimes be justified based on synchronic evidence – for example, *the river bank* versus *the bank of England* – in the case of a spatial particle, such as *over*, it demonstrably is not. For instance, Sandra and Rice (1995), and Rice *et al.* (1999) have found, based on a series of psycholinguistic experiments, that native speakers of both English and Dutch tend to recognize relationships between distinct meanings associated with the same spatial particle. The homonymy position ignores any shared similarities and interrelationships between the meanings of a form such as *over*, and would predict that native speakers would fail to find a relationship between the various meanings in a consistent inter-speaker way.

The second position, monosemy, assumes one highly abstract meaning, from which all other meanings are simply contextual variants. However, as we have already observed, some meanings associated with a particular form are context independent. That is, the range of meanings associated with an individual form such as *over* is so diverse that they cannot be straightforwardly inferred from a single abstract meaning as it occurs in context. This counts as evidence that contradicts the monosemy view, as we will see in detail in the next chapter. In addition, the experimental work by Sandra, Rice and their colleagues offers strong evidence that native speakers do associate distinct, conventionalized meanings with a single lexical form. As the monosemy approach predicts that there is simply a single, highly abstract meaning associated with each particular spatial form and that all additional interpretations arise from context, it fails to account adequately for these empirical facts. In other words, this view fails to distinguish adequately between contextual interpretations created on-line and conventionalized meanings, that is, distinct meanings represented in memory.

The position we advocate is principled polysemy. This position holds that a particular form, such as the English spatial particle *over*, is conventionally associated with a number of distinct but related meanings. However, principled polysemy also posits that not all contextually varying uses of a form constitute distinct senses. We will qualify precisely how distinct senses may be related during the course of this chapter. We suggested in chapter 2 that the distinct senses constitute a semantic network, such that the meanings linked with a particular lexical form constitute a semantic continuum. In essence, then, our proposal is that (the vast majority of) distinct meaning components associated with a lexical item, such as *over*, are related to each other in a systematic and motivated way.[1] The case of *over* will be taken up in detail in chapter 4.

The polysemy fallacy

Within the cognitive linguistic approach, treating lexical forms as being paired with a complex polysemy network fits with the more general assumption that as the lexicon and grammar consist of symbolic (form-meaning) pairings, they will necessarily be highly redundant (e.g., Goldberg, 1995; Langacker, 1987). This general position assumes that there cannot be a principled distinction between a highly productive rule-governed grammar and a lexicon that houses the arbitrary and the idiosyncratic. It further rejects the assumption that a putative rule-governed grammatical component could 'create' well-formed sentences by manipulating atomic elements from the lexicon in a recursive fashion. By assuming that linguistic knowledge consists of symbolic assemblies, a cognitive approach to grammar effectively treats the grammar and the lexicon as constituting a continuum (Langacker, 1987, 1991a, 1991b; Goldberg, 1995). As the grammar consists of a variety of symbolic assemblies, ranging from individual morphemes such as spatial particles, e.g., *over*, to constructions,

---

[1] We adopt a usage-based approach to the development of semantic networks as represented by our commitment to pragmatic strengthening. This entails the belief that inferences (which arise during the course of a spatial particle being interpreted in context), and potentially even other specific aspects of the context, can become associated with a spatial particle, eventually giving rise to a new sense being associated with the lexical form. When the new sense becomes associated with the particle, the context is likely to be apparent and readily recoverable by speakers of the language. Thus, the new usage is motivated and non-arbitrary. However, over time, the context that gave rise to a particular usage may become inaccessible to speakers. For instance, this is likely to take place when changes in custom and technology occur. At such a point in time, it is arguable that the sense is no longer part of the semantic network; although originally motivated, synchronically the sense may seem arbitrary to the native speaker. The two senses of *base* (i.e., the noun meaning one of the four 'stations' in a baseball diamond or the adjective meaning morally low or ignoble) represent such an example. Historically, the two senses are related; synchronically, native speakers appear to treat them as unrelated homophones. We suggest that certain seemingly anomalous uses of spatial particles are likely to be the result of the particular context that originally motivated the use no longer being accessible to native speakers. The ultimate consequence is that although there is much of polysemy that is systematic and motivated, there are also 'messy', arbitrary elements.

e.g., the 'Let Alone' construction, as in: *I couldn't run 5 laps let alone 10*, (Fillmore, *et al.*, 1988), and the 'What's X doing Y' construction, as in: *What are your feet doing on the table?* (Kay and Fillmore, 1999), to idiomatic expressions such as: *He kicked the bucket*, there will necessarily be a large amount of redundancy. That is, by assuming that a grammar does not consist of a series of rules, plus a lexicon, but rather that the grammar is co-extensive with symbolic assemblies, a cognitive approach posits that a grammar consists of a massive inventory of morphemes and constructions. Put another way, a cognitive grammar is a construction-based grammar. However, while accepting redundancy as an inevitable and important consequence of the flexible and creative nature of language, such an approach does not assume that a lexicon-grammar continuum need be inefficient. As Goldberg observes, if we treat the lexicon-grammar as an interconnected network, such a 'connectionist system can capture the redundancy without inefficiency by allowing inherited information to be shared information' (1995: 74). Hence, by treating the symbolic assemblies which comprise the grammar as being (more or less) related by virtue of semantic networks, the redundancy entailed does not imply inefficiency. Moreover, as Langacker notes in his discussion of the 'exclusionary fallacy' (1987: 28), there is no logical contradiction or inherent inefficiency in positing that a form can be both part of permanent memory and motivated by defined principles or identifiable processes.

This position contrasts, for instance, with linguists working in the generative tradition since the time of Chomsky (1957). Linguists working within this framework have made an a-priori assumption that the lexicon and grammar should be devoid of redundancy (cf. Chomsky's, 1995, Minimalist Programme, for a highly underspecified approach to grammatical organization). While we firmly agree with the cognitive linguistic position that language consists of symbolic assemblies (form-meaning pairings), and is highly redundant (as we will demonstrate in detail), there has been a tendency among some cognitive linguists, especially those working on lexical polysemy, to exaggerate the number of distinct senses associated with a particular form, generating more redundancy than is warranted (Evans, 2000; Sandra, 1998; Sandra and Rice, 1995; Tyler and Evans, 2001b). In deriving a theoretical model of polysemy, it is crucial to relate the model constantly to what the linguistic evidence is actually telling us. That is, a model is only useful to the extent that it provides a reasonable approximation of how language users might mentally represent the semantic network associated with a particular form (Sandra and Rice, 1995). Despite its utility in demonstrating the interconnected nature of conceptual structure, a model of polysemy is open to abuse.

Sandra (1998) has argued that some models of polysemy are methodologically unconstrained, and hence commit what he terms the *polysemy fallacy*. To commit the polysemy fallacy is to exaggerate the number of distinct senses associated with a particular form vis-à-vis the mental representation of a native speaker. That is, it constitutes fallacious reasoning in assuming that because a highly granular account may be plausible such an account is warranted. Yet, just because a linguist can come up with a highly elaborate, and indeed logically possible, semantic network for a particular lexical form does not entail that this is how language users represent the meanings associated with such forms. One reason why the number of distinct senses has been exaggerated is that too much importance has been ascribed to the lexical representation, and not enough to the context in which specific interpretations arise. Overemphasizing the information supplied by a particular lexical entry fails to recognize that lexical forms are merely prompts (or in Langacker's terms 'access points') for highly elaborate inferencing and meaning-construction processes.

One scholar who has argued that polysemy is more fine-grained than may be the case is George Lakoff in his (1987) case-study of *over* (Kreitzer, 1997; Vandeloise, 1990; Tyler and Evans, 2001b). To give a sense of the problem with Lakoff's approach, consider the following sentences:

(3.1)   The helicopter hovered over the ocean

(3.2)   The hummingbird hovered over the flower

Lakoff observed that, in a sentence such as (3.1), *over* describes a relation between a trajector (TR), *the helicopter*, and a landmark (LM) which is extended, *the ocean*, while in (3.2) the relationship is between a TR, *the hummingbird*, and a LM which is not extended, *the flower*. Lakoff argued that such differences in dimensionality of the LM should be represented as distinct senses (or distinct mental representations) in the semantic network associated with *over*. He termed this approach *full-specification* (see Lakoff, 1987 for full details and copious examples). From this view it follows that for a word such as *over*, there would be a vast number of distinct senses explicitly specified in the semantic network, including many of the metric characteristics of the variety of TRs and LMs which can be mediated by the spatial relation designated by *over*. While not in principle inconceivable, in practice, as observed by Kreitzer (1997), the fine-grained distinction between instances of *over* as in (3.1) and (3.2) provides a semantic network which is so unconstrained that 'the model . . . [allows] . . . *across*, *through* and *above* all to be related to the polysemy network of *over*' (p. 292).[2] Sandra and Rice (1995), based on their experimental findings, call into question whether the actual polysemy networks of language users are as fine-grained as suggested by models of the sort proposed by Lakoff. This is a view echoed forthrightly by Vandeloise (1990). Kreitzer (1997) observes that

---

[2] Future empirical analysis might find evidence that speakers make such fine-grained distinctions but, to date, the evidence does not bear this out. Although we cannot definitively prove Lakoff's full-specification model is wrong, it does result in questionable consequences, in terms of both its linguistic representations and the little experimental evidence that is available.

it is not so much the metric attributes of the TR or LM which are important, for example whether or not the LM is extended and vertical, but that the relative relation between them remains similar across uses of *over*. On this view, a spatial particle, such as *over,* does not denote a metrically ascertainable relation between the TR and LM, but rather, its use in sentences such as (3.1) and (3.2) is possible because the TR–LM configuration in both sentences is qualitatively the same. In both (3.1) and (3.2) the spatial configuration between the TR and the LM involves the TR being higher than the LM,[3] regardless of the metric properties of the TR and LM.

Moreover, a Lakoff-type analysis fails to consider that the detailed metric properties of LMs and TRs are often not specified by the lexical forms used by speakers in their utterances. For instance, the lexical form *flower* does not specify whether the entity should be construed as [+ vertical], as a tulip or calla lily might be, or [− vertical], as a lobelia or a water lily might be. Thus, in a sentence such as (3.2), *The hummingbird hovered over the flower*, it appears that the LM is not specified for verticality. This indicates that there must be a sense of *over* in which the TR is higher than the non-extended LM and the verticality of the LM is not specified. Thus, Lakoff's account results in the highly questionable consequence of positing three senses of *over* in which the TR is located higher than a non-extended LM – one which specifies for a vertical LM, one which specifies for a non-vertical LM, and one which does not specify for verticality and hence subsumes the first two senses. Similarly, Lakoff's model would posit three additional senses involving a LM which is extended, one which specifies for verticality (e.g., *a mountain range*), one which specifies for non-verticality (e.g., *an ocean*), and one which does not specify for verticality (e.g., *the area)* and hence subsumes the first two.[4]

Analogous arguments can be made for specification of the exact, metric relationship between the TR and LM in terms of the presence or absence of contact. Krietzer (1997) underscores this point with the example *Sam went over the wall* in which the precise manner in which Sam passes over the wall, either

---

[3] We will refine this representation of *over* in chapter 4.

[4] The variations among just the two attributes of +/− or unspecified extended and +/− or unspecified vertical results in nine distinct senses. Each time another attribute is added to the model, the list of distinct senses multiplies accordingly. Consider diagram n.2:

	+Vertical	−Vertical	Unspecified
+Extended	/	/	x
−Extended	/	/	x
Unspecified	x	x	x

Figure n.2

The predictions become even more questionable when one considers that five of the nine senses involve attributes being unspecified.

by jumping or crawling, is unspecified and hence the presence or absence of contact is unspecified. This indicates that there must be a representation of *over* which does not specify for the presence or absence of contact and only represents the spatial configuration of the TR being located higher than the LM. In sentences such as *Sam crawled over the wall* versus *Sam jumped over the wall*, even though the exact metric nature of the relation differs, the spatial relation between the TR and LM is conceptually the same as in the sentence *Sam went over the wall*.

In essence, by attempting to build too much redundancy into the lexical representation, Lakoff's model vastly inflates the number of proposed distinct meanings associated with a spatial particle such as *over*. An implicit consequence of this representation is that discourse and sentential context, which is utilized in the conceptual processes of inferencing and meaning construction, is reduced in importance, as much of the information arising from inferencing and meaning construction is actually built into the lexical representation.

Methodology for determining distinct senses

One of the problems noted by Sandra and Rice (1995) is that there appear to be as many different approaches of how best to model a semantic network as there are semantic network theorists. While we accept that all linguistic analysis is to some extent subjective, we propose here to introduce methodology in order to minimize the subjective nature of our analysis. We do so in the hope that other scholars can employ our methodology and test the analyses deriving from our model. That is, our aim is to provide the basis for replicability of findings, a prerequisite for any theoretically rigorous study. Such a methodology has been lacking in previous attempts to identify what counts as a distinct sense. Hence, our intention is that such a methodology may provide a useful starting point for other theorists in their attempt to conduct systematic studies of the polysemy exhibited by other lexical forms.

In view of the foregoing, we suggest two criteria for determining whether a particular instance of a spatial particle counts as a distinct sense. First, for a sense to count as distinct, it must contain additional meaning[5] not apparent

---

[5] By this we mean that the interpretation of the particle must involve meaning which is not strictly spatial in nature, and/or in which the spatial configuration is changed with respect to other senses. It is important to note that some primary (most basic, to be explicated) senses associated with spatial particles will crucially involve a coordinate system along the vertical or horizontal axes, while others will not. In chapter 4, we will argue that the primary sense associated with *over* does involve such a system in which the spatial relation of the TR being located higher than the LM is essential. But this should not be interpreted as a claim that ALL spatial particles prompt for such a system. While the English spatial particles *over* and *under* regularly code respectively for the TR being in a 'higher-than' or 'lower-than' position relative to the LM, the particle *out* appears to be insensitive to this dimension. Thus, we find sentences such as *The rain poured out*

in any other senses associated with a particular form, that is, a distinct sense must involve non-spatial meaning or a different configuration between the TR and LM than found in the proto-scene. Second, there must be instances of the sense that are context independent, that is, in which the distinct sense could not be inferred from another sense and the context in which it occurs.[6] In order to see how this would work let's reconsider the sentences in (3.1) and (3.2). In the sentence in (3.1) *over* designates a spatial relation in which the TR, coded by *the helicopter*, is located higher than the LM. In the sentence in (3.2) *over* also designates a spatial relationship in which the TR, *the hummingbird*, is located higher than the LM, coded by *the flower*. Hence, neither of the uses of *over* in (3.1) and (3.2) adds additional meaning with respect to each other. That is, the same basic TR–LM configuration holds in both and no additional non-spatial meaning is prompted for by one and not the other. By our proposed methodology, these instances of *over* have failed one of the two assessments and cannot be treated as two distinct senses.

In order to contrast the foregoing with an example that does appear to constitute a distinct sense, consider the following examples:

(3.3)   Joan nailed a board over the hole in the ceiling
(3.4)   Joan nailed a board over the hole in the wall

In these sentences the relation designated by *over* does not appear to be primarily spatial, in the sense that a relation along the vertical (up–down) axis is relevant. That is, the TR, *the board*, does not enter into a consistent spatial configuration vis-à-vis the LM, unlike the examples in (3.1) and (3.2). Rather, in the scene prompted for in (3.3) the TR and LM are horizontal with respect to the vantage point, while the TR, *the board*, is located physically below the LM, *the hole in the ceiling*. In the scene prompted for in sentence (3.4), the TR and the LM are vertical with respect to the vantage point and the TR is located next to the LM, *the wall*. In these instances, the meaning of *over* appears to be that of covering the hole and hence obscuring it from view. Clearly, this notion of covering and obscuring represents an additional meaning not apparent in examples such as those in (3.1) and (3.2). The fact that the usage in (3.3) and (3.4) brings additional meaning meets the first assessment criterion for whether this instance counts as a distinct sense.

In terms of the second, we must establish whether the covering or obscuring meaning can be derived from context. If it can be, then this instance would fail the second assessment criterion and so could not, on the basis of the present

---

of the sky (in which the TR is lower than the LM) and *The water bubbled out of the hot springs* (in which the TR is higher than the LM) which do not affect the basic TR–LM configuration associated with *out*. Whether or not a particular spatial particle is sensitive to the horizontal or vertical dimensions is part of its basic lexical entry.

[6] We will sharpen this criterion later in this chapter and in chapter 4.

methodology, be deemed a distinct sense. Assuming that the primary sense of *over* involves a unique spatial configuration between a TR and LM and that this configuration involves some sense of the TR being higher than the LM,[7] we see no way that the covering meaning component associated with *over* in (3.3) and (3.4) can be derived from context. In order to see why this is so, let us contrast this instance with the example in (3.5) in which the covering meaning is derivable from context:

(3.5)   The tablecloth is over the table

In (3.5), the TR, the *tablecloth*, is higher than (and in contact with) the LM, *the table*. As tablecloths are typically larger than tables, and the usual vantage point from which such a spatial scene would be viewed involves a vantage point higher than the table, the result would be that a substantial part of the table would be covered and so obscured from view. That is, the interpretation that the table is covered/obscured could be inferred from the fact that the tablecloth is *over* and hence higher than the table, in conjunction with our knowledge that tablecloths are larger than tables and that we typically view tables from above the top of the table. Such an inference is not possible in the example in (3.3) as the spatial relation holding between the TR and the LM is one which would normally be coded by *below* (i.e., *the board is below the hole in the ceiling*) rather than by *over*. Similarly, in (3.4) the spatial configuration between the LM and TR would normally be coded by something like *next to*. In short, unless we already know that *over* has a covering/obscuring meaning associated with it, there is no ready contextual means of deriving this meaning in sentences such as (3.3) and (3.4). From this, we conclude that the covering/obscuring meaning associated with *over* in (3.3) and (3.4) constitutes a distinct sense.

The two assessment criteria being proposed are rigorous, and in the light of future empirical research may be shown to exclude senses that are legitimately instantiated in the language user's mental lexicon and hence would have to be adjusted.[8] Nonetheless, without prejudging future findings, we suggest that

---

[7] Although there has been disagreement concerning the appropriate representation of the primary sense associated with *over*, all published analyses accept these two basic assumptions. Synchronically, evidence that the basic spatial configuration prompted for by *over* is something like a TR in a 'higher-than' position relative to the LM comes from sentences such as *The picture hung over the sofa*. In addition, the clear contrast between sentences such as *Nicole decided to walk **over** the bridge* versus *Nicole decided to walk **under** the bridge* provides strong evidence that it is plausible to take the basic spatial configuration prompted for by *over* to be something like 'the TR is higher than the LM'. Having argued that the primary sense for *over* involves a spatial configuration in which the TR is higher than the LM, we readily acknowledge that in many instances this spatial configuration is NOT prompted for by *over*. Our analysis attempts to model how these non-canonical spatial configurations have come to be associated with the form *over*.

[8] For instance, many native speakers assign an interpretation of 'crossed to the other side' to a sentence such as *Jane walked over the bridge*. We argue that this interpretation arises from the particular context which involves: (1) an animate, purposeful TR; (2) a LM whose typical function

this methodology predicts many of the findings which have already come to light, and hence represents a reasonable approximation for assessing where we should draw the line between what counts as a distinct sense conventionalized in semantic memory and a contextual inference, produced on-line for the purpose of local understanding. Moreover, given the current state of the field, which has hitherto failed to produce consensus as to how fine-grained a polysemy network should be, we suggest that the present approach represents an important step in the right direction. The appeal of such methodology is that it provides a rigorous and relatively consistent way of making judgements as to whether a sense is distinct or not, and provides methodology which can be used in an inter-subjective way.

Methodology for determining the primary sense

An equally thorny problem is the question of what counts as the primary sense associated with a polysemy network. In previous studies of semantic networks it has been assumed that there is a single primary sense associated with a spatial particle, and that the other senses are derived from this primary sense in a principled way. We share this assumption, which derives from our polysemy commitment (the view that speakers employ particular forms to prompt for new meanings because they perceive such new usages as being related to antecedent meanings already associated with the particular lexical form in question). However, one of the problems has been in deciding which is the primary sense, and even how 'primariness' should be defined. It is to this issue which we now turn.

In previous studies, scholars have often disagreed over which sense should be taken as primary or central. For instance, in terms of *over*, Lakoff (1987) following Brugman ([1981] 1988), argued that the primary sense for *over* is 'above and across', which Lakoff argued included a path along which the TR moves, as represented by sentences such as *The plane flew over the city*. Kreitzer (1997) disagreed, suggesting that the primary sense (*over1*) is something akin to an *above* sense, as in *The hummingbird hovered over the flower*. These decisions were primarily asserted rather than being argued for and were posited largely due to the notion of prototypicality.

Prototype theory derives from cognitive psychology and is most often associated with the work of Eleanor Rosch (e.g., 1975, 1978). This research was

is to facilitate passage across an obstacle (such as a river); (3) a verb which codes forward motion occurring; and (4) the occurrences of the spatial particle *over* (which we argue involves the functional element of the TR and LM being within each other's sphere of influence). However, it may be that this frequently occurring, contextualized use of *over* is represented in semantic memory as a chunk or construction (Goldberg, 1995) and as such has the distinct meaning of 'crossed to the other side' associated with it. How best to model such instances is, in the final analysis, an empirical question that awaits further investigation.

concerned with the categorization of objects. According to this theory, a prototype is the best exemplar of a particular category. For instance, for people
from the United States a robin might be the prototype of the category bird,
while a penguin which cannot fly but swims in the sea is likely to be perceived
as less prototypical. Cognitive linguists (e.g., Lakoff, 1987; Taylor, 1989) saw
the notion of prototypicality as a highly useful means of explaining some of
the inherent fuzziness in the way in which linguistic categories are delineated,
and argued that it underlies much of linguistic structure. In particular, Lakoff
(1987) argued that lexical categories and polysemy networks could be thought
of in terms of being structured with respect to prototypical meanings. On this
view, the distinct meanings or senses associated with a particular word, such
as *over*, are related in a principled way to a prototype. Lakoff modelled his
semantic network for *over* in terms of a radiating lattice structure, in which the
prototypical sense was positioned as central, while other senses were depicted
as being more peripheral.

If, then, we rely on the notion of prototypicality for determining the primary
sense from which others are derived, we have the problem of establishing what a
prototype is or should be. For instance, is a prototypical sense the most frequent
usage? Or is the prototype the usage which native speakers reach consensus
on as being 'most basic', whatever 'most basic' might mean? Or is it the one
which provides the richest specification from whose various elements extended,
'peripheral' senses can be derived? Or is the prototype determined by some other
criterion? Moreover, the criteria for relative centrality and peripherality, that is,
labelling the relative conceptual distances between a lexical prototype and its
various related senses, have been left wholly unaddressed. As linguists have
simply asserted what constitutes the prototype for a particular lexical category,
based on intuitions and assumptions which they have often failed to explicitly
articulate, we are in the unfortunate position that Lakoff (1987) and Kreitzer
(1997) can offer equally plausible yet conflicting views as to what the primary
sense of *over* should be.

While the notion of prototypicality has been useful in thinking about object
categorization, and the relationship between perception and cognition, it is less
clear that it represents a useful heuristic when thinking about lexical categorization (Evans, 2000;[9] Wierzbicka, 1990), particularly for non-objects, such
as relations and processes. Herskovits (1986) avoided using this terminology
altogether, preferring the term *ideal* rather than prototype, in her treatment of
spatial particles.

Some scholars (e.g., Sandra, personal communication) have suggested that,
although desirable, it may not be possible to show that one analysis of a primary
sense associated with a polysemy network is superior to another. The claim

---

[9] See Evans, 2000: chapter 3 for a critique of prototype theory in cognitive linguistics.

is that, given the current state of theoretical development, any analysis of a polysemy network, including what constitutes its primary sense, is relatively arbitrary, reflecting each analyst's own preferences or imagination. However, Langacker (1987: 376) has persuasively argued that we do have various types of evidence which can help us discover and verify the structure of a complex category. Building upon his suggestions, we advance a set of criteria that we believe can provide a more principled, inter-subjective method of determining the appropriate primary sense for individual spatial particles. As with our criteria for determining distinct senses, we see this set of criteria as beginning to build a plausible methodology leading to replicability of findings in an inter-subjective way. Advanced experimentation may eventually prove the criteria inadequate, but for the present, we believe they provide an important move in the right direction. We hypothesize that some of these same criteria may also be useful for other classes of words. However, it is important to note that because of the particular nature of spatial particles – that they code for spatial relations which may not have changed over the last many thousand years (i.e., the way humans perceive space may not have changed), and that they are a closed class – the nature of the primary senses associated with lexical forms is likely to be at least somewhat distinct from the primary senses associated with other word classes, such as nouns, adjectives and verbs.

We suggest that there are two major types of evidence that can be used to narrow the arbitrariness of the selection of a primary sense – linguistic and empirical. We suggest that no one piece of evidence is criterial but that when used together, a substantial body of evidence can be gathered. This *converging evidence* points to one sense among the many distinct senses being what Langacker terms the 'sanctioning' (1987: 157) sense, from which other senses may have been extended. We turn first to the linguistic evidence. The linguistic evidence includes the following criteria: (1) earliest attested meaning, (2) predominance in the semantic network, (3) use in composite forms (Langacker, 1987), (4) relations to other spatial particles, and (5) grammatical predictions (Langacker, 1987).

Given the very stable nature of the conceptualization of spatial relations within a language, one likely candidate for the primary sense is the historically earliest sense. The historical evidence shows that for the English spatial particles we have examined (with the possible exception of two particles), the earliest attested uses have to do with a spatial configuration holding between the TR and the LM (as opposed to a non-spatial configuration as in: *The movie is over* [= complete]). Since English has historically drawn from many languages, not all spatial particles entered the language at the same time and there are instances of competing near synonyms, for instance, *beneath, below* and *under*. In such cases, over a period of time, the semantic territory has been divided among such competing particles, but even so, they retain a core meaning that directly involves the original TR–LM configuration. Unlike words from many other word classes, the earliest attested sense for many spatial particles is still a major, active component of the synchronic semantic network of each particle. In the case of *over*, it is related to the Sanskrit *upari* 'higher' as well as the Old Teutonic comparative form *ufa* 'above' (OED).

Turning to the notion of predominance within a semantic network, we interpret predominance to mean the unique spatial configuration that is involved in the majority of the distinct senses found in the network. So, for instance, we have found, based on our articulated methodology, fifteen distinct senses of the particle *over*. Of these, eight directly involve the TR being located higher than the LM; four involve a TR located on the other side of the LM vis-à-vis the vantage point; one, covering, involves multiple TR–LM configurations (this is discussed in the section: 'Methodology for determining distinct senses', and, more extensively, in chapter 4); and two involve spatial reflexivity (this is discussed extensively in chapter 4). Thus, the criterion of predominance suggests that the primary sense for *over* involves a TR being located higher than the LM.

Spatial particles are involved in at least two types of composite lexical units – compound forms, such as *overcoat*, and verb particle forms, such as *look over* as in *Would you look over this letter and get it back to me as soon as possible?* Our examination of English spatial particles has revealed that many different senses in a semantic network can participate in these composite lexical units; however, there are some senses which do not participate. We suggest that participation in composite forms cannot directly determine which sense is primary, but failure to participate can be taken as suggestive that that particular sense is probably not primary in the network. Again, considering *over*, according to *Webster's New International Dictionary Unabridged* and the *Collins Cobuild Dictionary of Phrasal Verbs*, we have found no attested composite lexical unit for the On-the-other-side-of Sense which is found in a sentence such as *Arlington is over the river from Georgetown*. Complex lexical units involving this sense might be something like *overhouse* which would mean something like 'the house on the other side' or *kick over*, which would mean something like 'kick something to the other side'. As these composite forms do not exist with these meanings, based on this criterion, we would argue that the On-the-other-side-of Sense is an unlikely candidate for the primary sense. In contrast, a number of composite units involve the sense of a TR being located higher than the LM, as in *overhang*. This criterion, then, suggests that the 'TR is higher than the LM' sense is a more plausible candidate for the primary sense than the On-the-other-side-of Sense.

Within the entire group of spatial particles, certain clusters of particles appear to form compositional sets that divide up various spatial dimensions. For instance, the particles *above, over, under* and *below* appear to form a compositional set which divides up the vertical dimension into four related subspaces. (In later chapters we provide extensive evidence for this analysis, terming such groupings a *contrast set*: see chapter 5 for the contrast between *over* and *under*, and *above* and *below*.) Other contrast sets include *up* and *down, before* and *after*, and *in front of* and *behind* (chapter 6), and *in* and *out* (chapter 7). The linguistically coded division of space and spatial relations is relativistic in nature, depending largely on construal of the particular spatial scene being prompted for (Talmy, 1988a, 2000; Langacker, 1987). To a large extent, the label assigned to denote a particular TR–LM configuration is determined in relation to other labels in the contrast set. So, for instance, what we label as *up* is partially determined by what we label as *down*. In this sense, the meaning of a particle that participates in a contrast set is partially determined by how it contrasts with other members of the compositional set. The particular sense used in the formation of such a contrast set would thus seem to be a likely candidate as a primary sense. In the particular case of *over*, the sense that distinguishes this particle from *above*, *under* and *below* involves the notion of a TR being located higher than but potentially within reach of the LM.[10]

The choice of a primary sense gives rise to testable grammatical predictions. So, for instance, given our assumption concerning the communicative nature of language discussed in chapter 1, if we recognize that what are now distinct senses were at one time derived from and related to a pre-existing (i.e., an earlier) sense and became part of the semantic network through routinization and entrenchment of meaning, we would predict that a number of the senses should be directly derivable from the primary sense. This is consistent with Langacker's (1987) discussion of a 'sanctioning' sense giving rise to additional senses through extension. Any senses not directly derivable from the primary sense itself should be traceable to a sense that was derived from the primary sense. This view of polysemy explicitly acknowledges that language is an evolving, usage-based system. Grammatically, for any distinct sense that is represented as directly related to the primary sense, we should be able to find sentences whose context provides the implicature that gives rise to the additional meaning associated with the distinct sense. We have already discussed this notion briefly in the section 'Methodology for determining distinct senses' when we considered the additional meaning of covering/obscuring associated with *over* in sentences (3.3), (3.4) and (3.5). Recall that we argued that the use of *over* in sentences (3.3) and (3.4) revealed additional meaning which could not be derived from sentential context, while the additional meaning of covering/obscuring could be derived from context in sentence (3.5). We discuss this in

---

[10] In addition to the linguistic evidence, it might be possible to design experiments which tap native speakers' intuition concerning these compositional sets. Thus, this criterion should help establish an empirically testable theory.

greater detail later in this chapter in the section entitled 'Pragmatic strengthening'. By the criterion of grammatical prediction, sentence (3.5) constitutes evidence that a likely candidate for the primary sense associated with *over* involves the TR being located higher than the LM as the distinct, Covering/obscuring Sense can be derived from this primary sense and certain sentential contexts. Of course, the Covering/obscuring Sense is only one of fifteen; all other senses would have to be tested against this same criterion.

In terms of empirical evidence, much more experimental testing along the lines of that done by Bietel, Gibbs and Sanders (1997), Cuyckens, Sandra and Rice (1997), Frisson, Sandra, Brisard and Cuyckens (1996), Gibbs and Matlock (1997), and Sandra and Rice (1995) should eventually provide evidence which would help us judge the superiority of one analysis over a competing one.

The proto-scene

A basic tenet of our approach is that the spatio-physical world which we inhabit and the spatial relationships which hold therein are inherently meaningful for us. Focusing this notion more specifically on TR–LM configurations, we argued in chapter 2 that the spatial configuration associated with a TR being surrounded by a LM, as represented in figure 3.1, does not merely represent a neutral TR–LM configuration, but also a meaningful notion of containment. This spatial configuration is meaningful because there are typically real-world consequences which result from entities being involved in such a configuration. For instance, when a parent places an infant, the TR, *in* a playpen, the LM, the playpen (LM) serves to limit the infant's (TR's) activities, to locate the infant (TR) and to provide a certain amount of protection for the infant (TR).

In chapter 2, we also introduced the notion of a spatial scene. This notion constitutes the essence of this book; after all, we are attempting to account for the experiential and conceptual interactions which result in (and indeed form) spatial scenes. For our purposes, a spatial scene is an abstract representation of a recurring real-world spatio-physical configuration mediated by human conceptual processing. It consists of both configurational and functional elements. The configurational elements include: a trajector (TR), which is the locand (i.e., the element located) and is typically smaller and movable; a landmark (LM), which is the locator (i.e., the element with respect to which the TR is located) and is typically larger and immovable; and a conceptual spatial relation

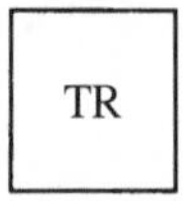

TR

Figure 3.1 Spatial configuration of containment

which denotes the TR and the LM. Returning to the example we just discussed, in the spatial scene described by the English sentence: *The infant is in her playpen*, the TR is *the infant*, the LM is the *playpen* and the conceptual spatial relation which mediates the two is prompted for linguistically by the spatial particle *in*.

The functional elements reflect the interactive relationship between the TR and the LM in a particular spatial configuration (Herskovits, 1986; Vandeloise, 1991, 1994). For instance, the spatial relationship described by the spatial particle *in* designates a relation in which the TR is enclosed by the LM. Put another way, the kind of LM associated with this spatial scene is one which is three-dimensional in nature, and the TR is located within the bounded area of the LM. As we have noted, such an interactive spatio-physical relation has non-trivial consequences; for instance the LM delimits the nature and extent of the TR's experience, such that the functional element is that of containment. It is in this sense that spatial scenes are inherently functional. Hence, spatial relations (coded linguistically by spatial particles; in English these are often, but not always prepositions) are conceptual in nature, rather than objectively existing in the world. Throughout this book, one functional element is identified for each proto-scene. However, we see no reason why, in principle, a proto-scene may not be associated with more than one functional element. It seems reasonable that human experience with a particular spatial configuration may be meaningful in multiple ways and thus be associated with more than one functional element. For instance, Beitel *et al.* (1997) argue that a number of meaningful physical interactions occur between the TR and LM in the spatial configuration coded by *on*. So in a situation described by the sentence *The boy sat on the table*, the table supports the boy, the table constrains the action of the boy (by not allowing him to move lower than the table top), the boy places pressure on the table, the boy's body physically obscures or covers part of the table, and the boy is more visible than the portion of the table with which he has contact. Although we are not convinced that multiple functions are necessary for the analysis of *on*, it seems plausible that these functional interactions (or a subset of them) might be best modelled by a cluster of functions, rather than a single functional element. In sum, in the analyses presented in this book, we will posit one functional element for each spatial particle, but we remain open to the possibility that multiple functional elements (or a cluster of functional elements) may be associated with a single particle.

In the previous chapter, we introduced the notion of perceptual analysis which, following Mandler (1992), we suggested constitutes the redescription of sensorimotor perceptual information into a form accessible to the conceptual system. That is, given that certain kinds of recurring experiences are meaningful, these can be redescribed as conceptual structures or concepts. Mandler argues that the 'accessible format' is probably not propositional in nature. For instance, in chapter 2 we provided diagrams for caused motion and containment. In order to distinguish the primary sense in a semantic network from the other senses that are ultimately (i.e., diachronically) derived from it, we use the term *proto-scene*.

A proto-scene is an idealized mental representation across the recurring spatial scenes associated with a particular spatial particle; hence it is an abstraction across many similar spatial scenes. It combines idealized elements of real-world experience (objects in the guise of TRs and LMs) and a conceptual relation (a conceptualization of a particular configuration between the objects).

Proto-scenes are instantiated in memory due to their frequency and utility in human interaction with the world. In our label proto-scene, the term *proto* captures the idealized aspect of the conceptual/mental relation, while the use of the term *scene* emphasizes spatio-physical and hence perceptual (e.g., visual) awareness of a spatial scene. For ease of explication we will diagram proto-scenes. Nonetheless, it should be noted that our diagrams do not make any serious claim about the neurological or indeed psychological basis of such conceptual representations. In our discussions of the variety of proto-scenes analysed in the remainder of this book, we will diagram the proto-scene for each spatial particle. Our purpose will be to attempt to identify, based on synchronic evidence, while informed by diachronic development, the way in which other distinct senses may have become derived from the proto-scene. For instance, the proto-scene for spatial scenes described by the following sentences:

(3.6)   The cat is in the box
(3.7)   The convict is in his cell

can be diagrammed as in figure 3.2. The TRs, *the cat* and *the convict*, respectively, are represented by the shaded sphere, while the LMs, *the box* and *the cell*, respectively, are diagrammed by the dark lines. The conceptual spatial relation holding between the TR and LM, coded linguistically by the spatial particle *in*, is represented in the proto-scene by the diagrammatic configuration holding between the sphere and the dark lines. The functional element of the configuration reflects containment. Moreover, the vantage point for construing

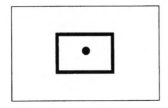

Figure 3.2 Proto-scene for spatial scenes involving the relation *in*

(i.e., viewing) the spatial scene is 'off-stage' (Langacker, 1987, 1991a) with respect to the spatial scene. That is, the vantage point, the construer, is external to the spatial scene. Crucially, the linguistic form *in* prompts for the conceptual spatial relation captured by the proto-scene. This relation places certain maximal constraints on what can count as *in*. In other words, a spatial relation should only be prompted for using the spatial particle *in*, if the spatial relation subsumes a configuration in which the TR is conceptualized as being contained by the LM, regardless of whether or not the TR and LM are in contact with each other.[11]

The notion of a vantage point mentioned in the preceding paragraph suggests that how a particular spatial scene is viewed will in large part determine the functional nature of a particular spatial scene, and thus in what way it is meaningful. We seek here to identify four distinct issues which affect the functional nature of a particular spatial scene, based on the different ways in which such scenes can be construed (i.e., 'viewed').

Ways of viewing spatial scenes

1. Every spatial scene is conceptualized from a particular vantage point. The conceptualizer represents the default vantage point. Accordingly, the same TR–LM configuration can be construed from many different vantage points (see Langacker, 1992: 288, who divides this phenomenon into two aspects, *perspective* and *vantage point*).
2. Certain parts of the spatial scene can be profiled (see Langacker, 1987, 1992). Thus, in the sentence *The cat is sitting in the middle of the circle*, the TR, *the cat*, is conceptualized as being surrounded by the LM, described by *the circle*; here the LM is being conceptualized as a container, and the space encompassed by the LM is being profiled. In contrast, in the sentence *Okay everybody, get in a circle*, the outer edge, or shape, of the LM is being profiled.[12]

---

[11] As we will see in chapter 7, for instance, the relationship between the TR and the LM turns out to be more complex than a simple geometric model would suggest. The consequences of the TR–LM configuration represented in the proto-scene, which we represent with the functional element, appear to contribute crucially to native speakers' interpretation of the containment relationship. For instance, entities involved in a *partial enclosure* relationship, which also involves support (e.g., a flower in a vase), can be construed by English speakers as being in a containment relationship.

[12] Cruse (1986) discusses this in terms of modulation of a lexical item. For instance, various parts of *the car* are highlighted in the following sentences: *The car needs to be washed* (where *car* is interpreted as 'the exterior body of the car') versus *The car needs to be serviced* (where *car* is interpreted as the engine) versus *The car needs vacuuming* (where the car is interpreted as the interior), etc. This constitutes modulation or highlighting different parts and backgrounding others.

3. Related to 2 above is the fact that the same scene can be construed in different ways. For instance, in a spatial scene in which a large cloth is positioned in relation to a table such that the cloth covers the top of the table, the scene can be construed by focusing on contact between the cloth and the table. In this case, the scene is likely to be coded in English by the sentence: *The tablecloth is on the table*. Alternatively, the relationship between the cloth and the table can be viewed as the cloth occluding the table from the observer's view. In this case, the spatial scene might be coded as: *The cloth is over the table*. A less typical, but perfectly acceptable, construal would be to place the table in focus, in which case the coding would be something like: *The table is under the tablecloth*.

4. The exact properties of the entities that are conceptualized as TR and LM can vary. In the sentence: *The present is in the box with the blue lid*, the LM is conceptualized as closed on all six sides; whereas in the sentence: *She peeked in at the kittens in the box*, the container is closed on only five sides.

Atemporality

In advancing our model of word meaning upon which we will base our analysis of spatial particles throughout this book, we note, following Langacker (1987, 1992) and Talmy (1988b, 2000) that spatial particles profile (i.e., designate) a spatio-functional relation which is scanned (i.e., apprehended) in summary fashion.[13] That is, they do not profile a relation that evolves through time, as is the case, for example, with verbs. Verbs typically profile processes that are scanned in serial fashion. For instance, in the sentence: *The boy runs home from school*, the process profiled by *run* constitutes a process that integrates all the points occupied by the TR, *the boy*, which intervene between school and home; hence the process evolves through time by integrating these sequential components. The result is a process that is sequential in nature. This contrasts with the relations described by a spatial particle that does not profile a relation which evolves through time. Spatial particles represent a conceptualized relation holding between two entities (a TR and a LM), independent of sequentially

---

[13] Langacker (1987, 1992, and elsewhere) discusses the atemporal nature of spatial particles in terms of the relationships they profile. As he observes:

> With *before* and *after*, time functions as the domain in which the profiled relationship is manifested. Its role is consequently analogous to that of space in the basic sense of *in, on* or *near*. A verb, on the other hand, is said to be temporal in a very different way ... the profiled relationship is conceived as evolving through time and is scanned sequentially along this temporal axis. It is by incorporating this further level of conceptual organization that *precede* and *follow* differ from the prepositions *before* and *after* ... [Verbs] specifically track [a process] through time ... A preposition can thus be characterized as profiling an atemporal relation that incorporates a salient landmark. (Langacker, 1992: 292)

evolving interdependencies. In this sense, spatial particles can be considered to profile atemporal relations.

On-line meaning construction

We have argued that some previous approaches to polysemy have been too fine-grained. As already intimated, a notable example is Lakoff's (1987) analysis of *over*. By attempting to fully specify all possible contexts in which the form *over* can appear, Lakoff failed to take account of the crucial role of context and infer-encing abilities based on context of use (cf. Green, 1989; Grice, 1975; Levinson, 1983; Sperber and Wilson, 1986; for detailed critiques of Lakoff's analysis see Kreitzer, 1997; Tyler and Evans, 2001b; Vandeloise, 1990). In short, such a fully specified approach fails to acknowledge that linguistic elements, while crucially important in the meaning-construction process, are merely prompts for conceptualizations which are far more complex than the conventionalized representations encoded by lexical forms. That is, the distinct senses associated with a form such as *over* are not 'fully specified', in the sense of Lakoff. Rather, they are sufficiently abstract representations, such that when integrated at the conceptual level with contextual cues, a range of on-line interpretations can be derived. These interpretations, which are created for the purposes of local un-derstanding, fill in the relevant details of the scene being specified. For instance, Lakoff argues that the uses of *over* in examples (3.8) and (3.9) represent two distinct senses below because in (3.8) the LM is extended while in (3.9) the LM is not extended:

(3.8)   The plane flew over the city
(3.9)   The bird flew over the wall

Lakoff further argues that the sense of *over* in (3.8) is distinct from the sense of *over* in sentences such as (3.1), *The plane hovered over the ocean*, and the sense of *over* in (3.9) is distinct from the sense of *over* in (3.2), *The hummingbird hovered over the flower*, because in (3.8) and (3.9) there is a path associated with *over* while in (3.1) and (3.2) there is no path.[14]

As in the argument we presented concerning sentences (3.1) and (3.2), we suggest that the interpretations that the TR in (3.8) moves above and across a horizontally extended LM, while in (3.9) the TR moves above and across a non-extended LM, derive from such information being filled-in by context, rather than the semantic representations associated with the lexical form *over* specifying prescribed contexts of use. While *over* prescribes a configuration

---

[14] Specifically Lakoff associates path with a moving trajector. For instance, in explaining his diagram for the sentence *The plane flew over* he states: 'The arrow in the figure represents the path that the TR is moving along' (1987: 419).

between a TR and a LM, the exact metric details of the TR and LM derive, we suggest, from contextual inferencing.

Similarly, we will argue in chapter 4 that the Above–across Path Sense posited by Lakoff is not explicitly coded by the lexical representation associated with *over*, but is constructed on-line, a consequence of integrating contextual cues and the encyclopedic knowledge we possess concerning planes, birds and the kinds of activities they can engage in. Thus, we take the position that while some spatial particles can include a representation for path in their proto-scene (cf. *through*, for instance, discussed in chapter 7), in the case of *over*, this form does not have a Path Sense associated with it. For instance, we will argue that in sentences such as:

(3.10)   The cat jumped over the wall

just because the sentence prompts for an interpretation in which the TR, *the cat*, is conceptualized as undergoing motion such that it moves from one side of the wall to the other (and thus follows a trajectory), it does not follow that the sense of motion is being explicitly coded for by the spatial particle.

We suggest that an interpretation of motion typically derives from the verb (although not always inevitably, e.g., *The plane is over the Atlantic right now*, where the inference of motion derives not from the stative *be*, but rather our knowledge of planes), as interpreted in a sentential context. Linguistic support for this position comes from sentences such as:

(3.11)   I can tell from all the noise that the helicopter is over my building right now

Parallel to the sentence *John went over the wall*, which is unspecified for presence or absence of contact between the TR and the LM, the sentence in (3.11) is unspecified for whether or not the helicopter is moving along a trajectory (or if it is moving along a trajectory, what the shape of the trajectory might be). We can think of at least three possible scenarios: (1) The helicopter is flying above and across the building; (2) The helicopter is hovering and thus in a relatively stable position above the building; and (3) The helicopter is circling above the building. Thus, it appears that there must be a distinct sense of *over* which does not specify for a path and hence would subsume both a sense which specifies for an above-and-across path and a sense in which there is no path, not to mention senses involving a zig-zagging path or a circular path. We take the position that the precise nature of motion involved is a consequence of on-line meaning construction, for the purposes of local understanding, rather than a Path Sense being associated with *over*.

In our previous discussions, we have used the term conceptualization in a non-technical way. In order to distinguish our non-technical usage from a more sharpened operationalization, we here introduce the term *complex conceptualization*. Informally, a complex conceptualization is the mental representation that results from the interpretation of an utterance. A complex conceptualization is a constructed representation,[15] typically (but not inevitably) produced on-line. A complex conceptualization represents our projection of reality (see Jackendoff, 1983) and can represent static spatial scenes, for example *The picture is over the mantel*, or spatial scenes involving dynamic phenomena, for example *The cat ran over the hill and ended up several miles away*. Our claim is, then, that the integration of the semantic representations associated with linguistic forms, contextual cues and encyclopedic knowledge prompts for the construction of a complex conceptualization.

Inferencing strategies

In deriving on-line interpretations, there are a number of inferencing strategies which listeners employ. Owing to constraints on space we will mention just three of the most important. In chapter 4 we will provide a detailed illustration of how these strategies enable us to produce meaning on-line.

1. BEST FIT: Only a tiny fraction of all possible spatial relations are coded by discrete lexical items. In linguistic terms spatial particles represent a closed class. That is, English speakers have a limited set of linguistic choices to represent a virtually unlimited set of conceptual spatial relations. Speakers choose the spatial particle which offers the best fit between the conceptual spatial relation and the speaker's communicative needs. The notion of best fit represents a crucial means for allowing us to fill in information regarding a particular spatial scene, as will be illustrated in the next chapter. To our knowledge, no other linguists have specifically discussed this notion, but it seems to be a logical extension of the notion of relevance (Grice, 1975; Sperber and Wilson, 1986).

2. KNOWLEDGE OF REAL-WORLD FORCE DYNAMICS: Although a spatial scene is conceptual in nature, in the creation and interpretation of an utterance, the speaker and hearer will assume that all elements in a spatial scene are subject to real-world force dynamics.[16] For instance, in the interpretation of a sentence such as *The cat jumped over the wall*, it is assumed the interlocutors will apply their knowledge of the world, which includes the knowledge that most entities cannot float in midair, unless they possess the means or ability for doing so. General knowledge of cats includes that they cannot hover above walls and that they are subject to gravity, and that walls cannot be jumped through, etc. Hence, any responsible account of

---

[15] This is essentially the kind of cognitive construction Fauconnier (1997: 36) represents as taking place at the level 'C' or cognitive level.

[16] Unless the world being discussed is explicitly designated as science fiction.

the conceptual system and meaning extension must recognize the large body of real-world knowledge we bring to bear (often unconsciously) when constructing meaning. Vandeloise (1991) discusses this in terms of a naïve theory of physics which applies to how humans conceptualize spatial relations and use language to express those conceptualizations.

3. TOPOLOGICAL EXTENSION: This concerns the notion that the principles of Euclidean geometry do not hold at the level of conceptual structure (Talmy, 1988b, 2000). Conceptualized space and spatial relations are not held to be metric notions of fixed distance, amount, size, contour, angle, etc. Rather conceptualized space and spatial relations are topological in nature, that is, they 'involve relativistic relationships rather than absolutely fixed quantities' (Talmy, 2000: 170). Thus, a TR–LM configuration can be distorted conceptually, as long as the relation denoted by the proto-scene remains constant. Informally, a way to think about this is that conceptual space is stretchy. This is analogous to the surface of a balloon, which can be deflated and inflated. Consider a face drawn on a deflated balloon. In that drawing, the eyes, nose and mouth all have established relationships to each other. When the balloon is inflated, the precise distance between the eyes, nose and mouth changes; by squeezing more air into one part of the balloon, it is possible to distort the distance between the eyes, nose and mouth in various ways. However, the general relationship between these elements still holds. In terms of how this principle applies to spatial particles, we will argue in the following chapter that the spatial particle *over* denotes a relation in which the TR is above but within reach of the LM. The principle of topological extension allows us to account for examples in which, on first analysis at least, this relation does not appear to hold, for example: *The plane flew over the city* (i.e., the plane is a considerable distance above the city, yet is being conceptualized as within potential reach). This has sometimes been represented as the TR and LM being within each other's 'sphere of influence' (Dewell, 1994).

Pragmatic strengthening

Earlier in this chapter we presented a methodology for establishing when a sense is distinct and hence putatively instantiated in semantic memory. Given our assumption that the distinct senses associated with a particular spatial particle are related to one another in a principled way (our polysemy commitment), one of the purposes of this book is to understand both how and why new senses associated with a particular spatial particle came to be derived. In so far as what are now conventionalized senses at one time did not exist, we seek to explain how they are related to the proto-scene. Our hypothesis is that all the senses associated with the spatial particles we will analyse in this book were at one time derived from the proto-scene or from a sense that can be traced back to the proto-scene for each individual spatial particle.[17]

In terms of synchronic polysemy networks, the empirical work by Sandra, Rice and their colleagues, suggests that it may not be the case that a particular lexical form has a single primary sense from which language users perceive all other senses being derived.[18] Thus, their empirical work raises questions concerning the view that we can define polysemy as a strictly synchronic phenomenon in which there is a relationship that speakers are consciously aware of holding between distinct senses of a particular lexical form. This is an empirical question which we do not yet have sufficient evidence to address. If extensive experimental evidence shows that language users systematically and consistently fail to perceive some senses as being related, then we must call into question whether what we are terming polysemy constitutes a phenomenon that is wholly synchronic in nature. While we believe all the senses in a particular semantic network are diachronically related, in terms of the adult lexicon, there may be differences in the perceived relatedness between distinct sets of senses, due to routinization and entrenchment, obscuring the original motivation for the derivation of senses from pre-existing senses such as the primary sense for language users (cf. Rice *et al.*, 1999, in particular). Hence, one of the reasons we term our approach *principled polysemy* is to reflect the view that due to processes of language change, not all senses associated with a particular phonological form may be recognized by a language user as being synchronically related. (Other reasons for using the term *principled polysemy* include: (1) avoiding the polysemy fallacy by setting forth explicit criteria for determining distinct senses versus contextual uses of the proto-scene, (2) avoiding the intuitive approach to determining the proto-scene, and (3) explicitly articulating the cognitive processes, etc., that give rise to distinct senses.)

---

[17] All the senses we analyse in this book will be represented as part of a spatial particle's semantic network. Uses of forms whose interpretation can be derived from context are represented as instances of the proto-scene. However, as we have already indicated, this does not rule out the possibility that frequently occurring, contextualized uses of a form might be represented in permanent memory as parts of larger constructions. The answer to the question of how spatial particles found in frequently occurring contextualized chunks are represented in memory awaits empirical testing.

[18] As Sandra and Rice (1995) argue:

it is possible to hypothesize that: there is a one-to-one relationship between prepositional networks and their mental counterparts, with each linguistic node corresponding to a distinct local semantic representation in the mental lexicon of the language user . . . A weak version of the hypothesis would treat the networks as graphic representational devices for capturing aspects of language users' mental representations without the concomitant claim that they are a direct rendering of an underlying mental reality . . . The only claim would be that they are compatible with that reality, i.e., that they make correct predictions on actual language use. (1995: 102)

Lacking the requisite empirical evidence, we must remain agnostic on this question.

In chapter 2 we discussed the role of experience in deriving new meanings associated with particular lexical forms. For instance, as vertical elevation correlates in experiential terms in a tight way with quantity, forms which denote an increase in vertical elevation can come to provide conventional readings pertaining to an increase in quantity. It has been observed by a number of scholars that inferences deriving from experience can, through continued usage, come to be conventionally associated with the lexical form identified with the implicature (e.g., Bybee *et al.*, 1994; Evans, 2000; Hopper and Traugott, 1993; Fleischman, 1999; Svorou, 1994; Traugott, 1989; Tyler and Evans, 2001b). Following Traugott, we term this process *pragmatic strengthening*. This process results in the association of a new meaning component with a particular lexical form through the continued use of the form in particular contexts in which the implicature results. That is, new senses derive from the conventionalization of implicatures through routinization and the entrenchment of usage patterns.

By way of illustration, consider the following examples:

(3.12)   The picture is over the mantel
(3.13)   Mary bent down to look at the dead man's face, but there was a thick cloth over it

Let us assume for the moment that the proto-scene for *over* is that in which the TR is higher than the LM, as in the example in (3.12) (this approximation will be revised in the next chapter). At first pass, it seems that in the sentence in (3.13) *over* not only provides information about the spatial configuration between the TR, *the cloth*, and the LM, *the dead man's face*, which is to say that the TR is higher than the LM, but also adds the semantic element of covering and hence obscuring or occlusion. We argue that this additional meaning prompted for by *over* is a result of interpretation within the sentential context. That is, in the spatial scene described by (3.13), *the cloth* (the TR) is higher than *the dead man's face* (the LM) and the cloth intervenes between Mary and the face. Given what we know about the nature of thick cloth (that it is generally opaque) and human vision (that humans cannot see through opaque objects), then we understand that the cloth which is over the man's face covers and hence occludes the face from Mary, that is, prevents Mary from seeing the face. Thus, it is the context itself (via inference and our knowledge of the real world) which provides the implicature of covering/occlusion. If an implicature is recurring, it can be reanalysed as distinct from the scene of which it is a part. This reanalysis results in the conventionalization of the implicature as a distinct meaning component associated with the lexical form with which it is related, that is, *over* in this case. As a consequence, *over* has, in addition to its 'higher than' sense, that is, its proto-scene, a Covering Sense associated with it. Once instantiated in semantic memory this additional sense can be employed in new contexts of use unrelated to the context that originally gave rise to it. Thus, we will argue that *over* has developed a conventionalized sense of Covering which can be employed in contexts in which the original TR–LM configuration, which initially gave rise to the implicature, is no longer required.

Although we hypothesize that a conventionalized sense has become 'free' of its original context, this should not be taken as a claim that the existence of conventionalized senses somehow precludes novel uses of the experiential correlation, or larger metaphoric patterns of conceptualization, that originally gave rise to the sense. For instance, we will claim that there is an independent State Sense associated with *in* (chapter 7) which arose from an experiential correlation involving location and emotional states; when speakers use this sense of *in*, for example *I am in love*, they do not actually conceive of themselves as being physically contained or surrounded by the emotion. Although this particular lexical use no longer directly draws on the underlying experiential correlation between location and emotional state, the tight correlation between emotional states and location remains an important part of our everyday experience and continues to shape our understanding of the world. Therefore, it is still actively available to speakers as they create novel utterances such as *I felt completely engulfed by my fears; He felt trapped in his marriage*, etc. Thus, established senses are consistent with active correlation-based metaphors (cf. Grady, 1997a) that shape our thought and are, thus, reflected in our ongoing creative use of language. Nevertheless, these senses themselves are conventionalized and no longer involve the speaker actively drawing on metaphorical conceptualizations when the conventionalized sense is used.

Recurring implicatures that come to be conventionalized can result either from independently motivated experiential correlations (as discussed in chapter 2), or from construing a spatial scene in a certain way, that is, from a new vantage point. Examples will be presented of each of these in chapter 4.

The conceptual significance of syntax

Before concluding this chapter it is important to point out that we subscribe to the view that formal aspects of language, such as syntactic configurations, have conceptual significance. Given that syntax is meaningful, in principle in the same way as lexical items, it follows that differences in syntactic form reflect a distinction in meaning (Lakoff, 1987; Langacker, 1987, 1991b, 1992; Sweetser, 1997; Talmy, 1988b, 2000).[19]

In this book we are using the generic term *spatial particle* to describe the linguistic forms we are studying. However, this term subsumes a number of formal

---

[19] Langacker (1992) argues:

> An expression's grammatical class is determined by the nature of its profile. A noun profiles a thing ... The relationship [is] profiled by an adjective, adverb, or preposition [and] is said to be atemporal ... A verb profiles a process, defined as a complex relationship which is temporal in the sense that its evolution through time is scanned in sequential fashion rather than being viewed holistically. (Langacker, 1992: 289–90)

distinctions characterized by *prepositions, verb-particle constructions* (VPCs or phrasal verbs), *adpreps*[20] (to be defined), and *particle prefixes*. Prepositions are distinguished from particles, adpreps and particle prefixes (i.e., bound spatial particles as in *overflow, overhead, underspend,* etc.) by the notion of iconicity. That is, prepositions mediate a linguistic relationship in which the element in focus is coded by a form that precedes the preposition, while the non-focal element is coded by a form that follows the preposition. This formal organization, that is, TR + prep + LM sequence, iconically mirrors the conceptualization of a spatial scene, in which a spatial scene is conceived in terms of a TR which is perceptually more salient than a LM. In formal terms, the particle in a VPC is a more grammaticized preposition in that the LM is linguistically covert, that is, it is contextually understood without being linguistically coded (see Lindner, 1981; O'Dowd, 1998). Such particles form part of a verb-particle construction with a verbal element, and each unit (the particle and the verb) contributes to the meaning of the whole unit (see Goldberg, 1995, for a construction grammar approach; Morgan, 1997 for a study of verb-particle constructions). We introduce the term adprep to describe a spatial particle that has adverbial meaning. That is, certain usages of the form *over* are adverbial in nature, describing an aspect of a conceptual process, for example, *the movie is over* (= finished). Hence, each formal component: preposition, particle (in a VPC), particle prefix or adprep, contributes different kinds of meaning.

Conclusion

Our primary goal in this book is to account for the systematic, motivated network of senses associated with each spatial particle. In part this involves articulating replicable criteria and methodology for examining polysemy networks. Having set forth the goal of replicability, we add the caveat that language does not function like a logical calculus which would allow us to predict what senses will become conventionalized nor to establish absolutely a single, precise derivation for each sense (i.e., the 'path' of derivation). Our model attempts to set forth rigorous criteria for determining the primary sense associated with a spatial particle and for determining when an occurrence of a particle represents an independent sense in the network versus an interpretation created on-line for purposes of local understanding. In addition, we posit several general principles by which senses may be extended from the proto-scene. These principles are themselves constrained by our experientialist commitment. Hence, we provide a means of determining the range of senses a particular spatial particle may have

---

[20] The term *adprep* has been used previously in a related way by Bolinger (1971) and O'Dowd (1998).

and a principled way of identifying which of these senses should be deemed to be the primary sense.

In principle, a range of analyses for the derivation of extended senses are logically possible. But, if they do not adhere to the basic principles involving embodied experience and how humans experience the physical world (e.g., ways of viewing a spatial scene), they would be ruled out by our model. However, it is important to recognize that even with these constraints, different speakers may have somewhat different intuitions or conceptualizations concerning the precise relationship between the proto-scene and a particular 'extended' sense. This variability represents the fact that spatial scenes are complex and can be construed in many ways and hence that multiple motivations may exist for the derivation of some senses (cf. the multiple ways in which the Reflexive Sense for *over* may have been derived, discussed in chapter 4). Introspective responses from various native speakers of English suggest that, in certain cases, speakers do have different conceptualizations of how a particular sense is related to the proto-scene. In other words, language users when questioned do seem to posit different motivations for a particular sense, that is, different 'routes' of derivation. Hence, when we argue that our methodology aims for intersubjectivity and replicability, we claim that the proto-scene and the extended senses associated with a particular spatial particle are shared among language users, but that, in certain instances, there may be different experiential correlations or different construals of a scene that result in multiple motivations for an extended sense. Nevertheless, using our methodology, analysts should be able to agree on a delimited set of potential motivations for distinct senses.

In accordance with our basic assumptions laid out in chapter one, we advance the hypothesis that the synchronic network reflects many aspects of its diachronic development. The remainder of the book consists of application of the model of word meaning and meaning construction adduced in this and the two previous chapters. Chapters 4 and 5 present an analysis of spatial scenes of verticality. Chapter 6 concerns spatial scenes pertaining to orientation, while chapter 7 analyses spatial scenes involving what we term bounded landmarks (LMs).

We begin, in chapter 4, with an analysis of the spatial particle *over*. We do so as this has been one of the most studied words in recent history (Brugman, [1981] 1988; Brugman and Lakoff, 1988; Dewell, 1994; Kreitzer, 1997; Lakoff, 1987; Tyler and Evans, 2001b). Accordingly, it represents an excellent arena for demonstrating in detail exactly how the model adduced above applies to the analysis of natural language, conceptualization and meaning construction.

4. The semantic network for *over*

For a model of polysemy, it is not sufficient simply to describe the senses that exist in the network. We must also provide an explanation of how they came to be there and how they are distinct from locally constructed (i.e., on-line) meanings, which are not instantiated in memory. Our account will show how the model outlined in the previous chapter will achieve each of these objectives. For instance, we will employ our methodology for identifying distinct senses. We will illustrate how the notion of pragmatic strengthening serves to conventionalize implicatures that derive from language use and the nature of spatio-physical experience. We will also show how the inferencing strategies we discussed in chapter 3 serve to provide on-line interpretations, created for the purpose of local understanding. However, before proceeding with these issues, we must first identify the proto-scene for *over*, from which the other senses are derived diachronically in a principled manner. Accordingly, our discussion of *over* will serve as our primary illustration of how the model adduced in chapter 3 applies. Consequently, this chapter will be somewhat more detailed than most ensuing chapters.

The proto-scene for *over*

In chapter 3, we provided five linguistic criteria for adducing the primary sense associated with a semantic network. To illustrate the application of each of those criteria, we used *over* as our primary example. In that discussion, we essentially argued that all five of the criteria suggested that the proto-scene associated with *over* involved a spatial configuration in which the TR is located higher than the LM. Recall that evidence for this conclusion included the criterion that the diachronically earliest meaning associated with a particular spatial particle may constitute the primary sense (criterion 1).[1] According to the *Oxford English Dictionary* (OED), the earliest meaning associated with the form *over* relates

---

[1] Given our polysemy commitment (the view that speakers attribute new meanings to a specific lexical item due to perceiving the new meaning to be related to a meaning already conventionally associated with the particular form), it follows that we are assuming that the conventional association of meanings with lexemes is motivated rather than being arbitrary (although see our

to higher than, or above. The OED relates *over* to the Old Teutonic preposition and adverb *ufa*, 'above', a cognate of the Sanskrit *upari* 'higher'. The form *over* derives from an earlier form *be-ufan*, which was a comparative form of *above*. Synchronically, this 'above' sense is still quite apparent, as is attested by the following sentences that involve *over* and describe spatial scenes in which the TR is higher than the LM:

(4.1)   The picture is over the mantel
(4.2)   The bee is hovering over the flower
(4.3)   The tree is leaning over the river

In terms of the criterion of predominance (criterion 2), the analysis presented in this chapter will also provide substantial evidence that the majority of distinct senses associated with *over* involve a spatial configuration in which the TR is higher than the LM. In addition, the criterion of use in composite forms (criterion 3), the criterion of relations to other spatial particles (criterion 4), and the criterion of grammatical predictions (criterion 5) will be particularly helpful in providing evidence for a sharper, more accurate representation of the primary sense.

We suggest that at the conceptual level, the primary sense associated with *over* (and indeed, the primary sense associated with each of the spatial particles we shall be examining) is represented in terms of abstracting away from specific spatial scenes, such as those described by sentences in (4.1) through (4.3), resulting in an idealized spatio-functional configuration. This abstracted mental representation of the primary sense we term the *proto-scene*. In the proto-scene we do not have the rich details apparent in the individual spatial scenes. For instance, we do not have mental representations of pictures or bees or trees directly associated with *over*, rather our mental representation is a more schematic trajector (TR), which represents the focal element, allowing any kind of entity which can be construed as 'focal' to occupy this position. Similarly, rather than having a mental representation of a mantelpiece, a flower or a river directly associated with *over*, we have a schematic background element, a landmark (LM), which serves as the frame of reference for the TR. The proto-scene also captures configurational information, namely the conceptual-spatial relation that relates the TR and the LM. In each of the spatial scenes described by the sentences in (4.1) through (4.3), the spatial relation is one in which the TR is higher than but within potential contact of the LM. That is, the TR is close enough to the LM that, under certain circumstances, the TR could come into contact with the LM (e.g., bees typically land on flowers in order to gather nectar,

discussion of partial sanctioning, ch. 4, n. 4). This said, we believe that we are justified in taking the earliest meaning associated with *over* as an important criterion in deciding which sense should be taken as primary, as the other senses associated with the lexical item *over* must have (given our polysemy commitment) been derived from the proto-scene.

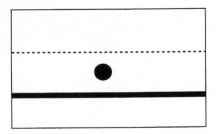

Figure 4.1 Proto-scene for *over*

trees might touch the river surface due to gusts of wind, and, over time, pictures may creep down the wall as their string-ties stretch with age). The functional aspect resulting from this spatial configuration is that the LM (or the TR) is conceptualized as being within the sphere of influence of the TR (or the LM) (cf. Dewell, 1994).[2]

This proto-scene is diagrammed in figure 4.1. In this figure, the TR is represented by the shaded sphere and the LM by the thick horizontal line. The area conceptualized as proximal to the LM (i.e., within potential contact of the LM) is delimited by the dashed line.

There are two claims that bear more thorough investigation resulting from the foregoing. The first is that the spatial configuration holding between the TR–LM is correctly captured by the description that *over* lexicalizes the proto-scene depicted in figure 4.1, namely that the TR is higher than but within a region of potential contact with the LM. The second claim warranting further scrutiny concerns the functional element: that the TR and LM are within each other's sphere of influence. Dealing with the first claim, the linguistic evidence suggests that *over* is at best marginally acceptable if the TR is not within a specifiably proximal range of the LM. The following sentence, from Kreitzer (1997), is only marginally acceptable:

(4.4)   ?The birds are somewhere over us

In sentences of this type (in which the TR is vaguely located in relation to the LM) it would be more felicitous to employ the spatial particle *above*.[3] As we will argue in chapter 5, this is because the proto-scene for *above* designates a spatial configuration in which the TR is higher than but not in potential reach of the LM; the vagueness of location, which is denoted by *somewhere*, implies that the TR is not within the LM's (*us*) sphere of influence. This point is even

---

[2] Recall that although we present only one functional element for each proto-scene, we are not in principle opposed to the possibility that more than one functional element or a cluster of functional elements may be associated with a proto-scene.

[3] Both Kreitzer (1997) and Lindstromberg (1998) note that *above* is more felicitous in situations in which the TR is vertically elevated and vaguely located in relationship to the LM.

clearer when, using the criterion of relationship to other spatial particles that form a contrast set, we contrast instances of *over* and *above* in sentences such as the following:

(4.5)   a. The cross-country skier skimmed over the snow
          b. ?The cross-country skier skimmed above the snow

In (4.5a) the conventional reading is one in which the TR, *the skier*, is higher than but within reach of the LM, that is, in this case, in contact with the snow. In contrast, in (4.5b), most native speakers of English would exclude possible contact from their reading. Since our understanding of the action of skiing involves contact with a surface, native speakers tend to find (4.5a) perfectly acceptable, while they find (4.5b) anomalous. These examples are strongly suggestive that we are right in positing that *over* does designate a spatial configuration in which the TR is in potential contact with the LM.[4]

Now, let's turn to the functional aspect of the proto-scene in figure 4.1, namely the claim that the TR and LM are within each other's sphere of influence. A consequence of being within potential reach of the LM is that the TR can affect the LM in some way and vice versa. For instance, due to an independently motivated experiential correlation, we conventionally understand power and control being associated with an entity who is higher than the entity who is being controlled (we will discuss the reasons for this in more detail when we deal with the Control Sense for *over*, later in this chapter). It is also clear that in physical terms, we can only control someone or something, and hence ensure

---

[4] Our focus is on uncovering the systematicity in the semantics associated with spatial particles. However, it is important to acknowledge that predictability and arbitrariness are graded in nature. Our investigation has led us to believe that the vast majority of instances of *over* (and the other particles we examine) are consistent with the parameters set by the proto-scenes we posit. However, we should not be surprised to find a small set of examples which fall outside the uses our model would predict. Whenever a speaker engages in the task of finding appropriate linguistic expression for a conceptualization, he or she faces a considerable challenge of considering a myriad of contextual factors involving (but not limited to) his or her interlocutor's background knowledge, social relations, physical setting in which the speech event is taking place, previous discourse, particular aspect of the conceptualization to emphasize, etc. The language produced in a particular context is, in Langacker's words:

a usage event, i.e., a symbolic expression assembled by a speaker in a particular set of circumstances for a particular purpose . . . [T]o the extent that [the language produced] accords with the conventional units in the grammar, these units are said to sanction this usage. It is crucial to realize that sanction is a matter of degree and speaker judgment . . . [Moreover] usage is not always so well behaved with respect to the canons of established convention. (Langacker, 1987: 67–69)

There can be a certain amount of conflict or strain between the specifications of the sanctioning form and the actually produced structures. In such cases, Langacker argues that the uses of the form are only partly sanctioned. Once a form is used in a particular way, even if it is only partly sanctioned, it has the potential of becoming part of the speaker's established repertoire, and hence, eventually a conventionalized use within the larger speech community.

compliance if we are physically proximal to the entity we seek to control. This notion that the ability to control something and physical proximity are related is attested by expressions such as: *When the cat's away the mice will play*. If, then, control and hence the ability to influence someone or something is dependent upon being higher than and physically close to the entity we seek to control, we would expect that these notions can be designated by *over* but not *above*. That is, while both *over* and *above* designate spatial relations which are higher than, only *over* also designates the functional relation of influence, which is a consequence of its spatial configuration involving the notion of potential contact between the TR and LM. In order to test this prediction, consider the following:

(4.6)   a. She has a strange power over me [Lakoff, 1987]
         b. ?She has a strange power above me

In terms of a control reading, while the use of *over* in (4.6a) is perfectly acceptable, the use of *above* in (4.6b) is decidedly odd. This is suggestive that the proto-scene for *over* does indeed have a functional element of influence between the TR and LM, as a consequence of its spatial configuration designating potential contact between the TR and LM. Further evidence for this functional element is evidenced by examples such as the following:

(4.7)   She watched the plane go over the city

In this sentence, while the plane is not within close contact of the city, *the plane* and *the city*, the TR and LM respectively, are within each other's sphere of influence. Hence, an inhabitant of the city can see the plane and presumably hear it, and its fuel discharge will fall on the city, leaving a grimy residue on windows, as any resident who lives under an airport's flight path will attest. We further hypothesize that this element of being within the sphere of influence of the TR (or LM) is reflected in native speakers' tendencies to use *over* in situations in which the LM is conceptualized as an obstacle or impediment to forward motion, thus influencing the TR's motion.

To this point, all the examples of lexical prompts for the proto-scene have involved an explicitly articulated TR and LM. However, the proto-scene is also apparent when the spatial particle is not a preposition, but has a different grammatical function. The following examples illustrate uses of *over* as a prefix. In these examples the non-*over* element constitutes a vertically elevated structure: *overarch, overbridge, overhead, overarm, overpass*.

The on-line construction of meaning

We have argued that not all meanings associated with a spatial particle such as *over* are stored as distinct senses. Before we consider some of the other distinct senses associated with *over*, we will first reconsider how on-line meaning construction might apply to the proto-scene (or indeed any distinct sense) in order to produce a contextualized interpretation of a particular utterance. In order to illustrate this process we will consider the Path Sense posited by Lakoff (1987) and Kreitzer (1997). Lakoff termed this the Above–across Sense, while Kreitzer called it *over2*. The intuition both scholars sought to capture was that *over* could be employed in order to designate a trajectory followed by a TR in which it moves from a position on one side of a LM so that it comes to be on the other side. Such a relation is illustrated in the following sentence first considered in chapter 1:

(4.8)   The cat jumped over the wall

Crucially, they suggested that *over* can participate in such a sentence because it codes a path as part of a distinct sense instantiated in semantic memory. Recall that in the previous chapter we introduced methodology for determining whether a sense is distinct or not. This methodology consists of two criteria: a sense can only be considered to be distinct if (1) it adds additional meaning not already available from other senses contained in the network, and (2) some instances of the meaning component in question are context independent. We suggest that in sentences such as (4.8) the interpretation that the TR follows a particular trajectory, described by 'above and across', is inferred from context. Hence, based on this methodology, *over* does not have a distinct Above–across or Path Sense associated with it.

The case for attributing an Above–across Sense to *over* in examples such as (4.8) relies on implied reasoning which runs as follows: (1) A spatial scene is conceptualized in which a cat starts from a position on one side of the wall and comes to be in a position on the other side; (2) there is nothing in the sentence, other than *over*, which indicates the trajectory followed by the cat; (3) therefore, *over* must prompt for an 'above and across' trajectory. However, this conclusion is a non-sequitur. Simply because a trajectory is not prompted for by specific linguistic forms (formal expression) does not entail that such information is absent. To reach this conclusion is to assume that the lack of formal expression coding trajectory information implicates a lack of trajectory information per se. On this view, all elements that are salient in the interpretation of a scene must be coded linguistically. This perspective fails to recognize the largely conceptual nature of meaning construction and the limited role in this process played by linguistic forms.

We offer an alternative account that argues that the meaning assigned to any utterance is radically underdetermined by the lexical items and the grammatical structures in which they occur. Rather, sentential interpretation is largely the result of various cognitive/inferential processes and accessing appropriate world knowledge. To illustrate this point let's consider the conceptualizations prompted for by the sentence in (4.8), and how it contrasts with the example below in (4.9):

(4.9)   The tree branch extended over the wall

Lakoff's full specification account for *over* would argue that sentences (4.8) and (4.9) represent two different senses of *over*. For sentence (4.9) he assumes that *over* has a meaning that can be paraphrased as 'above' while in sentence (4.8) *over* has a meaning of 'above and across'. The implied reasoning for adducing that *over* in (4.9) is associated with a Higher-than Sense runs as follows: In the interpretation prompted for by (4.9), (1) no motion is involved hence there is no trajectory; (2) the branch is located above the wall; and (3) the only element which indicates the location of the branch in relation to the wall is the word *over*; hence, (4) *over* must have an 'above' sense.

However, we suggest that the conclusion that sentences (4.8) and (4.9) represent two distinct senses is erroneous. Rather than representing spatial particles as carrying detailed information about each scene being described, we argue that they prompt for schematic conceptualizations (a proto-scene and other distinct senses instantiated in semantic memory) which are interpreted (or filled in) within the particular contexts in which they occur (recall our discussion of lexical forms being prompts for encyclopedic knowledge, in chapter 1). Under our analysis, while a Path Sense can sometimes be prompted for by a spatial particle, in the case of *over* it is not.[5]

In the sentence in (4.8), the verb *jumped* does prompt for a conceptualization involving motion, which entails a trajectory. Hence, the interpretation regarding the 'above–across' trajectory of the movement assigned to sentence (4.8) is not prompted for by *over* (i.e., the concept of 'across' is not a semantic attribute of the proto-scene, nor for any of the other distinct senses associated with *over*), but rather arises from the integration of linguistic prompts at the conceptual level, including the verb *jumped*. Most of the information required to integrate the linguistic prompts and construct a mental conceptualization of the spatial scene is filled in by inferencing and real-world or encyclopedic knowledge. In turn, this knowledge constrains the possible interpretations that *over* can have in this particular sentence. In the interpretation of (4.8), encyclopedic knowledge (as adduced in part by the inferencing strategy pertaining to real-world force

---

[5] In sentence (4.9) the lack of motion is the result of integrating what is coded by the verb *extended* with our knowledge of trees. In particular, the interpretation of lack of motion depicted by sentence (4.9) is the result of the interpretation of the verb *extended* as it relates to a tree branch. We understand trees to be slow-growing plants such that humans do not perceive the growth of a branch as involving motion. Thus, we interpret the verb *extended* to depict a state. Notice that the stative interpretation of *extended* is contingent upon the precise sentential context in which it occurs. *Extended* can also be interpreted to convey motion as in: *He extended his arm towards the door*. Since there is no sense of motion prompted for by the verb in the sentential context provided in (4.9), no trajectory is projected for the TR.

dynamics) includes (at the very least) the following: (1) our understanding of the action of jumping, and in particular our knowledge of the kind of jumping cats are likely to engage in (that is, not straight up in the air as on a trampoline and not from a bungee cord suspended from a tree branch extending above the wall), (2) our knowledge of cats (for instance, that they cannot physically hover in the air the way a hummingbird can), (3) our knowledge of the nature of walls (that they provide vertical, impenetrable obstacles to forward motion along a path), and (4) our knowledge of force dynamics such as gravity (which tells us that a cat cannot remain in midair indefinitely and that if the cat jumped from the ground such that its trajectory at one point matches the relation described by *over the wall*, then it would have to come to rest beyond the wall, providing an arc trajectory). Thus, we argue that the interpretation regarding the 'above–across' trajectory of the movement assigned in sentence (4.8) is not prompted for by *over*, but rather arises from the integration of linguistic prompts at the conceptual level, in a way which is maximally coherent with and contingent upon our real-world interactions.

But if the 'above–across' interpretation in (4.8) is not a distinct sense instantiated in memory, we must consider how this reading is derived. We suggest that part of the general understanding of this particular sentence involves the interpretation of *the wall* as an obstacle which *the cat* is attempting to overcome. Thus, there is an important conceptual connection between the TR, *the cat*, and the LM, *the wall*. Given this particular context and the functional element we have assigned the proto-scene, the salient point is that the cat jumped high enough to overcome the obstacle, *the wall*. The exact metric details of a spatial relation in a specific spatial scene are filled in by application of inferencing strategies, some of which were discussed in the previous chapter. These allow us to construct a likely interpretation, based largely on the extensive knowledge gained from our recurring daily interactions with our environment. To make this point more concrete, consider figure 4.2, which offers an approximate depiction of the complex conceptualization constructed in the interpretation of the sentence in (4.8).

In figure 4.2, the various positions occupied by the TR, *the cat*, along its trajectory are represented by the three spheres labelled A, B and C. Notice that

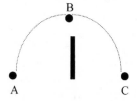

Figure 4.2 Schematization of *The cat jumped over the wall*

only point B, that is, the point at which the cat is higher than but in potential reach of the wall, is explicitly mentioned in the sentence (i.e., this point in the trajectory is explicitly prompted for by the occurrence of *over*). Points A and C are inferred from what we know about *jumping, cats* and *walls*. The verb *jumped* codes self-propelled motion using the ground to push off from. Thus, point A is implied as the initial point of the trajectory. Point B is explicitly coded by *over*. Accordingly, the prompts are integrated in such a way that the trajectory initiated by the verb *jump* intersects with point B. This being so, our knowledge regarding real-world force dynamics fills in position C. Put another way, if a cat begins at point A, and passes through point B, then given our knowledge of gravity and the kind of jumping cats are able to engage in, point C is entailed.

Many spatial relationships exist between the TR and the LM in the complex conceptualization represented diagrammatically in figure 4.2; thus, the speaker has many potential choices of which relationship between the TR and LM to mention. For instance, at both points A and C, the cat is beside the wall. The cat could also be described as jumping near the wall. However, none of these choices provides a sufficient cue for the construction of the relevant conceptualization that the cat jumped such that at one point in its trajectory, it was higher than, but crucially within the sphere of influence of, the wall. Thus, these alternative spatial particles fail to prompt for the key spatial configuration that prompts the listener to construct the complex conceptualization represented in figure 4.2. Given the conceptualization that the speaker wishes to convey, the speaker chooses among the closed class of English spatial particles the one which best fits the relevant (i.e., salient) conceptual spatial relation between the TR and LM at one point in the cat's trajectory, which will, in turn, prompt the appropriate entailments or inferences. This inferencing strategy we referred to in chapter 3 as pertaining to the notion of best fit. Accordingly, we reiterate that a serious flaw in Lakoff's full specification model is that it fails to distinguish fully between formal expression in language, on the one hand, which represents certain information, and on the other hand, patterns of conceptualization which integrate information prompted for by other linguistic elements of the sentence. *Over* does not itself prompt for an Above–across Sense, that is, for a 'path'. Following the notion of best fit, the relation designated by the proto-scene (and indeed other distinct senses) will not precisely capture a dynamic real-world spatial relation, which is constantly changing; in this case *over* provides a sufficient cue for conceptualization of the reading obtained in (4.8).

A number of native speakers have noted that a sentence such as: *The girl walked on the bridge* involves the interpretation that the TR was physically located higher than and in contact with the bridge, but did not necessarily pass from one side to another. In contrast, their interpretation of: *The girl walked over the bridge* entails that the TR traversed the bridge, passing from one side to the other. Lakoff, among others, would argue that a central sense that includes path, in conjunction with a transformation involving the assignment of end-point focus, provides the appropriate account for this difference in interpretation. The question for us is how our model, which does not posit a path component for *over*, accounts for this transversal interpretation. Following the model and methodology we have set forth, we hypothesize that the interpretation of traversing the bridge is a context-dependent implicature that arises from the particular nature of the verb, the TR and the LM as they are mediated by *over*. Specifically, we believe that the particular default function of bridges, that is, that they typically facilitate passage across obstacles such as rivers, contributes significantly to this interpretation.

Consider the following sentences in which the nature of the LM differs:

(4.10)   She walked over the ice/lawn/campus/picnic area/building site/familiar ground

Although all of these LMs are extended, none have a default function of facilitating passage across an obstacle. None of these sentences seem to entail that the TR traversed from one side of the LM to the other. Moreover, when contrasted with the spatial particle *on*, these sentential contexts do not appear to involve the same contrast as found in the 'bridge' sentences:

(4.11)   She walked on the ice/lawn/campus/picnic area/building site/familiar ground

With such LMs, only the spatial particle *across*, whose primary sense specifically involves path and traversing the LM, seems to entail the 'traversal' interpretation so strongly prompted for in *She walked over the bridge*.

Notice that sentences involving these LMs and other motion verbs whose interpretations indicate some contact with the surface also fail to prompt for the 'traversal' interpretation. However, in sentences where these same motion verbs occur with *the bridge* as the LM, a sense of traversal is implied:

(4.12)   a. She ran/twirled/hopped/danced/slid/scooted/skated over the ice
          b. She ran/twirled/hopped/danced/slid/scooted over the bridge

These data suggest that there is nothing inherent in the meaning of *over* which requires an interpretation of the TR traversing an extended LM when the spatial particle occurs with a verb coding for (generally) forward motion. The traversal sense seems only to arise with particular extended LMs (e.g. *bridge, railroad trestle, pedestrian walkway*).

Using the criteria we have posited for distinguishing between distinct senses and contextual interpretations, we argue that changes in the metric dimensions of the LM do not necessarily result in distinct senses. However, in real-world scenarios, entities construed as LMs obviously do have varying dimensions and default functions. The physical nature of the particular LM in conjunction with the particular action or activity coded by the verb can give rise to context-dependent implicatures. Some LMs, like bridges, are extended, pathlike entities which are regularly used for the purpose of getting from one side of an obstacle (like a river) to the other. Moreover, the functional element we have posited for *over* involves the TR and LM influencing each other. As we will argue in the following section, a common scenario associated with *over* involves the TR moving higher than and beyond an obstacle to forward motion. When such a LM occurs in sentential context with a verb of motion and an animate, purposeful TR mediated by *over* (with its strong usage-based interpretation concerning overcoming obstacles) one likely implicature is that the TR uses the LM for the purposes of passage. Since crossing bridges is a common experience, it is very possible that for many speakers the phrase *over the bridge* may be established in permanent memory with the interpretation that the TR used the bridge to cross to the other side.

The general position we have been putting forward is that the discourse and sentential context always determines whether or not *over* is interpreted as denoting a relation between a motile TR following a trajectory and a LM, rather than the path being conventionally associated with one (or more) of *over*'s distinct senses. By this argument, *over* fails our criterion for having a distinct sense based on the presence or absence of path. However, to this point, we have not offered any evidence that an analysis which posits distinct senses based on the presence or absence of path leads to inaccurate predictions. Using the criterion of grammatical prediction should provide such linguistic evidence.

If a path is conventionally represented in the proto-scene (or indeed as any distinct sense instantiated in memory) associated with *over*, we should be able to construct anomalous sentences in which there is conflict between the distinct path sense (or the distinct non-path sense) and the sentential context. In contrast, the position that a path is not conventionally associated with the proto-scene or any distinct sense leads to the following predictions: (1) We will never find a sentence in which the TR–LM relation is denoted by *over*, and the general sentential context prompts for an interpretation of the TR in motion, and the TR denoted by *over* is interpreted as not moving along a trajectory. (2) We will never find a sentence in which the TR–LM relation is denoted by *over*, and the sentential context prompts for an interpretation of non-movement, and the TR mediated by *over* is interpreted as moving along a trajectory. Support for this basic argument comes from the particle *across*, a spatial particle that does appear to code conventionally for a path. Consider the following:

(4.13)   #The helicopter hovered across the city

In this sentence, the interpretation involves a path, as prompted by *across*. Presumably a speaker would choose *across* only when the notion of path is salient. However, the sentential context contradicts the interpretation of a moving TR, and therefore the salience of a path, because of the meaning prompted for by the verb *hover*. Hence, the sentence (4.13) is judged as being semantically anomalous. We believe it is possible to create such anomalous sentences precisely because *across* does conventionally include a path as part of its proto-scene.[6]

However, we have not been able to discover similar anomalous sentences involving *over*. So in sentences such as in (4.14a) and (4.14b), whose sentential contexts involve a moving TR, it does not seem possible to interpret *over* as denoting a relation in which the TR is not moving along a trajectory:

(4.14) a. The Eurostar train, which is currently moving at 300 kilometres an hour, is over the bridge right now

      b. The Apache helicopter, which is at this moment flying north at 80 miles an hour, is over the crash site

We argue that this is because the sentential context prompts for a reading in which the TR is moving and over, and *over* is interpreted in a way that is consistent with the surrounding sentential context. However, we can force an anomalous reading by modifying the sentential context such that it also includes a reading in which the TR is not moving along a trajectory. In this case, the examples in (4.15) which are similar to the sentence in (4.13) are judged to be semantically anomalous:

(4.15) a. #The train, which is currently moving at 300 kilometres an hour, is **stalled** over the bridge

      b. #The Apache helicopter, which is at this moment flying north at 80 miles an hour, is **hovering** over the crash site

We note that this anomalous reading only arises when the verb (or some other elements of the sentence) explicitly prompts for a non-trajectory interpretation contradicting the information denoted in another part of the sentence (in these examples in the relative clause). Specifically, both the verbs *stalled* and *hover* indicate a lack of forward motion.

Similarly, it does not seem possible to form an interpretation of the following sentence in which the TR is following a trajectory:

(4.16) The helicopter hovered over the city

This sentence is in direct contrast with sentence (4.13). If the proto-scene for *over* involved an 'above–across' interpretation, we would expect that sentence

---

[6] *Across* can occur in sentences which do not involve a motile TR, but they generally involve a TR which perceptually resembles a path, as in: *John threw the rope across the table*, or *The clothes-line stretched across the yard*.

(4.16) should be ambiguous, with one reading ('above–across') – a near para-phrase for sentence (4.13) – being anomalous, and a second interpretation, involving a Non-path Sense of *over*, giving rise to a perfectly acceptable sen-tence. Since this ambiguity is completely absent, we argue that the linguistic evidence seems to point to the conclusion that the semantic network for *over* does not contain distinct senses based on the presence or absence of path.[7] Rather, the presence or absence of a trajectory interpretation is provided by the discourse and sentential context; only when *over* co-occurs with a verb of translocation (i.e., a verb which can be interpreted as designating motion from location A to location B translocating the intervening points) is there an inter-pretation of the TR moving along a trajectory, for example, *The plane flew over the city*. That is, the Path or Across component putatively associated with *over* may actually derive from the verb.

Following our methodology, a sense is recognized as distinct only if the read-ing occurs independently of contextual information that would prompt for that interpretation. As an Across reading is only apparent when it co-occurs with a verb of translocation, this suggests that *over* is not prompting for an inde-pendent Path Sense. While this conclusion falls out as a consequence of our methodology, we acknowledge that there is some evidence that senses may arise due to frequency of use (cf. Croft, 1998; Goldberg, 1995). To posit a distinct sense only when there is context-independent evidence for such may be overly stringent. However, the advantage of such stringency is that we have a clear lin-guistic 'decision-principle' for determining when a usage constitutes a distinct sense. It remains an empirical question, to be investigated via psycholinguistic experimentation, whether this criterion is too restrictive.

Despite the foregoing conclusion, there is at least some anecdotal evi-dence deriving from our analysis which is suggestive that there might be an

---

[7] It might be argued that this argument appears to be at odds with the psycholinguistic evidence. After all, psycholinguistic research indicates that when ambiguous lexemes appear in context, language users regularly select the contextually appropriate reading and automatically suppress any inappropriate readings. In typical processing, speakers rarely notice the potential, but anoma-lous interpretations of lexemes. So in a sentence such as *Jill took her jewels and other valuables to the bank*, the typical reading of *bank* would be 'financial institution' and the alternative 'side of a river or land' would never rise to consciousness. However, even though during normal pro-cessing speakers remain unaware of lexical ambiguity, upon reflection, naïve native speakers, as well as linguists, can evoke the alternative reading. So, it certainly is possible to come up with an interpretation that (for whatever reason), *Jill took her jewels to the river bank*. Furthermore, it is possible to imagine alternative but anomalous readings for other senses of *over*. For instance, in the exchange: *Do you know where Alexandria's house is? Yes, it's over the river*, the typical reading of *over* is something like 'on the other side of'. However, we can evoke the unusual interpretation of Alexandria's house being (somehow) suspended above the river. Thus, the in-ability to create anomalous readings involving the presence or absence of path associated with *over*, even when concerted effort is applied, seems to be a different situation from the normal suppression of an inappropriate sense during typical language processing of a sentence such as *Jill took her jewels to the bank*. Thus, we argue that this is a useful line of argumentation.

Above–across Sense associated with *over*. For instance, as we will see in our discussion of the A-B-C trajectory, certain distinct senses of *over* have developed from its frequent, contextualized co-occurrence with verbs of translocation. This strongly suggests that the correlation between the spatial relation described by *over* with translocation is salient in human experience. The fact that related senses have derived makes it appear plausible that an Above–across Sense might also be derived. One of the senses which derives from the A-B-C Trajectory Cluster is the Temporal Sense (e.g., *The relationship endured over the years*). As magnitude of duration correlates with journey length in human experience, it might appear a little unnatural that there should be a Temporal Sense and yet no Path Sense. However, we are dealing with linguistic (as opposed to psycholinguistic/psychological) evidence and to be rigorous we must base our conclusions on the data available to us. As a putative Above–across Sense would presumably necessarily co-occur with a verb of translocation, this situation means that we are unable to conclude that there is a distinct Above–across Sense, simply because there is no context-independent evidence of such, and we do not have direct recourse to language users' mental representations.

Thus far we have discussed the inferencing strategies of real-world force-dynamics and of best fit in deriving on-line interpretations. In order to illustrate application of the strategy that in chapter 3 we referred to as topological extension, consider the following sentence:

(4.17)   There are a few stray marks just **above** the line

This sentence provides, on first inspection at least, a counter-example to the spatial configuration we proposed for the proto-scene associated with *over*. Recall that we have been arguing that the proto-scene for *over* designates a spatial relation in which the TR is higher than but crucially within potential contact with the LM. On this view, then, we would expect *over*, and not *above*, to be employed in sentences such as (4.17), as this example is describing a spatial scene in which the TR, *a few stray marks*, is physically proximal to the LM, *the line*.

However, as we argued in chapter 3, the inferencing strategy of topological extension emphasizes that the absolute metric distance between the TR and LM is less significant than the functional element associated with a particular scene. That is, the metric distance between the TR–LM can be extended or contracted if the functional element holds. As already noted, the functional element associated with the proto-scene for *over* is that the TR and LM be within each other's sphere of influence. As we saw in a sentence such as (4.7) reproduced below:

(4.7)   She watched the plane fly over the city

the TR, *the plane*, cannot be thought of as within contact or even potential contact with the LM, *the city*, as the TR, *the plane*, may be several miles above the city in such scenes. However, as the plane can be seen, and perhaps even heard from the ground, and as residents under the plane's flight path may be affected by the plane, due to residue and debris, *the city*, the LM, is conceptually within the sphere of influence of the plane. Analogously, in (4.17), although the TR, *the few stray marks*, are metrically proximal to the LM, *the line*, there is no contact and no potential for contact. Hence, the stray marks are distinct from the line and the LM is not within the sphere of influence of the TR. As the functional element of the proto-scene for *above* (as we will see in chapter 5) places focus on the notion of non-bridgeable distance between the LM and TR, the relation in (4.17) is best designated by *above*. This analysis is supported if we attempt to employ *over* in place of *above*, *There are a few stray marks over the line*, which presents the ambiguous interpretation that the marks are in contact with the line and potentially obscuring parts of it. This interpretation arises from the Covering Sense, which we address later in this chapter.

Grice (1975) noted with his Maxim of Manner that in everyday conversation speakers generally try to avoid ambiguity, unless there is a purpose for the ambiguity. To avoid possible ambiguity, the inferencing strategy of attempting best fit in the choice of lexical item suggests that the speaker will choose the proto-scene (or particular sense) which best facilitates conceptualization of the scene he or she intends the listener to construct. Thus, in view of the strategies of topological extension and best fit, we argue that *above* is the most felicitous choice to prompt for the complex conceptualization that involves a LM (a *line*) and TR (*stray marks*) which are higher than and not in contact with the LM, as attested by (4.17).[8]

Beyond the proto-scene: additional senses in the semantic network

Our methodology for determining distinct senses, introduced in chapter 3, points to the conclusion that a number of other distinct senses must be instantiated in semantic memory (contra Ruhl's, 1989, monosemy framework).[9] We now turn

---

[8] We hasten to acknowledge that there are some contexts in which two spatial particles appear to be interchangeable and virtually synonymous. One of these is *Susan hung the picture over the mantel* versus *Susan hung the picture above the mantel*. We hypothesize that such substitutability arises because the semantic networks associated with each spatial particle represent continuums and that at certain points the interpretations of two continuums can overlap. Second, in the case of *over* and *above* we find a close diachronic relationship, with *over* initially being used as the comparative form of *above*. We suggest that the diachronic link may surface in these overlapping uses.

[9] Recall that we are using the term *sense* for distinct meanings instantiated in memory (i.e., in the semantic network associated with each spatial particle).

to a consideration of the distinct senses, other than the proto-scene convention-ally associated with the spatial particle *over*.

In our model, the primary sense associated with a spatial particle is the proto-scene. We hypothesize that the other senses in the semantic network are derived from the proto-scene in a principled fashion, a process that has been ongoing throughout the history of the language. Figure 4.2 (above) represents the complex conceptualization which would be constructed in the interpretation of sentences such as (4.8), and those given below:

(4.18)   The rabbit hopped over the fence
(4.19)   The boy stepped over the pile of leaves

We hypothesize that recurring, complex conceptualizations, due to their fre-quency, are likely to become entrenched and hence subject to reanalysis.[10] We suggest that distinct senses often arise as a result of the reanalysis of a par-ticular aspect of such a recurring complex conceptualization. In other words, the recurring complex conceptualization from which a distinct sense originally arises is derivable from the proto-scene and thus the resultant sense is related to the proto-scene in a principled manner. However, in many instances the dis-tinct sense is not directly derivable from the proto-scene within the sentential context in which the spatial particle occurs. In establishing whether a meaning component associated with *over* constitutes a distinct sense, we employ the methodology introduced in chapter 3 for identifying when a sense is distinct.

As a preview of the remainder of this chapter, we present figure 4.3 which represents our proposed semantic network for *over*, subsuming a total of fifteen distinct senses including the proto-scene. Each distinct sense is represented by a dark sphere or node in the network; the proto-scene occupies a central position which indicates its status as the primary sense. In some instances, our repre-sentation of the semantic network depicts a distinct, conventionalized sense arising from the conceptualization prompted for by another conventionalized sense, rather than directly from the proto-scene. For instance, in the network represented in figure 4.3, the Excess Sense I is represented as arising from the conceptualization associated with the More Sense rather than arising directly from a conceptualization in which the proto-scene of *over* occurs. This rep-resents the claim that reanalysis of conceptualizations is potentially recursive and that a distinct sense can be the result of multiple instances of reanalysis. Moreover, we believe that a complex conceptualization, such as the one repre-sented in figure 4.2, can be submitted to multiple instances of reanalysis and

---

[10] The reanalysis of an aspect of a particular complex conceptualization results in privileging a different aspect or perspective of the complex conceptualization. Yet, because the pertinent complex conceptualization is first prompted for by the proto-scene for *over*, as in the complex conceptualization in figure 4.2, the derived sense is coded by the same linguistic form, namely *over*.

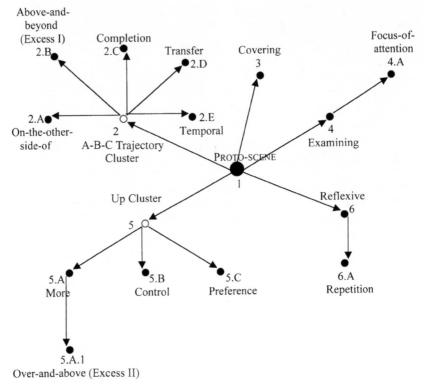

Figure 4.3 The semantic network for *over*

thus give rise to several distinct senses. When a complex conceptualization gives rise to multiple senses, we term the set of senses a cluster of senses. A cluster of senses is denoted in our representation of a semantic network by an open circle. A single distinct sense is represented by a shaded sphere.

The A-B-C Trajectory Cluster (2)

The five distinct senses in the A-B-C Trajectory Cluster (On-the-other-side-of, Above-and-beyond (Excess I), Completion, Transfer and Temporal) all derive from reanalysis of the complex conceptualization depicted in figure 4.2. This complex conceptualization, although profiling a sequentially evolving process, during reanalysis is subject to conceptualization in summary format. That is, although points B and C never exist simultaneously in the world, precisely because a TR such as a cat could not occupy two such positions simultaneously, by conceptualizing such a spatial scene in summary format, point C can be related to point B, and hence the lexical form which prompts for point B can come, through entrenchment, to be employed to reference senses related to point C.

The On-the-other-side-of Sense (2.A) An unavoidable consequence (i.e., an experiential correlate) of the unique trajectory prompted by sentences analogous to *The cat jumped over the wall*, that is, ones in which (i) the verb designates point A as a starting/push off point, (ii) TRs cannot hover and must return to ground, (iii) LMs are construed as impediments to forward motion, and (iv) *over* is used to designate the key spatial configuration, is that when the motion is complete, the TR is located on the other side of the LM relative to the starting point of the trajectory. Although point C in figure 4.2 and its relation to point A are not part of the proto-scene for *over* (and cannot be derived from the proto-scene in the absence of the particular properties of the verb and TR discussed above), the On-the-other-side-of Sense has come to be associated with certain uses of *over* which are not derivable from context. Consider the following sentence:

(4.20)   Arlington is over the Potomac River from Georgetown

Notice in this sentence that the verb, *is*, fails to indicate any sense of motion. In our model for *over*, it is the verb that typically codes for motion and hence prompts for a trajectory. Thus, the lack of motion coded by *is*, in turn, results in failure to prompt for a trajectory. If there is no trajectory, there is no beginning or end point. Hence, there is no principled way of deriving an On-the-other-side-of Sense from this sentential context. Nevertheless, native speakers will normally interpret this utterance such that Arlington is understood to be located on the other side of the Potomac River from Georgetown. Consequently, *over* must have associated with it a context-independent On-the-other-side-of Sense. Accordingly, the two criteria for establishing that a sense is distinct have been met. The On-the-other-side-of Sense adds meaning not apparent in the proto-scene and the use in (4.20) is context independent.

We hypothesize that this distinct sense came to be instantiated in memory as a result of reanalysis of the complex conceptualization represented in figure 4.2 and specifically, the privileging of the consequence of the jump, namely that the TR ends up on the other side of the LM. Additionally, this conceptualization involves a shift in vantage point from being 'off-stage' (Langacker, 1992), to being in the vicinity of point A (see figure 4.4). The default vantage point specified in the proto-scene for *over*, figure 4.1, is 'off-stage'. In chapter 3 we

Figure 4.4 On-the-other-side-of Sense

observed that spatial scenes could be viewed from a number of different vantage points, and these different vantage points could give rise to different construals of the same scene. In figure 4.4, the eye icon on the left represents the vantage point, the vertical line the impediment and the dark sphere the TR.

The following sentence:

(4.21)   The ball landed over the wall

is only felicitous if the construer (i.e., the vantage point) is located in the vicinity of point A (in figure 4.2) and the area beyond the wall is construed as point C. Thus, the reanalysis of *over* which results in the On-the-other-side-of Sense involves two changes vis-à-vis the proto-scene – the privileging of point C and interpreting it as the point at which the TR is located, and a shift in vantage point such that the construer is located in the vicinity of point A. While the On-the-other-side-of component, that is, point C in figure 4.2, is correlated in experiential terms with arc-shaped trajectories and jumping over (i.e., higher than) obstacles by TRs such as cats, without the shift in vantage point, this experiential correlation cannot be construed, that is, the TR can only be on the other side of the LM if the vantage point constitutes the opposite side. We hypothesize that through the use of *over* in contexts where On-the-other-side-of is implicated, this meaning has come to be conventionally associated with *over* as a distinct sense, a process we term pragmatic strengthening.

This sense is highly productive in English, as attested by the examples below. Notice that in none of the following do we conventionally obtain the reading in which the TR is physically higher than the LM or that jumping or moving is involved:[11]

(4.22)   The old town lies over the bridge
(4.23)   The mansion is situated over that wall
(4.24)   John lives over the hill

Moreover, examples such as (4.24), which have been described as having so-called end-point focus, are reminiscent of the examples posited in Lakoff's (1987: 423) analysis for *over* as attesting to an Above–across Sense.[12] Hence,

---

[11] At this point it is worth pointing out that sentences such as (4.20)–(4.24) offer strong evidence against a monosemy theory of word meaning. Monosemy (cf. Ruhl, 1989), as noted previously, posits that all interpretations of a linguistic form, such as a spatial particle, are contextually derivable from a highly abstract primary sense. However, as can be seen from the On-the-other-side-of Sense, neither of the original aspects of the spatial configuration hold – i.e., the TR is not above the LM and the TR is not proximal to the LM. The nature of a primary sense that would derive both these senses simply from contextual cues would need to be extremely abstract. We cannot see how a representation so abstract would also be constrained enough to distinguish among many other English spatial particles.

[12] Lakoff (1987: 422–23) represents *Sam lives over the hill* as an example of schema 1.VX.C.E (above–across, with a vertical, extended LM, contact between the TR and LM, and end-point focus).

we suggest that misanalysis of the On-the-other-side-of Sense contributed to an Above–across Sense, which explicitly involved a path, being posited by earlier analyses.

The Above-and-beyond (Excess I) Sense (2.B) In the following sentences, *over* is used as predicted by the proto-scene but with the additional implicatures that the LM represents an intended goal or target and that the TR moved beyond the intended or desired point.

(4.25)   The arrow flew over the target and landed in the woods
(4.26)   Lissa just tapped the golf ball, but it still rolled over the cup

Given general knowledge about people shooting arrows and targets, we believe most speakers would assume that whoever shot the arrow intended to hit the target, but aimed too high. Thus, the movement of *the arrow*, the TR, was above and beyond the LM, or in excess of, what the agent intended. Similarly, given general knowledge of the game of golf and the goals of people who engage in the game, we believe most speakers would assume that the agent (*Lissa*) intended that the movement of *the ball*, the TR, which she initiated with a tap, would result in the ball going into *the cup*, the LM. Thus, the movement of the ball was above and beyond, or in excess of, what the agent intended.

The basic spatial configuration and trajectory followed by the TR is identical to that associated with the proto-scene in the context of a verb depicting forward motion. However, in sentences such as *The cat jumped over the wall*, the TR's movement beyond the LM is presumed to be intentional, while in sentences such as (4.25) and (4.26) the LM is construed as the target or goal and the presumed intention is to have the TR come into contact with the target. When the TR misses the target, it goes above and beyond the LM. Going above and beyond the target is conceptualized as going too far or involving too much. The implicatures of (1) the LM being construed as the target/goal and (2) the TR passing over the LM as going beyond the target/goal have been reanalysed, resulting in a distinct sense being added to the semantic network. Evidence for this sense being distinct comes from sentences such as the following in which the sense cannot be derived from context:

(4.27)   Your article is over the page limit

Note that in this sentence, *over* cannot felicitously be interpreted as physically 'higher than'. Rather the interpretation seems to be that there is an established or targeted number of pages for the article and that the actual number of pages went beyond (i.e., exceeded) that target. Similarly in the example in (4.28), *over* cannot be interpreted as referring to a spatial configuration as the LM is not a physical entity:

Figure 4.5 Above-and-beyond or Excess I Sense

(4.28)   Most students wrote over the word limit in order to provide sufficient detail

In this sentence, the word limit for an essay is construed as the LM, and the students who do the writing as the TR. That is, a TR and LM, as we outlined in chapter 3, profile any entities that are placed in focal and secondary prominence (focus and background) respectively, regardless of whether or not they constitute a physical entity. In this sentence the use of *over* can make sense only if we understand it to be prompting for an Excess Sense: the number of words employed to write the essay is construed as exceeding the permitted number. That is, examples such as (4.28) cannot be construed as designating a spatial configuration in which the TR is somehow physically above and beyond the LM. This illustrates how spatial scenes and spatial experience such as physically going above and beyond can give rise to distinct meaning components that are not primarily spatial in nature.

We diagram the Above-and-beyond (Excess I) Sense by representing the LM as a bull's-eye target and highlighting the salient 'beyond' portion of the trajectory (see figure 4.5).[13] At this point, we wish to emphasize that we are not claiming that the semantic network contains criterial senses. That is, we are not suggesting that all uses of *over* will absolutely reflect one sense or another. Often, specific uses of a spatial particle will contain 'flavours' of more than one sense, which imbues a reading with complex nuances of meaning, providing both intra- and inter-hearer differences in interpretation. We are also not suggesting that application of the model outlined in chapter 3 will mechanistically provide a single, unique 'derivation' for each distinct sense, based ultimately on the proto-scene. As we have argued previously, we believe that, in certain cases, there are multiple motivations for a particular sense. Accordingly, we do not want to posit a simplicity rubric that claims that there is one 'correct' derivation and deny that there may be multiple means of instantiating a distinct sense in memory. We feel there is no strong evidence that shows that human conceptualization and cognition is constrained by such a dictum (contra the widespread view adopted in formalist approaches to meaning in the generative tradition; for a critique of such views, see Langacker, 1991a: chapter 10, and the discussion of the generality fallacy in Croft, 1998). We do, however, claim

[13] Our analysis provides for a second source of an Excess Sense associated with *over*. This second sense and its implication for the model are discussed later in the chapter.

that the model outlined in chapter 3 will give a delimited number of motivations which analysts can agree upon.

At this point we see no principled reason for ruling out the possibility that an 'excess' interpretation might arise through an alternative route as represented in the network by the Over-and-above (Excess II) Sense (5.A.1), that is, we hypothesize that there are multiple motivations for this particular sense. In fact, we hypothesize that some speakers might represent an 'excess' interpretation as relating to the proto-scene through one route while others represent the relationship as deriving through another. Still other speakers may have representations that involve both routes; the two resultant senses would then serve to inform each other in various ways. We further argue that it is inappropriate to treat this flexibility (or redundancy) as evidence that our model is flawed. Nor should an alternative analysis of the precise derivation of a particular sense be taken to constitute a counter-example to the overall model being posited, assuming that the principles laid out in chapter 3 are adhered to in reaching the alternative analysis. Rather we see this flexibility (and redundancy) as an appropriate reflection of the complexity of spatial scenes, the richness of human cognition and the many ways in which experience is meaningful to us as human beings.

The Completion Sense (2.C) When *over* occurs in context with a verb, it crucially influences the inferred shape of the trajectory by contributing the information that at some point during the movement the TR is higher than the LM, and that there is some conceptual connection between the TR and the LM. Thus, when *over* is integrated into a complex conceptualization, such as described by figure 4.2, the inferred shape of the trajectory has an end point C. The inference of end point C is an unavoidable consequence (i.e., an experiential correlate) of construing the spatial relation described by *over* as part of a trajectory which occurs when entities like cats and movement like jumping are involved. The end point of any trajectory (which represents the process of moving) is commonly understood as representing the completion of the process.

We suggest that the Completion Sense associated with *over* has arisen as a result of the implicature of completion being reanalysed as distinct from the complex conceptualization represented in figure 4.2. Once reanalysis has taken place, the final location resulting from motion correlates with the completion of motion, and the distinct sense comes to be associated with the form *over* in the semantic network via pragmatic strengthening.

(4.29)   The cat's jump is over [= finished/complete]

Contextually independent usages of this particular sense are highly productive, as attested by the following:

(4.30)   The film/game/play is over [= finished/complete]

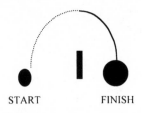

Figure 4.6 Completion Sense

Thus, we are suggesting that the meaning component of completion results from reanalysis of the spatial location of the TR as standing for an aspect of a process. For example, in the case of (4.29), the end point of the motion through space over an impediment (i.e., the location at which the TR comes to rest) is interpreted as the completion of the movement. Accordingly, in this instance, the Completion Sense is not describing a purely spatial relation, but rather an aspect of a process. As a result, the Completion Sense is adverbial in nature, that is, it refers to a process rather than a LM. This is reflected syntactically by the fact that the completion sense does not mediate a TR–LM configuration, in which the spatial particle is sequenced between the TR and the LM as illustrated by the example in (4.29). Hence, the Completion Sense, in formal terms, is not represented by a spatial particle, but rather by what we are terming an adprep (Bolinger, 1971; O'Dowd, 1998).[14]

The Completion Sense differs crucially from the On-the-other-side-of Sense in that the latter focuses on the spatial location of the TR when the process is completed (see figure 4.6). In contrast, the former focuses on interpreting point C as the end of the motion or process. We tentatively hypothesize that an adprep will always arise when the reanalysis involves interpreting the location of the TR as an aspect of a process. In figure 4.6 the dark ellipse on the left represents the location of the TR at the beginning of the process. The large sphere on the right, which is in focus, represents the end point or completion.

The Transfer Sense (2.D) A consequence of the conceptualization represented in figure 4.2 is what we term the Transfer Sense. Consider the following examples:

(4.31)   Sally turned the keys to the office over to the janitor
(4.32)   The bank automatically switched the money over to our checking account

---

[14] This is consistent with Langacker (1992) who argues that '[a]n expression's grammatical class is determined by the nature of its profile' (p. 279). The relationship profiled by an adverb crucially differs from the relationship profiled by a preposition in that an adverb takes a relationship as its TR and does not have a salient LM. In contrast, prepositions take an entity as their TR and elaborate a relational LM.

Figure 4.7 Transfer Sense

In these sentences, the conceptualization constructed is of a TR moving from one point to another. This follows from the conceptualization schematized in figure 4.2, in which an implicature of transfer arises. This is a consequence of understanding the spatial scene as one involving the transfer of a TR from one location, namely point A, to a new location, point C (see figure 4.7). We suggest that change in location of an entity is experientially correlated with transfer of entity; thus, change in position can often give rise to the implicature that transfer has taken place. Via pragmatic strengthening, this implicature is conventionalized as a distinct meaning component, and instantiated in the semantic network as a distinct sense. As with the Completion Sense, the Transfer Sense involves the reanalysis of the trajectory or process. Again, we see that, in formal terms, *over* is not represented by a preposition, or particle, but rather by an adprep. The TR has been transferred from the left side of the impediment to the right side, as represented by the dark sphere which is in focus.

As previously noted, non-physical entities can be identified as TRs or LMs, if they are construed as focal and backgrounded respectively, and if a relation holds between them. As *over* has a conventionalized Transfer Sense associated with it, the relation between non-physical TRs and LMs cannot be spatio-configurational, but as in (4.33) it can involve the notion of transfer. This further illustrates that transfer must be a distinct sense, as it could not be derived from context in such sentences:

(4.33)   The old government handed its power over (to the newly elected officials)

In this example, there is a conventional reading in which the members of the government transfer their authority, that is, their mandate to govern, to a new set of officials. In literal terms, nothing is physically transferred, as the TR, *power*, is a non-physical entity. Nonetheless, to say that power is a non-physical entity is not to say that the concept of power is without foundation in real-world experiences. In fact, the concept of power derives from a diverse plethora of very real experiences, consisting of physical forces, a series of socially constructed relationships and hierarchies, as well as social interactions such as taking, issuing and following orders, commands, edicts, etc. In this sense, we each experience power in a real way, although the variety of experiences that are subsumed by the concept of power does not have physical substance nor spatial dimensionality in the same way that a chair or a table has.[15] Nevertheless, the abstract concept of power can be mediated by *over*, due to a conventionalized Transfer Sense, rather than there being a literal spatial relation holding between the TR and the LM, as evidenced by (4.30).

The Temporal Sense (2.E)   In this sense, *over* mediates a temporal relation between a particular TR and a period of duration.[16] Consider some examples that are illustrative:

(4.34)   The festival will take place over the weekend
(4.35)   Their friendship has remained strong over the years

In each of these examples the TR is conceptualized as being manifested through time, and hence co-occurring with the temporal LM, *the weekend* and *the years*, respectively. For this reason we term this the Temporal Sense.

In order to understand how this sense is likely to have derived, consider the following:

(4.36)   The boy walked over the hill

The example in (4.36) is closely related to the A-B-C trajectory. By virtue of both walking and the speaker's choosing to prompt for a spatio-configurational relation denoted by *over* (i.e., above but within potential contact with the LM), versus, say 'to the top of', it is implied that the TR will traverse the hill. However, an important and indeed salient consequence of traversing an extended LM such as a hill is that a greater length of time is required than when traversing non-extended LMs. That is, the greater the distance traversed, the greater the amount of time required in order to do so. Put another way, there is a tight correlation in our experience between distance and duration. We suggest that due to this correlation, in such contexts duration is a salient implicature associated with *over*. Owing to pragmatic strengthening – in which a particular aspect of context becomes reanalysed as a distinct meaning component – the notion of temporality involving duration has been conventionally associated with the lexeme *over*. After all, if *over* did not have a Temporal Sense conventionally associated with it, there would be no way of predicting that the relations designated by *over* in (4.34) and (4.35) relate to time. This derivation of the Temporal Sense is

---

[15] The use of non-physical TRs and LMs constitutes a cline or continuum of uses. Some uses will be more figurative, some less figurative. Thus, we would expect inter-speaker variation in judgements about when a particular use is literal or figurative. For some speakers the sentence *Jeff and Kate hand the children over to the babysitter every morning* could be interpreted as either literal or figurative.

[16] Many of the spatial particles we have examined have temporal senses. For instance, *under, down, up, to, for, in, on, at, by, before, after* and *through* all have temporal uses. Because of space limitations, we will only address the Temporal Sense related to *over*.

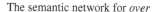

Figure 4.8 Temporal Sense

depicted in figure 4.8. The dashed line constitutes the passage of time, which correlates with the passage of the TR across the LM (in bold).

Two important points arising from this sense need to be considered. First, is the notion of atemporality. We argued in chapter 3 that spatial particles code conceptual relations which are atemporal, and yet we are now suggesting that *over* is associated with a Temporal Sense. However, the notion of atemporality relates to how particular spatial scenes are perceived and processed. While spatial scenes such as *The boy walked over the hill* can be processed in sequential fashion, as evolving through time, such spatial scenes can also be processed in summary fashion as a single conceptual gestalt. Processing of this kind captures the relational elements of the scene, rather than the scene as an evolving process. We suggest, following Langacker (1987, and elsewhere), that one way in which this atemporal format is coded for linguistically is via spatial particles. Hence, there is no contradiction in claiming that there is a Temporal Sense associated with *over*, and yet that this sense is scanned in summary fashion, and is hence atemporal. This follows as this particular meaning component, that of temporality, relates to the configurational relation holding between the TR and LM, which in this case happens to be that of duration.

The second point which arises from this discussion of the Temporal Sense is that by virtue of the principled polysemy viewpoint we have been advocating, experiential correlations give rise to implicatures which become strengthened through contextual association and use (i.e., pragmatically), such that they derive distinct meaning components. That is, the Temporal Sense associated with *over* is a conventional meaning component instantiated in semantic memory. This is an important point as it has been suggested to us that the Temporal Sense could simply be derived on-line by virtue of the cross-domain metaphoric mapping between time and space. By this argument, a well-established metaphor acts as general background knowledge which can be brought to bear in the interpretation of an utterance in the same way that knowledge about force dynamics is automatically brought to bear in interpreting a sentence like *The cat jumped over the wall*. We believe this argument is flawed for several reasons. Our goal is to account for word meanings, a much more specific level of conceptual organization than the cross-domain mappings of conceptual metaphor. In attempting to account for word meanings, we need to explain (1) why temporality comes to be associated with some spatial particles, but not all and (2) the exact character of the temporal meanings that are associated with various spatial particles. Our most basic argument is that

distinct senses associated with spatial particles arise through experiential correlation (the same correlation that motivates the metaphor) and strengthening of
implicatures that arise in the course of sentence interpretation. If we assume that
what we are calling the Temporal Sense is simply an online meaning derived
from, say, the proto-scene (which simply specifies that a TR is located higher
than the LM) in conjunction with the TIME IS SPACE cross-domain mapping,
we have no way of explaining why the Temporal Sense associated with *over*
has the specific character of duration while the Temporal Sense associated with
at, for instance, does not (e.g., *He arrived at 10 o'clock*).

Covering

The Covering Sense (3) In our definition of TR and LM, we noted that
the typical situation is for the TR to be smaller than the LM (when the TR and
LM are physical entities). All the senses and interpretations we have examined
so far have assumed that the TR is smaller than the LM. This default ascription
is also represented in the proto-scene we posited for *over*. However, there are
instances in the real world in which the object that is in focus (i.e., the TR) is
larger or perceived to be larger than the locating object (i.e., the LM). Such a
situation is described by the sentence in (4.37):

(4.37)   The tablecloth is over the table

In addition, given our normal interactions with tables and tablecloths, that is,
we typically sit at tables or walk past them such that both the table and the tablecloth are lower than our line of vision (i.e., we do not normally sit on tables
or underneath tables such that the tablecloth is over both us and the table), it
follows that our typical vantage point is such that when a tablecloth is over
the table, then we perceive it as covering the table. In such a scenario, the
vantage point is not that depicted in the default representation of the proto-
scene, in which the viewer/construer is 'off-stage'. Rather the vantage point
has shifted such that the TR is between the LM and the construer or viewer. The
perceptual effect of having the TR physically intervene between the viewer and
the LM is that the TR will often appear to cover the LM or some significant
portion of it. Again, following our argument that metric properties concerning
the relationship between the TR and LM are filled in on-line, *over* can be used
to prompt this covering interpretation when there is contact between the LM
and TR, as in (4.38), or when there is no contact between the TR and the LM
as in the following sentence:

(4.38)   The fibreglass protector was over the swimming pool

In accordance with the position outlined in chapter 3, in which we argued that
spatial scenes could be viewed in a number of different ways, and from different vantage points, the covering interpretation results from construing the

Figure 4.9 Covering Sense

situation in a certain way, that is, having a particular vantage point from which the situation is construed. When a shift in vantage point occurs, the conceptualization that is constructed is likely to involve an additional implicature which is not part of the interpretation when the default vantage point on the proto-scene is assumed. In sum, we are arguing that the conceptualization constructed in the normal interpretation of (4.37) involves two changes from the default representation of the proto-scene – first, the TR is perceived as being larger than the LM and second, the vantage point has shifted from off-stage to higher than the TR.[17]

The covering implicature can be reanalysed as distinct from the spatial configuration designated by the proto-scene, as illustrated in figure 4.9. In this diagram, the eye icon represents the vantage point, the elongated sphere the TR, which from the perspective of the vantage point covers the LM, represented by the horizontal line.

Accordingly, the 'covering' component comes to be instantiated in the semantic network, via pragmatic strengthening as a distinct sense. Further evidence for the instantiation of a Covering Sense component in memory comes from examples such as the following:

(4.39)   They put a transparent plastic sheet over the painted ceiling of the chapel during repairs

In the sentence in (4.39), the TR, *a transparent plastic sheet*, is physically lower than the LM, *the painted ceiling*. Yet, the form *over* (and not *under*, for instance) is being used to denote the relation between the TR and the LM. What is important in this sentence is the notion of covering. Unless *over* had

---

[17] These two changes are closely intertwined in everyday experience. We are often involved in real-world scenarios where the TR is physically larger than the LM and we normally view the TR–LM from above, as in the example: *The cloth is over the table*. Note that in this real-world scene, if the TR were smaller than the LM, the spatial particle of choice (best fit) would be likely to change:

    a. ?The small handkerchief was spread out over the table
    b. The small handkerchief was spread out on the table

However, there are also many real-world scenarios in which the TR is actually smaller than the LM but because of the construer's vantage point (in which the TR intervenes between the viewer and the LM), the TR appears larger than the LM. For instance, in the sentence: *The thick, dark clouds moved over the sun*, the clouds are not physically larger than the sun. But they do appear larger to the earth-bound viewer.

a distinct Covering Sense associated with it, we would expect this sentence to be semantically anomalous because the TR is not higher than the LM, a canonical part of the meaning of *over*. Thus, the covering reading in (4.39) is not derivable from context, precisely because the TR–LM spatial configuration is not one associated with the proto-scene for *over*.[18] Hence, the Covering Sense must exist independently in semantic memory.[19]

---

[18] Lakoff (1987) accounted for cases of the covering reading in which the TR is not higher than the LM by positing a Rotation Transformation. 'The covering schemas all have variants in which the TR need not be above (that is, higher than) the LM. In all cases, however, there must be an understood viewpoint from which the TR is blocking accessibility of vision to at least some part of the LM ... We will refer to these as *rotated* (RO) schemas, though with no suggestion that there is actual mental rotation degree-by-degree involved' (p. 429). An alternative way of articulating this analysis would be to say that the vantage point in the proto-scene can switch to the LM and that the LM then 'experiences' the TR (which blocks its perceptual access) as being physically higher than or above it. Under this analysis, any case in which the LM experiences the TR as blocking its perceptual access, even when the TR is not vertically higher than the LM, would count as an instance of the proto-scene denoted by *over* whose covering interpretation is filled in by context and inferencing.

Although we acknowledge the logical possibility of this analysis, our model rules out such mechanisms as the Rotation Transformation. This is primarily on the basis that the analysis does not reflect the way humans experience the world. Humans do not experience a room from the viewpoint of a spider walking on the ceiling or a fly on the wall. Because of the particular ways their bodies (and neural architectures) are constructed, spiders and flies may very well orient themselves to the surface located most proximal to the bottoms of their feet and thus might 'understand' the surface of a ceiling or a wall as being lower than they are (i.e., they may experience themselves to be 'over' such LMs). In contrast, humans consistently orient themselves from the perspective of the earth, under the influence of gravity. Thus, we argue that for humans the configuration between the TR and LM in many instances of the Covering Sense, such as the sentence (4.39), is not understood as being in a spatial configuration in which the TR is vertically elevated in relation to the LM.

Even if the vantage point in the scene were from a person peeking through a hole in the ceiling down into the room below or through a hole in the wall (in effect making the ceiling or the wall the vantage point), that person would not experience a board covering the hole, in either the ceiling or the wall, as being vertically elevated in relation to the LM, i.e., themselves or the ceiling or the wall. For instance, taking the vantage point of the ceiling peep-hole, the floor of the room is understood by the human viewer as being *under*, or vertically lower than, the LM (i.e., the viewer or the ceiling), not *over* the viewer. If this person were a detective reporting on the movements of a suspect, and the suspect were located in line with the hole in the ceiling, the detective would relay this information by saying something like: *The suspect is directly below me* or *The suspect is directly below my peep-hole*, not *The suspect is directly over my peep-hole*. *Over* would be used felicitously only if it specifically meant 'covering'. Hence, we argue that *over* has developed a distinct Covering Sense. This sense is no longer directly tied to the 'above–below' spatial configuration between the TR and LM which gave rise to the Covering Sense.

Finally we note that the Rotation Transformation is an extremely powerful mechanism which potentially affects all spatial particles whose primary sense involves either a vertical or horizontal orientation. The result is that, in a number of instances, the proto-scenes for *over, under, before* and *after*, etc., would be essentially indistinguishable. Moreover, the Rotation Transformation offers no explanation for why TR–LM configurations that do not match the proto-scene denoted by *over* would become associated with the lexeme *over* in the first place.

[19] A common consequence of the LM being covered by the TR is that the LM is occluded from the construer's view. Typically the scene described in the example in (4.37) is that the tablecloth

Above and proximal

The Examining Sense (4) As we have noted previously, any spatial scene can be viewed from a variety of vantage points. Furthermore, the default vantage point associated with the proto-scene is one in which the observer (or construer) is off-stage or external to the specific scene being construed. The construal which gives rise to the Examining Sense is the result of a shift in vantage point. In particular, we argue that in the scene associated with the Examining Sense, the vantage point is that of the TR, and further that the TR's line of vision is directed at the LM.

Let us consider how this construal might arise. Consider the following sentence:

(4.40)   Phyllis is standing over the entrance to the underground chamber

Here *over* is being used as designated in the proto-scene and is denoting a spatial relation between the TR, *Phyllis*, and the LM, *the entrance to the underground chamber*, in which the TR is higher than but proximal to the LM. A consequence of Phyllis being in this physical relation to the entrance is that she is in a position to observe the entrance carefully. An important way of experiencing and therefore understanding an object being examined is in terms of the examiner being physically higher than but proximal to the object being examined. Many recurring everyday examples of looking carefully at objects involve the human head (and therefore the eyes) being higher than the object being scrutinized, for example examining tools, jewellery, a written text, or wounds on the body. Further, if an object is not proximal to the viewer, it is generally not possible to see the object clearly and therefore not possible to

---

occludes the table top from the observer. As we see in example (4.38), occlusion is not an inevitable consequence of covering. Consider the following examples:

a   The mask is over her face
a′ She wore a transparent veil over her face
b   The dark, heavy clouds are over the sun
b′ There are a few wispy clouds over the sun

In a and b, a consequence of the LM being covered by the TR is that the LM is no longer visible. In a′ and b′, covering takes place without the additional consequence of occlusion. We have not been able to find any instances of occluding (which involve the use of *over*) that do not include a Covering Sense. We further note that in the examples in which we can tease apart covering from occluding, the physical attribute of transparency/opacity of the TR must be specified. If the TR is not specified as being transparent, the normal reading is that covering entails occlusion. Thus, we have concluded that the occlusion interpretation is a contextual implicature of the Covering Sense and our real-world knowledge of the properties of objects such as tablecloths and blankets. Given the absence of contextually independent examples of occlusion (i.e., linguistic examples of *over* in which occlusion is not an implicature deriving from covering), our methodological procedures suggest that an 'occluding' reading is an on-line interpretation.

examine the object thoroughly. The experiential correlation between proximity and potential thoroughness is reflected in sentences such as:

(4.41)   I'll give the document a close examination
(4.42)   I'll give the manuscript a close read

Thus, we argue that two experiential correlates of examining are the viewer being located above the LM and in proximity to the LM. Furthermore, the functional aspect associated with the proto-scene is that there is a conceptual connectedness between the TR and LM, that is, the notion of 'sphere of influence'. In this case, the connection is construed as that between the examiner and the examined. Because the proto-scene for *over* contains these elements – a TR higher than a LM, proximity between the TR and LM, and a conceptual connectedness between the TR and LM – which match the physical correlates necessary for examination, *over* is a likely candidate for developing an Examining Sense.

But this is not the entire story. Notice that the use of *over* in (4.37) does not prompt for the interpretation that Phyllis is examining the entrance, only that she is located such that she could examine it. For the Examining Sense to arise, the scene must contextually imply examination. Put another way, examination must be an implicature deriving from the particular linguistic prompts in a given sentence. Consider the following example:

(4.43)   Mary looked over the manuscript quite carefully

The normal interpretation of this sentence is something like: Mary examined the manuscript. In this sentence, the TR, *Mary*, is physically higher than and in proximity to the LM, *the manuscript*. Thus, the TR and the LM are in the spatial configuration associated with the proto-scene for *over*. In addition, the TR is construed as directing attention towards the manuscript. (This construal arises from our knowledge of the act of looking – that it involves looking at something – and our knowledge of humans: that when we do look it is typically for some purpose.) This additional meaning element of directing attention towards the LM is essential to the Examining Sense. This is illustrated in figure 4.10, in which the eye icon (vantage point) occupies the position of TR, and is above and proximal to the LM. The vantage point is in focus and not the LM.

Figure 4.10 Examining Sense

Now consider sentence (4.44):

(4.44)   The mechanic looked over the train's undercarriage

The normal reading is that the mechanic examined the train's undercarriage. However, for such examination to occur, *the mechanic*, the TR, must be physically underneath the train. In other words, in this conceptualization, the TR is **under** the LM. Clearly, in this situation, there is no way of predicting that *over* has associated with it an 'examination' reading, given that the TR–LM spatial configuration does not correspond with that normally associated with *over*, that is, the very configuration which motivated the implicature of examination in the first place. This is good evidence, therefore, that the contextual implicature of examination has been instantiated as a distinct sense in the network via pragmatic strengthening. Hence, examination results from construing a scene in a particular way. This being so, speakers are free to use this examination meaning component in the absence of the TR–LM configuration which gave rise to the implicature of examination initially. In some instances, utterances involving *over* are ambiguous because of multiple possible interpretations of *over* (the fact that the network constitutes a semantic continuum). Consider the following:

(4.45)   John looked over the book

In one reading, John looked past the book, viewing what is on the other side of it. In the second reading, John was examining the book itself. We argue that these two readings are available precisely because there are two distinct senses associated with *over*, an On-the-other-side-of Sense and an Examining Sense.

The Focus-of-attention Sense (4. A)   The following sentences illustrate what we call the Focus-of-attention Sense. Notice that in these sentences *over* can be paraphrased by *about*:[20]

(4.46)   a. The little boy cried over his broken toy
          b. The little boy cried about his broken toy
(4.47)   a. The generals talked over their plans for the invasion
          b. The generals talked about their plans for the invasion

In (4.46a) and (4.47a), the LM is the focus of attention. This sense is closely related to the Examining Sense from which it derives. In the Examining Sense, the vantage point is that of the TR, while the LM is physically below and proximal to the TR. We further posited that the TR must be construed as directing

---

[20] Dirven (1993) notes that in cases such as *talk over*, there is a verb-particle construction, as evidenced by the syntactic test: *We talked it over* versus **We talked over it*. In contrast, *talk about* is not a verb-particle construction: **We talked it about* versus *We talked about it*.

Figure 4.11 Focus-of-attention Sense

attention toward the LM. A natural consequence of the Examining Sense is that the object being examined, the LM, is the focus of the TR's attention. This natural consequence of examining has been privileged and reanalysed as distinct from the spatial scene in which it originally occurred, as diagrammed in figure 4.11, and via pragmatic strengthening, conventionalized as a distinct sense. Figure 4.11 differs in a minimal way from figure 4.9. Here the LM is in focus.

Once this sense has been instantiated in memory, non-physical TRs and LMs can be denoted by this sense, as evidenced by the following:

(4.48)   She thought over the problem
(4.49)   The search committee agonized over the decision
(4.50)   Niels Bohr mulled over a solution to Einstein's thought experiment

Figure 4.12 Up Cluster

The vertical elevation or Up Cluster (5)

Four distinct senses fall under this cluster, as can be seen from figure 4.3 (above). Each of these arises from construing a TR that is located physically higher than the LM as being vertically elevated or up relative to the LM. Being up entails a particular construal of the scene in which upward orientation is assigned to the TR, as illustrated in figure 4.12. In this cluster of senses, vertical elevation of the TR (shaded sphere) relative to the LM (vertical line) is privileged.

The construal of upward orientation being assigned to the TR arises frequently in real-world experiences associated with the conceptual spatial relation *over*. For instance, in order to move *over* and beyond many LMs, movement from a physically lower location to a physically higher location is often necessary, that is, vertical elevation of the TR occurs. Furthermore, an upward orientation is not typically construed in a neutral way. As Clark (1973) and Lakoff and Johnson (1980) observed, an upward orientation is meaningful in human experience. For instance, an element in a vertically elevated position is experienced as being positive or superior to an element in a physically lower position. Notice that there is nothing in the proto-scene of *over*, that is, of a TR being higher than the LM, which entails this construal. For example, in the scene described by: *The picture is over the mantel*, the picture is not construed as being in a better or superior position vis-à-vis the mantel.

The More Sense (5. A) As we observed in chapter 2 when we discussed experiential correlation, vertical elevation and quantity are correlated in our experience. Hence, when there is an addition to the original amount of a physical entity, the height or level of that entity often rises. Because *over* can be construed as relating a TR which is physically up with respect to a LM, and vertical elevation correlates in experiential terms with greater quantity, an implicature associated with being *over* is of having more of some entity. This implicature is conventionalized (via pragmatic strengthening) as attested by the following example:

(4.51)   Jerome found over forty kinds of shells on the beach

The normal interpretation of *over* in this context is 'more than'. The LM, *forty kinds of shells*, is interpreted as some kind of standard or measurement. The TR is not actually mentioned; in interpreting the sentence, we infer that the TR is shell types forty-one and greater. If *over* were interpreted in terms of the proto-scene in this sentence, we would obtain a semantically anomalous reading in which the additional shells would be understood as somehow being physically higher than the forty kinds actually mentioned in the sentence. Again, we see no direct way in which this interpretation can be constructed from the proto-scene and the sentential context alone. Moreover, in this sentence, there is no direct correlation between the concept of more types and vertical elevation. The concept here is more variety not more shells. Thus, we argue that the More Sense which is associated with *over* has arisen because of the independently motivated experiential correlation between greater quantity and greater elevation. Owing to this experiential correlation, the implicature of greater quantity comes to be conventionally associated with *over* (which, in terms of the designation prompted by the proto-scene, has a greater height meaning, and hence also implicates greater quantity). The implicature of greater quantity, or more, comes to be reanalysed as distinct from the conceptualization of the physical configuration which originally gave rise to it.

Figure 4.13 illustrates this sense. In this configuration the TR (sphere) is higher than the LM, which correlates with greater quantity. Moreover, once reanalysis has taken place, the distinct sense comes to be associated with the form *over*, in the semantic network.

Figure 4.13 More Sense

As we noted above, additional evidence for the existence of a distinct sense is if a sentence is ambiguous. Consider the following:

(4.52)   From my seat in the theatre, I could see over twenty people.

This sentence has two readings: (1) I could see beyond the heads of twenty people (who were presumably sitting in front of the speaker); and (2) I could see more than twenty people. The first reading involves the interpretation based on the On-the-other-side of Sense. The second reading clearly involves the More Sense.

The following is an additional example involving the More Sense:

(4.53)   The buyer offered Matt $1,000 over the amount he was asking for his house

In this sentence, the TR ($1,000) is construed as a new, greater amount, which is being compared to the original amount represented by the LM. In this example, the amount of money corresponds to a physical entity.

As we have noted before, once a distinct sense is established, it is also available to mediate relations between non-physical TRs and LMs. Consider the relationship between metric measure systems and verticality in the following:

(4.54)   John is over fifty years of age

Age is a non-physical entity, as it does not directly correspond to physical amounts of a substance whose dimensions can be measured. Nonetheless, age can be quantified in other ways, such as counting the passage of pre-determined temporal intervals such as years. As *over* has a distinct More Sense associated with it, and as age-systems are quantifiable, John's age, the TR, can be related to the LM, the age of fifty, in terms of the More Sense.

Other kinds of measurement which are commonly described with *over* include weight, speed and duration, etc. as illustrated by the following:

(4.55)   He weighs just over 150 pounds
(4.56)   The car was going over ninety miles an hour
(4.57)   Mary has been in Europe for over five months

Over-and-above (Excess II) Sense (5.A.1) The Over-and-above (Excess II) Sense is closely related to the More Sense. It adds an interpretation

Figure 4.14 Excess II Sense

of 'too much' to the more construal. We believe that a likely origin for this sense involved reanalysing scenes involving containment, such as those described in the following:

(4.58)   The heavy rains caused the river to flow over its banks
(4.59)   Lou kept pouring the cereal into the bowl until it spilled over and onto the counter
(4.60)   My cup runneth over

In these scenarios, the LMs are containers and the TRs are understood as the entities held by the container. When the amount of liquid or cereal (or whatever) which has been placed in the container is such that its level is higher than but within reach of the top of the LM, then the amount constitutes more than the container can hold. A consequence of the capacity of a container being exceeded is that more of the TR becomes an excess of the TR, which results in spillage. In sum, more of the TR, for instance, *the river* in (4.58), equals a higher level of water. Too much more of the TR results in a mess, as illustrated in figure 4.14. In this configuration, greater height of quantity results in greater volume than the LM has capacity for, hence excess.

A number of compounds involving *over* prompt for this Excess Sense. In many cases, the lexical item prompts for the conceptualization of containment, such that the state, attribute or process prompted for by the non-over element is construed in terms of a container, e.g., *overflow, overfill, overfeed* and *overeat* (the body is a container). The conceptualization of going beyond the capacity of the container is evident in the following, which evidence the notion of going beyond the normal: *overtired, overdevelop, overreact, over-anxious, overdo*. This node in the semantic network represents a second potential source for the general notion of excess associated with certain uses of *over*. We see subtle but distinguishable differences between the Above-and-beyond (Excess I) Sense, which seems to us to be more closely tied to motion along a trajectory and the interpretation of going beyond a designated point, and the Over-and-above (Excess II) Sense, which seems to be more closely related to exceeding the capacity of containers and exceeding what is normal. For instance, in a compound such as *overtired*, it seems that the conceptualization involved is not that

an expected level of tiredness is a goal that is missed but rather that an expected
or normal capacity for tiredness has been exceeded.

In some cases, we do not see a clear way to determine which source is most
appropriate. As we noted in our discussion of the Above-and-beyond Sense,
specific uses of *over* (or any spatial particle) seem to contain 'flavours' of more
than one sense, which imbues a particular reading with complex nuances of
meaning. For instance, consider the following:

(4.61)   Hey! Why are you bringing in so many cases of motor oil? There must
be a dozen cases here. That's well over the two cases I ordered.

In this example we might construct a 'more' conceptualization for *over*, or we
might construct an 'excess' interpretation (which provides not just a 'more'
meaning, but the additional 'too much more' meaning) for *over*. In this latter
case, the example could be derived from either the Above-and-beyond
(Excess I) Sense or the Over-and-above (Excess II) Sense. On the one hand,
two cases could be conceptualized as the target the customer was aiming for,
and bringing in ten additional cases could be construed as going beyond the
designated target. On the other hand, *two cases* could be conceptualized as
the expected amount or level of goods, and the additional ten cases could be
construed as going above the expected amount or level.

Alternatively, the hearer may construct a complex conceptualization in which
all three senses are influencing the interpretation. This reflects our claim that
there is a semantic network linking distinct senses, and that conceptualizations
reflect the continuous nature of meanings. Accordingly, our network should be
thought of as a semantic continuum, in which complex conceptualizations can
draw on meanings from distinct nodes as well as the range of points between
nodes, which provide nuanced semantic values. In addition, an important consequence of our claims, namely that: (1) the principles of meaning construction
in conjunction with a distinct sense such as the proto-scene (or any other distinct mental representation or sense) can be used to construct a wide range of
conceptualizations, (2) any one conceptualization is subject to multiple construals (through, for instance, privileging a particular aspect of the scene or shifting
the vantage point from which the scene is viewed), (3) distinct senses can be extended to include non-physical entities when such are perceived as focal (TRs)
and backgrounded reference points (LMs), and (4) semantic networks form an
interrelated continuum of interpretations (rather than just a series of absolutely
discrete points of meaning), is that the model predicts that a particular sense
may arise from more than one source.

In forms such as *overachieve, overkill, overdo, overdress* we do not see a
clear basis for arguing for the superiority of the Above-and-beyond interpretation versus the Over-and-above interpretation. As we noted earlier, we do not
consider this a flaw in our model; rather, we see it as testimony to the richness

and complexity of conceptualization. Although our model does not provide a straightforward identification procedure for the 'correct' derivation of each sense, it is constrained and allows for only a limited range of derivations. The hypothesis that there are multiple motivations for some senses makes testable predictions, that is, we expect to find that native speakers vary in their intuitions about cases for which we ascribe multiple motivations. These variations should be verifiable through psycholinguistic experimentation.

Control Sense (5.B) A third experiential correlate associated with vertical elevation is the phenomenon of control or power. This meaning component associated with *over* is illustrated by the following sentence (from Lakoff, 1987):

(4.62)   She has a strange power over me

Clearly this sentence does not mean that the TR, *she*, is higher than but within reach of *me*, the LM. Rather, the conventional interpretation derived from such an example is that the TR exerts influence or control over the LM (as observed earlier in this chapter). This meaning could not be derived from context, and is therefore suggestive, given our methodology, that this constitutes a distinct Control Sense instantiated in semantic memory. The question then is, how did the Control Sense derive from the semantic network associated with *over*? We suggest that this sense is due to an implicature which arose from an independently motivated experiential correlation between control and vertical elevation, that eventually became conventionally associated with *over*. This analysis is in contrast with Lakoff's (1987) conceptual metaphor analysis.[21]

For most of human history, when one person has been in physical control of another person, control has been experienced as the controller being physically higher. In physical combat, the victor or controller is often the one who finishes standing, in the up position; the loser finishes on the ground, physically lower than the controller. Hence an important element of how we actually experience control (and presumably from where the concept itself is derived) is that of being physically higher than that which is controlled:

(4.63)   The fight ended with John standing over Mac, his fist raised

Further, within the physical domain, the physically bigger, up, often controls the physically smaller, down. Within the animal kingdom, a widespread signal of the acknowledgement of power or status is for the less dominant animal to

---

[21] Our claim is that 'control' is a conventionalized meaning component associated with *over*, and hence, while this sense may be associated with other concepts/domains within the conceptual system, this sense is not motivated by virtue of a fixed knowledge structure inhering in long-term memory. For a critique of metaphor approaches to conceptual structure, see Evans (2000), especially chapter 3.

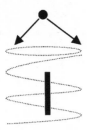

Figure 4.15 Control Sense

put itself in a position in which its head is physically lower than the head of the dominant animal. In experiential terms, then, control and vertical elevation are correlated. In short, we suggest that due to an independently motivated experiential association between control and being vertically elevated, there is an implicature of control associated with *over*.

Nonetheless, if control were understood only in terms of vertical elevation, we would expect that the English spatial particle *above* should also implicate control. However, as the following example demonstrates, this is not the case:

(4.64)   #She has a strange power above me [Control reading]

In experiential terms, a correlate of control is vertical elevation, as noted. In addition, to be able to exert control, one must be physically proximal to the subject, in order to affect the subject's actions and thus guarantee compliance. This suggests that in experiential terms, there are two elements associated with the concept of control; the first is up, and the second is physical proximity. As we argued above, the proto-scene for *over* designates a TR being physically higher and proximal to the LM, and, as we will see in chapter 5, there is good evidence for supposing that *above* designates that the TR will be physically higher but precludes physical proximity. Hence, in linguistic terms we would expect *over* to develop a control reading. The linguistic usage, then, accords with how we actually experience control. The Control Sense is depicted in figure 4.15. The spiral shape denotes that the TR (sphere) controls the LM (vertical line).

As we have been arguing, distinct senses such as the Control Sense, once instantiated in semantic memory, can be employed in situations which did not originally motivate them. This is a consequence of being instantiated as a distinct component within the semantic network. Accordingly, the Control Sense can be employed to mediate relations between non-physical TRs and LMs. Some examples are given below, in which either or both the TR/LM are non-physical entities:

(4.65)   Camilla has authority over purchasing (= the act of deciding what will be purchased)

Figure 4.16 Preference Sense

(4.66)   The Prime Minister holds sway over all the important decisions
(4.67)   Personality has more influence over who we marry than physical appearance

The Preference Sense (5.C) In this sense, that which is higher is conventionally understood as being preferred to that which is lower. Consider the following examples:

(4.68)   I would prefer tea over coffee
(4.69)   I like Beethoven over Mozart
(4.70)   I favour soccer over tennis

We suggest that the Preference Sense derives in the following way. Being physically up in experiential terms can implicate greater quantity, which generally is preferred to a lesser quantity. There is a further experiential pattern in which being physically up is associated with positive states such as happiness (e.g., *He's feeling up today*), being awake (e.g., *Is she up yet?*), etc., while being physically down is associated with being unhappy (e.g., *I'm feeling down today*), etc. (see Lakoff and Johnson, 1980). Given that states such as happiness are normally preferred to those such as unhappiness, this experiential correlation results in states associated with positions of vertical elevation being preferred to those associated with a lower position. Hence, being *over* implicates a preferred state (see figure 4.16, where the TR, which is higher, is to be preferred to the LM, which is hence not in focus). This implicature of preference is conventionalized, allowing a preference interpretation (rather than a higher-than reading) in the examples in (4.68)–(4.70).

Reflexivity

The Reflexive Sense (6) Spatial reflexivity (first noted by Lindner, 1981) is the phenomenon whereby a single entity that occupies multiple positions is conceptualized such that two salient positions occupied by the entity are integrated into a TR–LM spatial configuration. A spatial particle such as *over* is then utilized to mediate a spatial relation between the two positions, even though the same entity cannot simultaneously occupy two distinct spatial

Figure 4.17 Reflexive Sense

positions in the world. Hence, the dynamic, evolving character of experience is reanalysed as a static spatial configuration. As already discussed in chapter 3, and above in the Temporal Sense, Langacker (1987) discusses such gestalt-like static conceptualizations of a dynamic process as summary scanning. Consider the following example:

(4.71)   The fence fell over

In (4.71), the TR, that is, the initial (upright) position of the fence, is distinguished from the final position, in which the fence is lying horizontally on the ground. In our experience we see the fence fall through a 90-degree arc. From this experience, a conceptual spatial relation is abstracted (via summary scanning) integrating the two temporally situated locations into a single spatial configuration. In the world, no such spatial configuration exists. However, by conceptualizing the fence reflexively, an entity can be both the TR and the LM. By way of illustration, consider figure 4.17. The dark horizontal line is both the TR and the LM (i.e., the dashed vertical line). The dashed arrow demonstrates path. The two temporally distinct positions of the same entity are captured in this configuration.

Additional examples of the Reflexive Sense are given below:

(4.72)   He turned the page over
(4.73)   The log rolled over
(4.74)   The tree bent over in the wind

Note that this sense arises from reanalysis of a process. As noted previously, when *over* is used to profile a process, it is coded as an adprep.

The Repetition Sense (6.A) The Repetition Sense adds an iterative meaning component to the use of *over*. Again, this meaning component could not be predicted from the proto-scene (or any other sense so far considered) alone. Consider the following example in which *over* can be paraphrased by *again* or *anew*:

(4.75)   After the false start, they started the race over

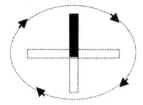

Figure 4.18 Repetition Sense

Further examples of the Repetition Sense are given below:

(4.76)   After exercising on all the weight machines, Edna began the circuit all over

(4.77)   He played the same piano piece over

(4.78)   This keeps happening over and over

It is also interesting to note that the Repetition Sense is limited to complex conceptualizations involving a particular set of process verbs. Specifically, the Repetition Sense does not occur with processes (prompted for by the verb) that cannot be readily conceptualized as iterative and/or voluntary (i.e., under conscious control). The following for instance are semantically anomalous with the Repetition Sense:

(4.79)   #She died over

(4.80)   #He ate the meal over

(4.81)   #She won this afternoon's tennis match over

Many native speakers have informed us that sentences involving this sense prompt for a conceptualization of a wheel or cycle, which seems to be evoked by the notion of repetition. We hypothesize that the repetition meaning component associated with *over* may be the result of iterative application of the Reflexive Sense (i.e., the 90-degree arc is repeated such that the TR passes through 360 degrees returning to its original starting point).

This analysis concurs with the intuition that repetition is conceptualized as cyclical in nature, see figure 4.18, which captures the iterative effect of the Reflexive Sense resulting in repetition. An alternative derivation may be due to an iterative application of the A-B-C Trajectory, such that when the end point or completion of the trajectory is reached the process begins again.[22] A third possibility may be that the notions of completion and reflexivity are conceptually integrated forming a conceptual blend (in the sense of Fauconnier and Turner, 1998, 2002). We remain agnostic as to which of these

[22] Lindstromberg (1998) offers a very similar explanation.

possible routes led to the instantiation of the Repetition Sense in the semantic network for *over*.

Conclusion

In this chapter we have provided a detailed analysis of the principled polysemy of *over*. In doing so, we employed criteria for distinguishing fifteen distinct senses associated with this form, which were introduced in chapter 3. We have also employed five criteria for distinguishing the primary sense of *over*, which we have termed the proto-scene, represented in figure 4.1. This chapter has been considerably more detailed than ensuing chapters, as we have attempted to illustrate how the model adduced in the first three chapters applies to a relatively complex conceptual category such as a single spatial particle.

5   The vertical axis

In this chapter we will consider three additional spatial particles that involve verticality – *above, under* and *below*. The analysis of spatial scenes related to these forms, in conjunction with *over*, will demonstrate that this subset of spatial particles acts as a particular lexical contrast set. Hence, in semantic terms, the four English lexemes *over, above, under* and *below* represent a systematic means of dividing up the vertical axis into four distinct spatial locations. Moreover, the analysis for each of these forms provides further evidence for our representation of proto-scenes for English spatial particles as most appropriately being characterized as involving both a functional component and a conceptual-spatial configuration between a TR and a LM. Our goal, then, in this chapter is to show that working out an appropriate analysis of the distinction between the proto-scenes associated with *over* versus *above* and *under* versus *below* underscores the efficacy of the model developed in the first four chapters.

Contrast sets

Linguists have long recognized that languages readily add new lexical items to the existing inventory of certain classes of words (open-class words), while being more resistant to adding a new lexical item to the existing set of other classes of words (closed-class words). We argued in chapter 3 that spatial particles represent a closed class of lexemes. They have this status because, in their spatial-physical uses, spatial particles operate within a stable, self-contained conceptual domain (Talmy, 2000).

Languages vary, both inter- and intra-linguistically, in their degree of granularity in dividing up various aspects of the spatial domain. Over millennia of communication, the speakers of what has evolved into present-day English have segmented and labelled the conceptual domain of space. While new inventions give rise to new lexical forms, for instance *the steam engine, the telephone, the digital computer*, etc., and new actions or activities may be invented, for example *bungee jumping*, which require additional lexemes being added to the lexical inventory, newly relevant spatial configurations are more difficult to imagine. As such, the closed-class status of spatial particles is a natural consequence of the nature of a relatively stable environment (gravity and the physical laws have remained in place for aeons), as well as the relative stability of our physiology (evolution in human morphology and neuro-anatomy is, relative to the timescale of language change, effectively unchanging).

Since spatial particles, in essence, delineate the meaningful distinctions within a stable, conceptual domain, at least part of their meaning is determined by the meanings of other spatial particles. To some extent, then, spatial particles contrast with one another in a systematic way. However, in making this claim we do not advocate the notion that the 'meanings' of spatial particles are limited to oppositional features, in the sense of Ferdinand de Saussure ([1915] 1983). The meaning of each particle is simultaneously semi-autonomous from and semi-dependent upon the conceptual space labelled by other spatial particles in the language. This is because while, on the one hand, the division of space by language is partially oppositional – in English a TR can be coded as being either in an enclosed relationship, vis-à-vis the LM, *in*, or not enclosed, *out* – on the other hand, the functional consequences of each particular spatial configuration are unique. For instance, if we consider the simplest representation of the spatial configurations between the TR and LM coded by *over* and *under*, they appear to form an oppositional pair, and indeed they have traditionally been characterized as opposites (or antonyms).

Given the nature of human physiology – we stand erect and our heads, which represent our physical top, contain the primary sense organs – and the nature of the world we inhabit – we are, for the most part, located on the earth's surface which forms the most basic LM for orienting ourselves and the earth's surface is solid and opaque so that we cannot easily gain access to what is located under the surface – the way we experience many TR–LM relations designated by *over* is substantially different from the way in which we experience TRs which are designated by *under*. Some of the differences can be characterized as, in part, oppositional. But many are more appropriately understood as contrasting, that is, they are simply different.

Moreover, as we argued in our discussion of *over*, English spatial particles also involve a functional element; the meaningful consequences of the functional element associated with spatial 'opposites' are not necessarily in opposition. We have found that particles which code for near antonymy in terms of spatial configuration of the TR and LM can code for quite different functional elements, as we will see later in the book (particularly when we consider spatial particles relating to oriented LMs in chapter 6). We also find spatial particles that have traditionally been represented as antonyms, such as *over* and *under*, both developing some of the same extended senses. For instance, both *over* and *under* have developed both Control and Covering Senses that neither *above* nor *below* have developed. We will argue that this is due to the fact that while the TR–LM configurations for *over* and *under* represent an oppositional contrast, both particles denote the same functional element.

Accordingly, we posit that spatial particles make up a particular *contrast set*. As we understand it, a contrast set relates two (or more) spatial particles, such that in some respects they may form a system of meanings that are understood (and have developed) in terms of other members of the contrast set. However, from this it does not follow that *contrast partners* can be considered to be straightforwardly or simplistically oppositional. For instance, although the majority of uses seem to pair *above* with *below* and *over* with *under*, there are instances in which the conventional pairing is *above* and *under* (as in *keeping one's head above water* versus *going under water*). Our focus is to establish the systematicity to be found in the non-spatial uses of spatial particles, and our analysis shows that there is a good deal; nevertheless, an accurate model of language must also recognize the complexity and semi-systematicity as well.

The vertical axis

English has developed subsets of spatial particles whose proto-scenes privilege certain orientational axes or dimensions (Langacker, 1987; Talmy, 2000). One of the most highly developed subsets involves the vertical axis. The sets: (1) *over, under, above* and *below* and (2) *up* and *down* (see chapter 6 for a discussion of *up* and *down*), all crucially involve the vertical axis. After all, it seems clear that if we are to account for the regular interpretations of sentences such as: *Hillary walked **over** the bridge* versus *Hillary walked **under** the bridge*, it is necessary to recognize that these spatial particles do involve reference to the vertical axis.

Under the topic of *orientation*, Langacker (1987) discusses the need to recognize the vertical and horizontal axes with regard to the various ways a spatial scene can be viewed. 'Orientation ... pertains to alignment with respect to the axes of the visual field (or some comparable coordinate system)' (p. 133). Typical descriptions of spatial scenes presuppose 'the normal horizontal/vertical dimensional grid we calculated in relation to the surface of the earth; this in turn reflects the orientation of our visual field when we assume our canonical upright viewing ... We are accustomed to seeing most of the objects in our experience ... in a canonical alignment with respect to their surroundings ... To the extent that our conception of such objects includes a canonical viewpoint or alignment, this information is necessarily a part of an encyclopedic characterization of the predicates designating them' (ibid.). Langacker also discusses oriented space as a necessary element in our understanding of the distinction between particular spatial particles.

Having argued for the necessity to refer to the vertical or horizontal axis, our claim that the proto-scene for a particular spatial particle involves such a reference does not constitute the claim that **all** spatial particles prompt for such an orientation. So, while the English spatial particles *over, under, above* and *below* regularly prompt for a spatial configuration in which the TR is located along the vertical axis in relation to the LM, either in a 'higher-than' or 'lower-than' position, particles such as *in* and *out of* appear not to reference any axis. Whether or not a particular spatial particle references a vertical or horizontal axis is part of its basic lexical entry. This position is coherent with that presented by Langacker (1987) and Talmy (2000).

Above versus *over*

Above traces its origins to Anglo-Saxon *be + ufan*, which is related to the same Sanskrit root, 'upari', as *over*. In Anglo-Saxon, the antecedent of *over* was *ufa*, the comparative form of *above*. In Gothic, *be + fan* was interpreted roughly as 'being in an up position'. Thus, *over* and *above* have long been closely associated semantically.

Many previous accounts have suggested that *over* and *above* are synonyms, both of which designate a TR that is higher than a LM. For instance, Lakoff (1987) states that the Higher-than Sense of *over* 'is roughly equivalent in meaning to *above*' (p. 425). So in sentences such as the following:

(5.1)   a. The picture is above the mantel
         b. The picture is over the mantel

the interpretations are virtually synonymous.[1] However, these accounts have not addressed sentences such as the following:

---

[1] Although Brugman (1981), Dewell (1994), and Lakoff (1987) do not provide a detailed analysis for *above*, we can infer that the presence or absence of dynamism provides the primary distinction between *above* versus *over* under their approaches. This is so because they define the primary sense of *over* as 'above and across'; they further explain that this sense entails a TR that is higher than the LM and a path along which the TR moves. This definition implies that *above*, as an independent lexical item, does not prompt for an *across* (i.e., dynamic) reading. This representation is consistent with that offered by Lindstromberg (1998) and traditional definitions. However, the linguistic evidence shows that *above* cannot be appropriately distinguished from *over* on the grounds of its presence in sentences that express dynamism. Consider the following sentences:

a. As the British soldiers crouched on the beach of Dunkirk, they could hear the German war planes circling high above them.

b. The blimp sailed far above the stadium, barely visible to the crowd.

Clearly, the interpretation of each of these sentences involves a TR that is in motion. If the appropriate representation of *over* involved [+dynamism] while the appropriate representation of *above* involved [−dynamism], the example sentences should be anomalous. It would seem that analyses which assume this distinction have no explanation for the acceptability of these sentences. Hence, something other than dynamism must distinguish *over* from *above*.

(5.2)   a. The maid hung the jacket over the back of the chair
          b. The maid hung the jacket above the back of the chair

These sentences clearly reveal that the Higher-than readings associated with *over* and *above* are not synonymous. After all, in (5.2a) the TR is conceptualized as being higher than but crucially in contact with the chair. In (5.2b) contact between the TR and LM is precluded.

In attempting to tease apart the meanings of the two particles, Brugman ([1981] 1988) and Kreitzer (1997) argued that *above* is typically interpreted as indicating a less specific location than *over*. On this view, while for *over* the TR is represented as being in the same vertical axis as the LM, in their representation of *above* the TR is located in some 'indefinitely large region' or in an unknown location physically higher than the LM. Kreitzer illustrates the distinction with the following sentences:

(5.3)   a. The birds are somewhere above us
          b. ?The birds are somewhere over us

Krietzer argues that the supposed infelicity of (5.3b) is caused by a clash between the semantics of *somewhere*, which denotes a vagueness of location, and *over*, which is claimed to denote a relatively specific location of the TR.

Careful examination of the evidence demonstrates that this characterization of the TR–LM spatial configuration does not accurately distinguish these particles. First, it fails to explain the seeming synonymy of sentences (5.1a) and (5.1b). Second, it fails to account for the acceptability of sentences such as (5.2b) and (5.4):

(5.4)   There were several stray marks just above the line

Clearly, the interpretation of the location of *the jacket* in relation to *the chair* or the *stray marks* in relation to *the line* cannot involve some infinitely large region or unknown location.

We suggest that the linguistic evidence supports the conclusion that it is the functional element that distinguishes these two particles. Recall that the functional element we posit as being associated with *over*'s proto-scene is that the TR is 'within potential reach of' the LM. This results in a conceptual connectedness between the TR and the LM. In contrast, we suggest that the functional element associated with *above* emphasizes an unbridgeable distance between the TR and the LM, such that the TR is 'not within potential reach of' the LM. Figure 5.1 diagrams the proto-scene for *above*.

As in chapter 4, the TR in figure 5.1 is diagrammed as the dark sphere and the LM as the bold line. The dashed line distinguishes the spatial region that is conceptualized as being proximal to the LM from that which is conceptualized

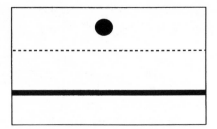

Figure 5.1 The proto-scene for *above*

as being distal. Owing to its location, the TR in the figure is being conceptualized as not within potential reach of the LM.

Now let us examine some linguistic evidence that supports distinguishing the semantic representation of *above* from *over* in this way.

(5.5)   a. Nora twirled over the polished floor
        b. Nora twirled above the polished floor

The examples in (5.5) are characteristic of the distinction in English between *over* and *above*. In the spatial scene described by (5.5a), the TR, *Nora*, uses the *polished floor* as a surface upon which to twirl. Our understanding of the spatial scene described is based on our human experience of dancing, which requires physical contact between the person dancing and the surface being danced upon. In the spatial scene described by (5.5b), we cannot interpret the polished floor as the surface being twirled upon. One possible interpretation is that the TR, *Nora*, refers to some fantastical creature, perhaps a fairy, capable of dancing in the air without actually touching the floor. A second possible interpretation of (5.5b) is that the TR, *Nora*, is located on a balcony overlooking the polished floor. In this case, the surface on which the TR, *Nora*, is located is physically higher than the floor in the scene referred to in (5.5b).

Key to each of these interpretations is the notion that *above* prompts for a relation between the TR and LM which precludes the potential for contact. This contrasts with the relation prompted for linguistically by *over* in which potential for contact is a central part of the interpretation. The point is that speakers of English interpret sentences (5.5a) and (5.5b) differently, and that these meaning distinctions result from the particular spatial particle selected and the distinct spatial-functional relation prompted for by each proto-scene associated with these spatial particles.

Returning to sentence (5.4), as we argued in chapter 4, the use of *above* in this sentence emphasizes the fact that the *stray marks* are not and never could be in contact with *the line*. The distance between the *stray marks* and *the line* is unbridgeable, even if it is metrically very small. This use of *above* is sanctioned through the functional element associated with its proto-scene. Again we note that the sentence in (5.6):

(5.6)   There were several stray marks **over** the line

introduces the possible interpretation of *the marks* being in contact with (and the implicature of covering) the line.

Now let's reconsider the apparent synonymy of the sentences in (5.1). We emphasized in chapter 3 that there are a plethora of ways in which a spatial scene can be viewed or construed. If we consider the various spatial scenes involving *over*, we find that in many instances there is no contact between the TR and the LM; similarly, the spatial scenes described by *above* do not allow contact between the TR and the LM.[2] Thus, in describing a scene in which the TR is higher than the LM and there is no contact between the two, a speaker would conceivably have a choice between the two spatial particles. The basis of the choice would seem to hinge on how the speaker construed the physical distance between the TR and the LM. In other words, in many instances the same spatial scene could efficaciously be described by the use of either particle; the choice would seem to have to do with subtle differences in the speaker's perspective, that is, whether or not the speaker interpreted the distance between the TR and LM as distal or proximal.

Moreover, given that conceptual space is topological in nature rather than Euclidean (recall the discussion in chapter 3), then the conceptualization of, and hence the linguistic representation of, the precise metric measurement between the TR and LM is quite subjective. In certain instances, one speaker's proximal interpretation of the space between the TR and the LM (as signalled by the use of *over*) might be another speaker's distal interpretation (as signalled by the use of *above*). The proto-scenes we posit for *over* and *above*, in conjunction with the inferencing strategy of topological extension discussed in chapter 3, allow for a certain amount of overlap in use of the two particles and predict that either spatial particle can, in some contexts, be used to locate a TR which is higher than and not in contact with the LM. Hence, the proto-scenes posited for *above* and *over* account for several sentence types for which previous accounts have no apparent explanation.

---

[2] This may be too strong a statement. An anonymous reviewer has pointed out that certain TR–LM spatial configurations denoted by *above* do allow contact. For instance, consider the situation in which there is a stack of boxes and two interlocutors. Interlocutor A points to a box: 'Is this the one you want?' Interlocutor B responds, 'No, the one just above it.' Clearly, in this scenario, there is contact between the TR and LM. Such seeming counter-examples potentially point to the reality that our proto-scenes are only an approximation of how the semantics of spatial particles are represented in memory. While the notion of distance between the TR and LM accounts for the majority of uses of *above*, we fully concur with Langacker's analysis of partial sanctioning which ultimately means that certain uses of lexical items are not predictable and only partially motivated.

However, we acknowledge that there are some contexts in which the two prepositions do appear to be interchangeable. For instance, Grice (1975) has argued that one of the guiding principles of communication is that speakers say only as much as is necessary to convey the message they intend (the Maxim of Quantity). In many instances, the speaker may deem that it is communicatively sufficient to identify an entity (TR) by indicating that the entity is higher than the second, locating entity (the LM), in which case the speaker's communicative needs can be met by either form. Consider the following dialogue:

(5.7)   A: Which picture are you planning on selling?
          B: The one hanging above/over the mantel.

In this situation, the relevant information for locating the picture in question is that it is the one located higher than the mantel, rather than, say, to the right of the mantel or in the hallway. Either spatial particle provides the relevant information for the communicative purposes at hand.

Finally in this section, we return to the intuition associated with previous scholars such as Brugman ([1981] 1988), Kreitzer (1997) and Lindstromberg (1998), that the spatial scene prompted for by *above* involves a vaguer relationship between the TR and the LM, one in which the location of the TR is less clearly specified or known, than the scene prompted for by *over*. It seems intuitively clear that humans can more distinctly perceive and observe those entities in their environment which are proximal and with which they have potential physical contact than those entities which are distal and with which they have no potential contact. We find systematic uses of language across a wide range of experiential domains that support this intuition. For instance, language conventionally used to indicate emotional intimacy, a strong degree of knowledge, and salience all draws on the notion of physical proximity:

(5.8)   Colleen is a *close* friend

In contrast, entities which are perceived as being less well known or less important are represented by language indicating a physical distance:

(5.9)   Suzanne and I have grown *apart*

Sweetser (1990) offers an extensive discussion of the relationship between knowing and physical touch (which obviously involves proximity and contact) in her examination of perceptual verbs. She notes that words like *grasp* when used in sentences like:

(5.10)   Chris quickly grasped the idea

reveal the embodied connection between physically holding and manipulating objects and humans' sense of having knowledge of entities. Given the importance of physical proximity in human experience, it seems quite predictable that a TR that is represented as being distant from the LM versus one that is represented as being proximal would be understood as being less clearly located. Thus, we argue that the proto-scenes we have posited for *over* and *above* also account rather neatly for the intuitions of scholars such as Kreitzer, Brugman and Lindstromberg concerning vagueness of location being associated with *above* relative to *over*.

The semantic network for *above*

Beyond the proto-scene, the semantic network for *above* contains only four distinct senses, many fewer than the number contained in the network for *over*. Given that meaning is embodied (derived from human interaction with spatial scenes), this follows naturally. As discussed in the foregoing, in many ways the most salient elements in our environment are those that are close to or in potential contact with. These are accordingly the entities we are most likely to interact with and have first-hand knowledge of. For the young child learning about the world and learning how his or her language labels entities, actions and relations in the world, the here and now, that is, the immediately perceivable, is what is crucial. Moreover, the primary spatial domain for humans (i.e., the spatial domain with which we interact most frequently) is the ground. The fact that we have fewer kinds of formative, salient experiences with entities with which we are not in potential contact results, we suggest, in a spatial relation such as *over*, which relates to potential contact and hence proximity, giving rise to a greater number of distinct meanings than a distal relation such as *above*, which (generally) relates to non-contact, and hence distance.[3]

Figure 5.2 diagrams the semantic network associated with *above*.

The Up Cluster (2)

As we noted during our discussion of the Up Cluster associated with *over* in chapter 4, there are a number of common, everyday experiences in which the notion of being higher than another entity is experienced as being positive in some way. In this cluster, inferences of this kind, relating to the TR being up relative to the LM, give rise to two distinct senses, the More Sense and the Superior Sense.

The More Sense (2.A) In chapter 2 we observed that there is an independently motivated experiential correlation between quantity and vertical elevation. Because an increase in vertical elevation is frequently correlated with

---

[3] Interestingly, *Webster's New International Dictionary, Unabridged* lists many fewer compound forms using *above* than are found for *over*.

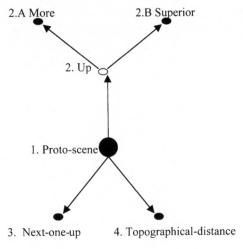

Figure 5.2 The semantic network for *above*

an increase in amount, the proto-scene can in some contexts implicate more. Through pragmatic strengthening this implicature has become conventionally associated with *above*.

Evidence for a distinct sense comes from sentences in which the additional interpretation occurs independently, that is, in the absence of a TR–LM configuration that can be construed as matching the proto-scene associated with the particle. Evidence for establishment of a distinct sense comes from uses of *above* in which there is no objective sense of physicality or of vertical elevation. Consider the following:

(5.11)   The price of that stock is now above $20

In this sentence, both the TR, *the price of that stock*, and the LM, *$20*, represent non-physical entities or concepts. As such, the TR cannot be construed as being located physically in relation to the LM; hence, the sentence cannot be interpreted as prompting for a TR being located physically higher than the LM. The interpretation involves a reading in which the stock price is more than $20.

Consider another example:

(5.12)   The temperature rose to above 100

Due to the experiential correlation between greater quantity and vertical elevation, measuring systems that 'count' quantity are often conceptualized as vertical systems. That is, we often conceptualize measuring systems as vertical scales. Evidence for this comes from thermometers, for instance, which are typically manufactured as vertical scales, consisting of mercury that rises up a thin glass stem as the temperature increases. By perceiving similarity between measurement and verticality, we speak of an increase in temperature as a rise in temperature. Yet, temperature is not in itself a physical entity that has height. Hence, we are utilizing the conventionalized More Sense associated with *above*.

Both *over* and *above* have developed a More Sense. However, the uses of each of these particles in their More Sense are constrained by their representative proto-scenes. For instance, we commonly find expressions such as *above reproach* and *above suspicion* as in the following:

(5.13)   a. Unlike many presidents, Lincoln's personal relations have always been considered above reproach
         b. Gandhi's simple lifestyle placed him above suspicion in terms of acting out of greed or desire to accumulate wealth

In these sentences, the focus is on the clear distinction in Lincoln's or Gandhi's character/actions and the character/actions which would be considered within the realm of *suspicion* or *reproach*. If someone's character or actions put them within potential reach of *suspicion* or *reproach*, then their character or actions are within the scope of *suspicion* or *reproach*. Thus, the choice of *above* seems semantically more felicitous than the choice of *over*.

Nevertheless, the uses of *over* versus *above* to prompt for a More Sense are often nearly synonymous. For instance, we see little difference in interpretation between the following pairs of sentences:

(5.14)   a. In Tuscaloosa, the temperature was above 100 for the tenth straight day
         b. In Tuscaloosa, the temperature was over 100 for the tenth straight day

In our discussion of the near synonymy of the sentences in (5.7), we hypothesized that synonymy is the result of the subjectivity of speakers' interpretation of what is distal and what is proximal. We appeal to this same notion of subjectivity when representing differences in concepts such as temperature. To one speaker, 101 degrees may seem like a big difference in temperature, whereas it may seem like a small difference to another speaker. The key element that both speakers can agree upon is that 101 degrees represent more heat than 100 degrees. Alternatively, it may be that in many situations either spatial particle sufficiently conveys the notion that the temperature is more than 100 degrees. Since both sentences express the fundamental notion of more, either may convey the speaker's intended message with sufficient precision for the communicative purposes at hand.

The Superior Sense (2.B) In many instances, a consequence of being vertically elevated is being superior in some way. In instances where physical elevation is associated with more goods, this is generally considered to be positive. For instance, possessing a higher mound of gold is generally considered to place the prospector in a superior situation. In terms of physical combat, positioning soldiers or an army on higher ground relative to the enemy puts one in an advantageous position, as this affords a better vantage point, and a more effective position from which to launch a mortar assault, etc. Equally, such a location can be more easily defended, as the enemy must climb a hill before attacking.

Analogously, there is a correlation between being physically taller and physical superiority. For instance, the taller, larger person is often the one who will win in physical combat. Moreover, the person who is left standing, in the vertically up position, is the winner in many physical contests. The implicature of superiority, which comes from being vertically elevated, has been conventionalized in the semantic network associated with *above*.

Consider the following example that evidences the Superior Sense:

(5.15)   Nancy's intellectual prowess is well above the other judges in her district

The interpretation of this sentence is that Nancy is a superior judge, not that her intellectual prowess is located physically higher than the other judges. Moreover, in this use of *above*, the concept of great distance seems to be highlighted, which is consistent with the proto-scene we have posited for *above*. Additional information for this claim is that a common paraphrase for a sentence such as (5.15) explicitly involves the notion of 'not within possible reach':

(5.16)   Nancy is such a good judge none of the other judges in her district can even touch her

The sense of superiority involved in sentence (5.16) has to do specifically with merit. We suggest that unless there were a distinct Superior Sense associated with *above*, there would be no contextually derivable way of predicting a superior meaning associated with *above* in (5.15).

Another aspect of the Superior Sense involves an individual's relative status within a hierarchical organization such as a company or a social system. Consider the following examples:

(5.17)   He's above me in the company

In the relation designated by this example, the sentence does not mean that the TR, *he*, is physically higher than the LM, *me*, but rather that the TR, *he*, is superior to the LM, *me*, in some way, for instance in terms of authority, seniority, salary, etc. Interestingly, examples such as (5.17) do not provide a control reading. This is apparent when we compare it to the minimally contrasting (5.18), employing *over*:

(5.18)   He's over me in the company

We suggest that this is the case because of the functional element of 'not within potential reach' associated with *above*. If someone is at a distance, even if they are in a superior position in the organization or society and hence may have nominal control, they are less likely to affect you directly. In contrast, an immediate supervisor, somebody to whom we directly answer, who is hence physically and hierarchically closer to us, is understood to control and affect us. Supervisors and (line-)managers with whom we are in direct contact are often represented as being *over* us. The chief executive or president of a company only indirectly affects lower-level employees, and, hence, is typically conceived as being *above* but not *over* them. Again, the functional element of *above*, which emphasizes distance between the TR and LM, determines the kind of relations that *above* can be used to describe.

As with the More Sense, both *over* and *above* have developed a Superior Sense. Again, we find that the Superior Sense associated with each of these particles reflects their respective proto-scenes:

(5.19)   William rose above his detractors' petty comments

The interpretation of this sentence is not that William physically moved to a position higher than the designated LM, *his detractors*. Rather, the interpretation of this sentence is something like: at one time, William suffered disparaging comments from certain individuals who sought to belittle him; at some later point in time, he behaved in a more morally laudable (= superior) way than his detractors such that he did not become involved in the petty behaviour associated with those who sought to do him ill. Hence, the Superior Sense associated with *above*, relates to no longer being affected by the comments or behaviour of the detractors. A paraphrase might be something like: 'William effectively distanced himself from his detractors' petty comments.' In experiential terms this reading is motivated, as to be *above* one's detractors' petty comments is no longer to be in contact or potential contact with them. This leads to the inference that *William* is no longer affected by these petty comments or the behaviour associated with them (due to the tight correlation between proximity and ability to affect/be affected). Notice the interesting contrast between this sentence and (5.20):

(5.20)   William overcame his detractors' petty comments

Although we can imagine that both sentences could describe the same set of circumstances, sentence (5.20), with its use of *over* in *overcame*, implies a stronger sense of the *detractors' petty comments* being an obstacle that required effort to get beyond. We account for the difference in the readings through positing a functional element associated with *over* that involves connectedness between the TR and the LM versus the functional element of *above*, which highlights an unbridgeable distance between the TR and the LM.

Two additional senses

There are two additional senses associated with *above*, which appear to directly derive from the proto-scene. These are what we term the Next-one-up Sense, and the Topographical-distance Sense. We will briefly deal with each in turn.

The Next-one-up Sense (3) In this sense, *above* relates to the next one up in a vertical sequence. In addition to the Higher-than reading associated with the proto-scene, it provides a more specific meaning component, in which the next element above the one currently in focus is identified. In order to make this concrete, consider some examples:

(5.21)   a. Be careful! The rung above the one you're standing on is broken
         b. His office is on the floor above mine
         c. See the window with the lace curtains? My window is the one just
            above it

In the example in (5.21a), the broken rung being referred to is not in a vaguely defined, general region higher than the one identified as *the one you're standing on*, but rather the next rung in sequence higher than the one identified.

We hypothesize that this sense most likely resulted from the ubiquitous experience of vertical sequences of items, such as rungs on a ladder, floors in a building, etc., in which a particular element within the vertical sequence is identified by virtue of the element beneath it, which serves as a reference point. Accordingly, through pragmatic strengthening, the Next-one-up Sense has become instantiated in memory, such that it can be applied to elements in any vertical sequence, including non-spatial scenes, such as those involving abstract sequences. For instance, this sense is often used to refer to sequenced classes in school, as attested by sentences such as the following: *My sister is in the class/year above mine/me*. It is interesting to note that while in the proto-scene *above* precludes contact between the TR and LM, in certain scenes involving the Next-one-up Sense, by virtue of elements being related in a vertical sequence, such as boxes stacked on top of one another, the next one up will necessarily be in contact with the one beneath, that is, there will be contact between the TR and LM. This use is illustrated in the following: *Is this the box you want? No, not that box, the one above it.*

The Topographical-distance Sense (4) There is a second sense beyond the proto-scene, which does not derive from the Up Cluster. This is the Topographical-distance Sense. To give an immediate indication of what this involves, consider the following:

(5.22)   The nearest bridge is about half a mile above the falls

This sentence does not mean that the bridge is located vertically above the waterfalls such that it is half a mile up in the air. Rather, the conventional reading associated with this sentence is that the TR, *the bridge*, is located half a mile distant upstream from the LM, *the falls*.

This being so, we must consider how *above* has developed this distal sense. In terms of geographical features such as rivers, water flows under the force of gravity. Hence, the source of the river is physically higher than the point at which the river reaches the sea. A second feature of landmarks such as rivers is that they typically extend over great distances, often hundreds of miles. Given that moving upstream correlates with covering geographical distance, then being *above*, in the sense of being at a part of the river which is physically higher than a lower part, entails having covered distance to reach the new location.

A further point of interest with regard to this sense is that the use of *over* is infelicitous: *??The bridge is half a mile over the falls*. Our analysis suggests that *over* was less likely to develop this sense than *above* because of the differences in their proto-scenes. In (5.22), for instance, the point is to emphasize the distance between one point on the river and another point. Our account represents *over* as involving a conceptualization between the TR and the LM which concerns relative proximity, whereas *above* involves relative distance.

Under and *below*

The divisions of the vertical axis higher than the LM represented by *over* and *above* are mirrored by *under* and *below* when the TR is conceptualized as being lower than the LM. Parallel to *over*, the proto-scene for *under* denotes a conceptual spatial-functional relation between a TR and a LM, in which the TR is lower than and yet proximal to the LM. Parallel to *above*, the proto-scene associated with *below* denotes a relation in that the TR is lower than and distal with respect to the LM, and hence the possibility of contact between the TR–LM is (largely) precluded. Figure 5.3 provides the proto-scene for *under*, while figure 5.4 gives the proto-scene for *below*.

In figures 5.3 and 5.4, the LM is designated by the bold line, the TR by the shaded sphere and the region experienced and conceptualized as within reach of the LM by the dashed line. Hence, the region of potential contact is between the LM and the dashed line. In figure 5.4, the TR is outside this region and

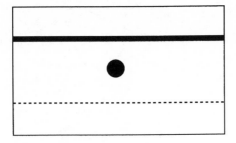

Figure 5.3 Proto-scene for *under*

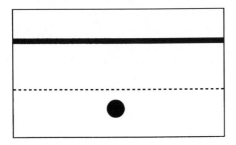

Figure 5.4 Proto-scene for *below*

hence the TR and LM are not in potential contact with respect to one another. The following example evidences this distinction:

(5.23)   a. ??The valley is far under the tallest peak
          b. The valley is far below the tallest peak

In (5.23a) the TR and LM are distant from each other. However, *under* denotes a proximal relation. Hence, *under* is infelicitous in spatial scenes involving great distance between the TR and LM. In contrast, *below* precludes proximity and hence provides the best fit to indicate a distal relation between the TR and the LM. Felicitous examples for *under* are provided in (5.24):

(5.24)   a. The life jacket is kept under the seat
          b. The lumberjacks put skids under the felled logs
          c. The nurse deftly slipped the pillow under the patient's head

Notice in the interpretation of (5.24a) the TR, the *life jacket*, is not necessarily in contact with the seat, but is in proximity to it. In (5.24b) and (c) the interpretation is that the TR is in contact with the LM. As we noted in our discussions of *over* and *above*, we find that in spatial scenes in which there is no contact and no emphasis or assumption of an unbridgeable distance, the choice of either form is acceptable. So, we find the choice of *below* acceptable (although perhaps not as natural as *under*) in the following:

(5.25)   The life jacket is kept **below** the seat

In contrast, in scenes in which contact is highlighted or assumed, *below* is less felicitous:

(5.26)   ??The nurse slipped the pillow **below** the patient's head

Hence, spatial scenes that allow for subjective interpretation of distance allow the use of either *under* or *below*. This is in accordance with the inferencing strategy of Topological Extension and the view that spatial particles can be construed in a number of different ways. In such instances, the two particles seem to be near synonyms. However, in scenes in which presence or absence of contact between the TR and the LM is highlighted, the two particles are clearly distinguished.

Etymologically, *under* is related to Sanskrit *adhara*, which translates roughly to 'lower'. *Below* is directly related to Gothic *be + low*. Thus, both particles retain their diachronically earlier spatial sense. As with *over* and *above*, what distinguishes the two is their contrasting functional elements, being within potential reach (*under*), versus not being within potential reach (*below*).

The semantic network for *under*

Under is analogous to *over* in that both spatial relations prompt for conceptualizations in which the TR is proximal to, and hence in potential contact with, the LM. Accordingly, the patterns found with *over* are to some extent repeated with *under*. However, the semantic network associated with *under* is far less extensive than that of *over*. This may be because in many of our interactions with the world, objects and entities which are higher are often more accessible. For instance, as we are vertically elevated, and do not crawl along the ground in the way that animals such as snakes do, entities and actions which occur higher than ground level may be more accessible than those which occur at ground level, and hence in a lower position. The semantic network for *under* is given in figure 5.5.

The Down Cluster (2)

This cluster represents the mirror of the Up Cluster for *over*. Owing to experiential correlation, a TR that is lower than the LM implicates less. Equally, a TR that is both vertically lower than and within potential reach of the LM can be

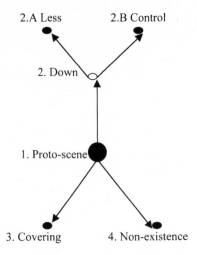

Figure 5.5 Semantic network for *under*

conceptualized as being subject to the control of the LM. These implicatures have been conventionalized and instantiated in the semantic network for *under*.

The Less Sense (2.A) Evidence that less is a distinct sense in the semantic network comes from sentences in which the TR and LM cannot be construed as being physically lower than the TR:

(5.27)   The government decided to exempt incomes under $4,000 (*Webster's Unabridged Dictionary*)

In this sentence, we do not conventionally understand that there is a spatial relation that holds between incomes higher than $4,000 and those lower than $4,000. Rather, *under* has a conventional meaning of less than. Unless there were a distinct sense instantiated in memory, there would be no way of predicting this non-spatial reading.

As we have already seen with our discussion of *over* in chapter 4, and *above* earlier in this chapter, this sense comes to be associated with *under*, due to an independently motivated experiential correlation between vertical elevation and quantity. Being lower correspondingly implicates having less of something. This sense is highly productive, as illustrated by the following:

(5.28)   a. Sorry, you can't drink here if you're under 21
          b. It's impossible to run the marathon in under one hour

The Control Sense (2.B) The second sense deriving from the Down Cluster is the Control Sense. An important insight offered by the principled polysemy approach is that both *over* and *under*, which are traditionally represented as opposites, should both develop a similar meaning component, a Control Sense. We will argue that representing the primary meaning of the spatial particles as including both TR–LM configurations (which indeed are 'opposites' for *over* and *under*) and functional elements (which we represent as being 'within reach of the LM' or proximal for both spatial particles) allows for a motivated account of this phenomenon.

Because *under* prompts for a relation which includes both being physically lower than and within potential contact with the LM as meaning components (recall the discussion of control in chapter 4 in which contact emerged as a key component of control), it is ideally suited to developing a Control Sense. Consider the following:

(5.29)   The boy had trapped the fly under his hand

In the spatial scene designated by this sentence, the proto-scene is denoted. However, by virtue of the TR, *the fly*, being located *under* the LM, *his hand*, the fly is thereby trapped, and the boy has the fly in his control. Through pragmatic strengthening this control implicature has become conventionally associated with *under*, as evidenced by the following:

(5.30)   George works under his father's close supervision at the family business

The sentence in (5.30) does not have a conventional interpretation that George is physically lower than his father, but rather that George's actions at work are scrutinized and controlled by his father. In fact, almost any kind of physical and/or abstract condition that can be conceptualized as influencing and hence controlling one's actions can be related via the Control Sense:

(5.31)   a. He was caught driving under the influence of alcohol
         b. We're under contract
         c. They put her under general anaesthetic
         d. Philip felt himself under obligation to attend the new boss's party

Two additional senses

The Covering Sense (3) The semantic network for *under* has two senses that do not derive from the Down Cluster. The first of these is the Covering Sense. As with the Control Sense, a simple oppositional representation of *over* versus *under* would not predict that these two particles would develop the same sense. However, as was the case with *over*, a consequence of adopting a certain vantage point on a spatial scene involving a TR that is within potential reach of the LM is a construal in which one element in the spatial relation intervenes between the construer and the second element. If the intervening element is opaque, the inevitable consequence is that the second element is obscured. In the case of *under*, the LM intervenes and obscures the TR from view.

By way of illustration consider the following:

(5.32)   My diary is somewhere under all this paperwork

In (5.32) the TR, *my diary*, is physically lower than the LM, *all this paperwork*. The interpretation of the sentence is that the papers are covering the diary and obscuring it from the speaker's line of vision. However, in (5.32) the Covering reading is a contextually derived implicature, based on the proto-scene.

Evidence that the Covering Sense has become a distinct sense comes from sentences in which a vertical relation does not exist between the TR and the LM:

(5.33)   The decorated walls were draped under plastic sheeting while the floor was being sanded

In (5.33), the TR, *the decorated walls*, is not actually physically lower than the LM, *plastic sheeting*. Without a distinct Covering Sense, there would be no way of correctly predicting the conventional reading of covering associated with this sentence.

Sentence (5.34) provides a second example:

(5.34)   The curator keeps the pictures hanging in the gallery under glass to protect them

Here the spatial configuration between the TR and the LM is a horizontal one. The interpretation assigned to the sentence is that the LM, *the glass*, is covering the TR, *the pictures*, not that the pictures are physically lower than the glass.

As with *over*, when the LM is opaque, some usages of *under* give rise to an on-line interpretation of occlusion, as in the following:

(5.35)   The RAF kept their planes under camouflage tarps

The assumed vantage point is such that the LM, *camouflage tarps*, intervenes between the viewer and the TR, *their planes*. Because of what we know about *camouflage tarps* and human vision, we interpret the tarps as obstructing the view of the planes. We find a 'covering-and-thereby-occluding' reading in sentences in which the LM is not necessarily in vertical alignment with the TR.

(5.36)   As Esmerelda stared at the painting on the wall, she explained, 'Van Gogh's distinctive brush strokes can't be seen under all this old varnish!'

As with *over*, we have been unable to find any context-independent examples of occlusion with *under*. That is, occlusion seems not to be a distinct sense, but a contextualized implicature deriving from the Covering Sense when the LM is opaque.

Further evidence that the Covering Sense constitutes a distinct sense comes from the following examples. As these relate to non-physical entities, there is no contextually available means of predicting a reading of Covering:

(5.37) a. He hid his yawn under a cough
        b. The Germans often bombed London under the cover of darkness

The Non-existence Sense (4) A salient aspect of human experience is death. In many cultures, and traditionally in western cultures, the dead are buried underground. This gives rise to a recurring correlation between being *under* and no longer being alive. For instance, dead people are often buried underground; drowning, resulting in death, correlates with disappearing under the water's surface, etc. We suggest that this correlation in experience has given rise, in certain contexts, to an implicature of non-existence having become associated with *under*.

By way of example, consider the following:

(5.38) Typically, to prevent animals from disturbing the grave, the dead person is buried under six feet of dirt

In this sentence there is a correlation between being located under and death (hence non-existence). Hence, the use of *under* in this context implicates non-existence. However, there are also instances of this sense that cannot be predicted from context. This suggests that the implicature that being *under* is no longer to exist has been conventionalized within the semantic network for *under*:

(5.39) The business went under

In (5.39) the conventional reading associated with the sentence is that the business no longer exists. Clearly, this interpretation cannot be derived from the context, primarily because the business is a non-physical entity. As such, the spatial configuration designated by *under* is not available. This counts as evidence that a distinct Non-existence Sense must be instantiated in memory.

The semantic network for *below*

The origins of *below* can be traced to Old Norse *be* + *lagr*, 'to be prostrate' and Anglo-Saxon *bi* + *low* 'be in a lower place'.

As with *above*, which constitutes its contrast partner, *below* denotes a conceptual spatial-functional relation in which there is no possibility of contact between the TR and the LM. The senses associated with the semantic network for *below* closely mirror those associated with *above*, as illustrated in figure 5.6.

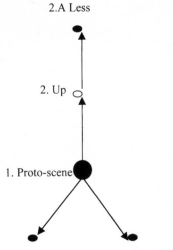

2.A Less

2. Up

1. Proto-scene

3. Next-one-down   4. Topographical Distance

Figure 5.6 Semantic network for *below*

The Down Cluster (2)

Below has two distinct senses subsumed under the Down Cluster. These are the Less Sense and the Inferior Sense.

The Less Sense (2.A) In this sense, *below* denotes a relation in which the TR constitutes less vis-à-vis the LM. Evidence for this sense comes from examples such as the following:

(5.40) a. The temperature dropped below freezing
        b. The European stock markets fell below their lowest levels for half
           a century

As with the More Senses associated with *over* and with *above*, this sense is motivated by the tight correlation in experience between quantity and vertical elevation. When an entity is vertically lower, there is less quantity. It is likely that this sense derived from examples of the following kind, in which this correlation is apparent:

(5.41) a. The water level is far below what is needed to supply the district
           during the summer months
        b. Ian's head was still below the mark made for his brother when he
           was twelve.

In these examples, the spatial relation of being below strongly implicates less. Due to strengthening of this implicature, we suggest that *below* has derived a conventionalized Less Sense, which has come to be instantiated in memory. It is due to this conventional sense that a reading of less is designated by the examples in (5.39).

The Inferior Sense A consequence of being lower and hence having less quantity is that one is in a disadvantaged position, and hence an inferior situation. By way of illustration, consider the following:

(5.42)   I don't interact with Alan much, as he is below me in the law firm

The interpretation of this sentence is not that the TR is located physically lower than the LM, but that the TR, *Alan*, is in an inferior position in the law firm relative to the speaker. Consider some additional examples of this sense:

(5.43)   a. Her reading comprehension is below average compared to that of
             other twelve-year-olds
          b. Year on year, the company is performing below par

As these examples do not directly relate to spatial scenes, but rather involve non-physical entities, such as average reading ability and a company's financial performance, unless there were an Inferior Sense conventionally associated with *below*, there would be no other means of predicting that these sentences prompt for a reading of inferiority.

Two additional senses

The Next-one-down Sense (3) The semantic network of *below* has a mirror-image of the Next-one-up Sense, associated with *above*, namely the Next-one-down Sense. Here, *below* serves to identify precisely the next element in a vertical sequence below the TR, as evidenced by the following:

(5.44)   a. Not that one, the box below it!
          b. His office is on the floor below mine

As we observed in our discussion of the Next-one-up Sense for *above*, this sense allows the TR and LM to be in potential contact, by virtue of participating in a vertical sequence. Moreover, evidence that this sense is stored as a distinct sense in semantic memory comes from the fact that it can be used in non-spatial scenes, that is, contexts of use from which this meaning could not otherwise be contextually derived: *She's in the year/class below me.*

Topographical distance

The Topographical-distance Sense (4) As with *above, below* conventionally designates distance. As we saw previously, distance correlates with elevation in terms of geographically extended landmarks such as rivers. The following are illustrative of this sense.

(5.45)   a. The hydroelectric station is five miles below the dam
         b. They stood a mile or so below the falls

In each of these examples, *below* conventionally prompts for a reading of distant from, rather than lower than. In (5.45a) *the hydroelectric station* is five miles distant from the dam, while in (5.45b), *they* are located a mile distant from the falls. The view that both *above* and *below* are associated with similar sense, albeit in a different direction relative to the direction of the flow of water (above versus below the LM, e.g., the dam/falls, etc.), provides further evidence that these two forms are contrast partners.

Conclusion: the semantics of verticality

One important conclusion that has emerged during our analysis of *over, above, under* and *below* in the course of this and the previous chapter, is that English makes certain locational distinctions in dividing up the vertical axis. Each of the four particles considered selects a slightly different range within the vertical axis. However, as we have seen, these distinctions are not criterial, that is, we cannot pinpoint metrically established necessary and sufficient conditions for determining when a relation is properly *over* rather than *above* or *under* rather than *below*. There are elements of subjectivity or 'plasticity' in what can count as proximal or distal and hence what can count as *over* and what *above*. To an extent, conventions of usage dictate in which collocations *above* rather than *over* can be felicitously used. However, there are nonetheless clear semantic distinctions between *over* and *above*, as there are between *under* and

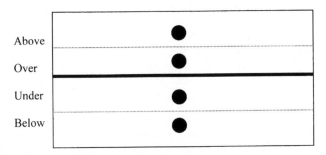

Figure 5.7 Vertical axis in English

below. These distinctions manifest themselves in the way that each particle can be extended in its development of other distinct senses. For instance, the fact that *above* and *below* generally preclude the possibility of contact between the TR and the LM while *over* and *under* do not has clear and consistent consequences, for instance, in the Control Sense, which requires the possibility of contact.

In chapter 3 we introduced the inferencing strategy of topological extension. This notion reflects the view that the human conceptual system for space does not seem to deal in metric distances, but rather in conceptually flexible judgements, which are nonetheless well motivated and systematic. Figure 5.7 provides a summary, based on the linguistic analysis adduced, representing how the vertical axis in English is segmented.

6   Spatial particles of orientation

In the previous two chapters we have argued that the semantics of *over, under, above* and *below* differentially reference the vertical axis (or what Langacker, 1987, terms 'oriented space'). As such, these spatial particles serve to partition conceptual space in terms of verticality. In this chapter, we turn to a subset of spatial particles whose semantics crucially involves an additional element, the orientation of either the LM or the TR. We will deal with four forms which relate to an oriented TR: *up, down, to* and *for*, and four which relate to an oriented LM: *in front of, before, behind* and *after*.

Orientation is a designation of a conceptual front/back, top/bottom, or lateral[1] partitioning of either the TR or the LM. This conceptual partitioning has its basis in a perceived asymmetry of the partitioned entity. Such asymmetry can arise as a result of the way the entity typically stands or sits, its shape (e.g., if an object has a pointed end, it is typically understood as its 'front') (Talmy, 2000), its perceived parts (Talmy, 2000),[2] its perceived 'directedness' (Talmy, 2000: 199), its movement (Fillmore, 1971), or the way it is used by humans (e.g., the 'front' of a building is the side which is accessible for general entry) (Langacker, 1987), as well as its perceived resemblance to human beings or animals (Fillmore, 1971; Herskovits, 1986; Svorou, 1994). Clearly, the attributes which give rise to an object being conceptualized as asymmetric involve how humans both perceive and interact with the object. Accordingly, the concept of orientation underscores the importance of embodied experience (rather than 'objective reality'; recall our discussion in chapter 2) in the semantics of natural language.

In many spatial scenes, the orientation of the TR and/or LM is not salient for the speaker's purposes. For instance, the sentence *The cat is in the box* involves a TR, *the cat*, which has a clear front. However, in this scene, the orientation of the cat is inconsequential to the interpretation of the spatial configuration between the TR, *the cat*, and the LM, *the box*.

---

[1] In a full analysis of spatial particles, lateral orientation also must be included in order to account for the semantics of particles such as *next to, along, beside*, etc. We do not directly address these particles in our presentation.

[2] In certain cases, asymmetry and recognition of parts is crucial (Talmy, 2000: 197).

Nevertheless, an examination of the semantics of English spatial particles indicates that a number of forms crucially involve conceptualizing either the TR or the LM (or both) as being oriented. The motivation for linguistically coding such conceptual partitioning presumably lies in its usefulness in allowing the speaker to articulate a sufficiently precise description of the spatial scene being prompted for. We assume the purpose of such a description is to allow the listener to locate a specific entity either actually or 'imaginally' (Talmy, 2000: 185). Talmy argues that as speakers attempt to provide a kind of conceptual map of the spatial scene through language, they tend to be concerned with locating a smaller area of focal interest within a broader scene. ' "[L]ocalizing" an object (determining its location)... involves processes of dividing a space into subregions or segmenting it along its contours, so as to "narrow in" on an object's immediate environment' (ibid.).

The notion of orientation of the TR or the LM is not new. For instance, even traditional accounts (e.g., Frank, 1972; Quirk *et al.*, 1985) represent the prepositions *to* and *from* diagrammatically with arrows pointing towards or away from a particular location. Although they do not explicitly discuss the notion of orientation, it is implicit in these 'arrow' characterizations. However, these authors also represent a number of other prepositions which we do not believe have inherent orientation, such as *out* (see chapter 7), with arrow diagrams. Thus, while traditional accounts recognize orientation at some level, its characterization has been unclear and its assignment to individual particles inconsistent.

Many cognitive linguists (e.g., Fillmore, 1971; Herskovits, 1986; Heine, 1997; Langacker, 1987, 1991; Svorou, 1994; Talmy, 1983, 2000; Vandeloise, 1991) have recognized, with varying degrees of explicitness, the necessity of designating front/back, top/bottom, or side regions for TRs and LMs in particular configurations. Heine (1997), Svorou (1994), Talmy (2000) and Vandeloise (1991), in particular, discuss the importance of the front/back designation based on both anthropomorphic and zoomorphic models. In addition, they also discuss the top–bottom axis not only in terms of its basis in human and zoomorphic forms but also in terms of the earth's surface in relation to the sky. (The effect of gravity also figures in this designation.)

However, our analysis is distinct from these previous approaches, given that we assume the perspective and methodology of the theory of principled polysemy outlined in chapter 3 and illustrated in chapters 4 and 5. Notably, while previous analyses have primarily focused on the polysemy of spatial senses associated with spatial particles, we will show in this chapter how spatial orientation, through experiential correlation, gives rise to new experiences and inferences. Moreover, the proto-scene we posit for each particle involves not only a conceptual spatial relation between a TR and LM (at least one of which is oriented) but also a functional element, which, with the particular particles considered in this chapter, also reflects the meaningfulness of spatial orientation. Hence, the spatial particle *to*, for instance, which historically had a spatial meaning of a TR being oriented towards an unoriented LM, has derived a Comparison Sense, which is non-spatial in nature, for example *The design of this sweater is inferior to that one*. Consequently, we will be in a position to explain how such meanings, grounded in the nature of our interaction with spatial scenes, give rise to non-spatial meanings which, in turn, become conventionally associated with forms such as *to*, enriching the semantic network of this form.

Another important way in which the analyses to be presented in this (and the next) chapter differ from previous research is that we will argue a full analysis of spatial particles involves distinguishing orientation and path and motion. Previous analyses (e.g., Lakoff, 1987; Talmy, 2000) have assigned path to the primary sense associated with particular spatial particles because the spatial scenes that are prompted for by the contextualized use of a particle often involve motion. As such, these analysts have tended to conflate orientation and path. We will argue in our discussion of *through* in chapter 7 that a path is a conceptual construct, derived from a series of spatially contiguous locations, mediating a starting point and an ending point. The concept of path derives from a spatial relation, independently of a TR in motion (although motion does often correlate with a path). Some spatial particles (e.g., *through* discussed in the next chapter) code path as their functional element.

However, as will become clear in this chapter, the notion of orientation, while often associated with motion or with path, is distinct from both. Motion is designated typically by verbs, as it involves a relation that evolves through time; in contrast, spatial particles are atemporal, designating a spatial snapshot via summary scanning (recall the discussion in chapter 3). As such, although spatial particles can designate *orientation* – which pertains to asymmetry of the TR (or LM) in relation to the LM (or TR) – or *path* – which pertains to a spatially contiguous series of locations – or both, they cannot designate motion. (It is worth pointing out that the concepts of orientation, path and motion can also be distinguished from a *trajectory*, discussed in chapter 4, which relates to the path followed by a trajector (TR), canonically a motile entity.) Hence, the present approach clearly distinguishes the notions of orientation, path and motion.

In terms of the analyses we will present in this (and the next) chapter, our objective, in contrast to chapters 4 and 5, is not to provide an exhaustive characterization of the semantic network associated with each form. Although we have conducted detailed analyses of each of the spatial particles we will address, to characterize the entire network for each would be very lengthy and the argumentation would be highly redundant. Rather, we select a limited number of senses associated with each form. These have been chosen in order to illustrate the proto-scene for each spatial particle and extensions from it to non-spatial meanings. Our purpose in proceeding in this fashion is twofold. First, such an overview will provide a means of exploring the range of ways in which spatial particles can code for orientation. This, in turn, reflects the way in which we as human beings experience orientation through interacting with our environment. Second, such an overview will illustrate how orientation has non-trivial consequences giving rise, via correlations in experience, to new meanings and inferences, which come to represent distinct and conventional meanings. Such meanings, while derived from a particular spatial scene, are often non-spatial in nature. Hence, this analysis will further elaborate the view that spatial experience plays an important, if not fundamental, role in deriving many non-spatial senses.

Vertical orientation of the TR: *up* and *down*

In this section we examine the semantics of *up* and *down*, two spatial particles involving orientation of the TR and the LM along the vertical dimension.[3] Unlike the four spatial particles of verticality discussed previously, *up* and *down* do not code relative vertical **location** of the TR in terms of partitioned space vis-à-vis a LM. Rather, they represent the linguistic means of expressing **orientation** of the TR in reference to an asymmetric LM along the vertical axis.

In an early, groundbreaking analysis of the importance of interaction with spatial scenes in structuring non-spatial conceptualization, H. Clark (1973) noted that, given that our legs are at one end of our bodies and our head at the other, and that we walk in an upright fashion, then these distinctions provide a reliable means for distinguishing *up* from *down*. Put another way, our bodies are asymmetric, and this asymmetry has non-trivial consequences for our interaction with our environment. Moreover, in terms of our environment, the vertical axis is also asymmetric, as gravity provides a natural direction, which can be established at any location on the Earth. Hence, spatial orientation in the vertical axis is inherently meaningful, by virtue of the seemingly unremarkable fact that we interact with our environment. Yet, what may appear to be nothing more than a truism is anything but trivial, as it has the most profound consequences for conceptual structure and the development of a semantic (and hence linguistic) representational system.

Through an examination of the complex polysemy exhibited by the English forms *up* and *down*, we will see how the asymmetric orientation of verticality is meaningful to us, and, in conceptual terms, extends far beyond the purely spatial notion of vertical orientation.

---

[3] Other particles such as *on top, at the top, on the bottom, at the bottom,* etc. involve vertical orientation of the LM. We do not address these particles in our present discussion.

The semantics of *up*

The semantics of *up* is particularly complex. However, in the ensuing we will primarily limit ourselves to a discussion of the proto-scene and one cluster of senses. In particular, the analysis provides an elegant illustration of the way in which experiential correlations based on the proto-scene can give rise to meanings or senses that, in some cases, are wholly non-spatial in character. Moreover, more than one experiential correlation may contribute to a particular concept. This point is made clear when we study the complex nature of the concept of completion, illustrated in our discussion of the Completion Sense associated with *up*.

The proto-scene

We propose that the proto-scene for *up* denotes a relation in which the TR is directed towards the top of an oriented LM. Thus, the LM is conceptually partitioned and construed as having a top and bottom; what counts as *top* is determined by the LM. The TR is also conceptualized as being oriented; in this case, the asymmetry arises as a result of the direction in which the TR is directed. What constitutes *up* is the relation between the asymmetric LM and the oriented TR. Thus, we posit a proto-scene for *up* (as well as *down*) which involves an oriented TR and an asymmetric LM, partitioned into top and bottom components.

Given the importance of embodied experience and the asymmetrical nature of the human body, we suggest that the human anatomy offers a plausible schematization for the LM, and employ this in the proto-scene for *up* (cf. Heine, 1997; Svorou, 1994 for a cross-linguistic perspective). In a study of fifty-five languages, Svorou (1994) found that over 50 per cent actually used a term for 'head' to indicate the spatial relation denoted by *up*. A number of uses of the word *head* in English seem to draw on the notion that the head is the highest body part when a person is in upright position, for example *head of the stairs, head of beer, head of steam*. One of the motivations for the use of the lexeme *head* to describe the person or entity at the 'top' of hierarchically structured organizations (which are metaphorically conceptualized as vertical) may derive from the head being located at the top of the human body.[4] Our proto-scene for *up* is diagrammed in figure 6.1.

In figure 6.1 the 'stick-person' represents the asymmetrical LM; the head or 'top' is in focus and hence highlighted, which is represented by the shaded sphere, constituting the TR. The TR is represented by the dark sphere. The

---

[4] Another important motivation may be that the head of the body is conceptualized as being the centre of our faculties of reason, and hence controls our bodies and the actions associated with them. Analogously, the head of a school, or of an organization, controls the organization.

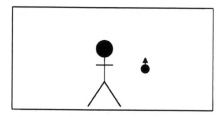

Figure 6.1 Proto-scene for *up*

orientation of the TR is represented by the direction of the arrow emerging from the sphere. Some linguistic examples of spatial scenes containing this relation are as follows:

(6.1)   a. The bird flew up the chimney
          b. Jennifer climbed up the mountain
          c. Frankie threw the stone up the well-shaft

While none of the LMs in the sentences in (6.1) are necessarily asymmetrical, a vertical asymmetry, not unlike the asymmetry of the human body, appears to be projected onto these structures, even when they are perfectly symmetrical, such as well-shafts and chimneys. For instance, we can speak in terms of the top of a well-shaft, as easily as we speak of the top of someone's head. Further examples involving adpreps and participles in verb-particle constructions (VPCs) rather than prepositions (recall from chapter 3, that adpreps and particles in VPCs do not overtly signal a LM) are given below:

(6.2)   a. The kite is up in the air
          b. The child picked up the shell from among the seaweed
          c. The cat pricked up its ears
          d. He set the jar the right way up

We hypothesize that the functional element[5] associated with the proto-scene denoted by *up* is one of positive value, in the sense that entities which are physically elevated are more visible as in (6.2a), more accessible (6.2b), in a state of readiness (6.2c), or in a normative position (6.2d). This is consistent with the work of H. Clark (1973), who observes that:

[F]acts of perception also suggest how we could assign positive and negative values to the directions away from the ... [plane] ... of asymmetry ... where *positive* is taken in its natural sense to mean the presence of something, and *negative* the absence ... since everything above ground level is perceptible and nothing below it is, upward is naturally positive and downward naturally negative. (Clark, 1973: 33)

---

[5] Grady (personal communication) has noted that given the range of concepts covered by the term 'positive', it might be more useful to characterize these as a set of functions rather than a single function.

As our model would lead us to predict, not all extended senses of *up* highlight the functional element and therefore not all the extended senses denote a positive value. For instance, in a sentence such as *Shackleton's men broke up the furniture to use for firewood*, the form *up* appears to stem from human observation of an upward motion which occurs when downward pressure is placed on two ends of a rigid object until the object snaps (upward) in the middle. Contrary to the meaning denoted by the functional element, the result of *breaking up* an object is to make it less functional and less in a state of readiness.[6]

The Quantity Cluster for 'up'

The cluster of senses that we are terming the Quantity Cluster derives from the familiar experiential correlation between quantity and vertical elevation. In the following sections, we discuss three distinct senses that derive from this correlation. This discussion illustrates how a particular orientation towards the vertical axis can become meaningful to us as human beings because of the consequences it entails. Spatial axes are far more than merely locational/spatial denotations; they necessarily give rise to subjective (in the sense of humanly lived) responses, which provide non-spatial concepts. What is interesting about the senses subsumed under the Quantity Cluster is that there is nothing inherently spatial about these meaning components, although they ultimately derive from experiential correlations grounded in spatial scenes closely related to the proto-scene, which is spatial in nature.

The More Sense As we have already seen, quantity and vertical elevation come to be associated at the conceptual level, not due to any perceived similarity between them, but rather due to their pervasive and recurring correlation in experience. It is often the case that an increase in vertical elevation correlates with an increase in quantity. This association causes *up*, which hence implicates more, to give rise to a conventionalized More Sense. Consider some examples:

(6.3)   a. The maid plumped up the cushions
          b. The farmer fattened up the calf
          c. Pump/turn up the volume/heat [= more volume/heat]

In each of these examples, the conventional reading associated with *up* is that there is an increase in quantity. In some examples, such as (6.3a), this is a

---

[6] We hypothesize that this use may also derive from experiencing an object moving away when it is thrown up into the air, giving rise to an experiential correlation between an object in an up position and separation between the object and the observer. In our full analysis we have posited a Separation Sense, which is based on this experiential correlation. Other examples of the Separation Sense include *tear up, split up, chop up, cut up*, etc.

contextually available implicature, as an increase in upward orientation correlates with greater quantity. However, in (6.3b) and (6.3c) this implicature is not available from context. The More Sense must therefore be instantiated as a distinct meaning component in the network for *up* if the More reading is to be available.

The Improvement Sense A consequence of obtaining a greater quantity, or more of something, is that it often implicates improvement or betterment. For instance, obtaining more food entails being less hungry, a desirable situation. Equally, obtaining more money for a particular job implicates a superior standard of living. Owing to the use of *up* in contexts in which an implicature of improvement or betterment occurs, *up* has developed a conventionalized Improvement Sense. This is clear from the following example in which there is no contextual means of predicting that *up* is associated with improvement:

(6.4)   a. I read up on British history after watching the film about Elizabeth I
          b. I brushed up my German before the conference in Landau
          c. Dave and Kirsten decided to get dressed up and go to a nice restaurant

In the first example, the conventional reading is that the speaker's knowledge of British history was increased and therefore improved. Note there is no implication of anything being physically elevated. In the second sentence, the conventional reading is that the speaker's language skills were increased and therefore improved. In the final example, the interpretation of improvement or betterment is particularly distinct from any sense of increase of amount. When people get dressed *up*, they put on clothing that they perceive to be more fashionable or elegant than their everyday attire; their goal in doing so is presumably to improve their appearance. However, this improvement does not necessarily involve putting on more clothing. If we contrast sentence (6.4c) to *Dave and Kirsten decided to get dressed*, we can see that the presence of *up* clearly adds an element of dressing in a culturally sanctioned 'improved' style.[7]

The Completion Sense A consequence of increasing quantity is that, in many circumstances, a limit is reached at which point there can be no further increase. This entails that the increase is complete. A common example of this relates to our everyday interaction with containers, ranging from cups of coffee, to baths, to glasses of beer. For instance, if liquid is poured into a glass, as the

---

[7] While it seems evident that there is an important connection between having more of something and improvement of one's situation, another plausible motivating influence on the Improvement Sense comes from the experiential correlation between being physically in an upright position and a general sense of alertness and well-being. These two motivations seem to mutually reinforce one another.

quantity of liquid contained increases, a point is reached where no more liquid can be contained, and hence the pouring activity is complete. Thus, there is a correlation between a liquid being up, with respect to a particular container, and the capacity of the container being completely used. For instance, in the following example, by virtue of filling up the container, the pitcher reaches its full capacity, hence the increase in the level of beer is complete and the action of filling the container is completed:

(6.5)   The server filled up the pitcher with beer

It might be argued that the verb *fill* entails completion in sentence (6.5). However, in (6.6a) we find the implication of carrying out an action until the container is filled to capacity even though the verb does not imply completion. In (6.6b) the implicature is that the filling will proceed until the task is complete.

(6.6)   a. Be sure to gas up the car for the trip
          b. Let's load up the truck and get going

Thus, in certain contexts, as filling a container to capacity correlates with an increase in vertical elevation, an implicature of completion comes to be associated with *up*. Through pragmatic strengthening this implicature has become a conventionalized sense. This is evidenced by the following examples, in which the meaning of completion is not derivable from context, strongly suggesting that there is a Completion Sense associated with *up*:

(6.7)   a. Let's finish up this work today
          b. They closed up the shop for the night

In each of these examples, unless *up* had a conventional Completion Sense associated with it, there would be no means of explaining how *up* is compatible with verbs such as *finish* and *close*.[8]

Parallel to our analysis of *over*, in which we argued for more than one Excess Sense, we suggest that *up* has two distinct Completion Senses, each stemming from a different experiential correlation and each denoting a somewhat different aspect of completion.

Consider the following sentences:

(6.8)   a. The flashlight won't work. We must have used up the batteries
          b. Students, turn in your papers; your time is up!
          c. The guests drank up the wine and promptly fell asleep.

---

[8] There are a number of examples which reflect the perception that the human body is a container that has reached capacity: 'How about some more cake? No, really, I'm **full**', 'I'm stuffed', 'If I take one more bite, I'll explode.' These expressions implicate that the eating is completed. We believe this conceptualization of the body as a container and the Completion Sense associated with *up* is the basis for the metaphoric expression in the sentence *I'm fed up with all this complaining*, which seems to draw on the image (through perceptual resemblance) of the human as a container that can be filled to capacity by the actions of others.

Notice that the sense of completion evoked in each of these sentences seems to involve the notion of depletion, rather than filling a container to capacity. In sentence (6.8a) the implication is that all the stored energy in the battery has been consumed. In (6.8b) the typical interpretation is that the students were allotted a specified amount of time to write their papers and that the time has elapsed, that is, the students have used all the allotted time. In (6.8c) the boorish guests have completely consumed the wine.

At first glance, the link between *up*, which generally denotes a TR in an elevated position, and the notion of depletion seems contradictory. However, we suggest that this link derives from the tight correlation between taking food and drink up to the mouth in order to consume it, and the subsequent depletion of food and drink from the relevant vessels. Indeed, a consequence of depletion is that the activity of eating or drinking will be complete, as in (6.8c). Owing to pragmatic strengthening the association between depletion (and hence completion) and *up* has become conventionalized, licensing the use of this completion meaning in contexts which are quite distinct from those which originally motivated it, as evidenced by the examples in (6.8a) and (6.8b).

The point of this discussion, then, is that different kinds of experiential correlation may provide motivations for a sense with slightly different nuances. Completion can arise due to a container being full (and hence the filling activity being complete), or due to the entity being depleted, and hence the uptake of food or drink being complete. In both cases the activity is complete. This discussion also emphasizes the point that a Completion meaning, which is non-spatial in nature, derives from spatial experience and understanding, that is, the correlation between an activity being complete and the upward trajectory of an entity central to the activity.

The semantics of *down*

As with *up*, in this section we will consider the proto-scene for *down*, and just one cluster of senses associated with it.

The proto-scene

Having considered *up* in some detail, we will now consider *down*, which with *up* constitutes a contrast pair. A number of the patterns found with *up* are inversely reflected with *down*. The proto-scene for *down* is given in figure 6.2.

In figure 6.2. the 'head' is unshaded while the 'legs' are in bold. This highlighting reflects the view that for *down*, the bottom half of the human form is profiled. The following examples illustrate the proto-scene for *down*:

(6.9)   a. The stone plunged down the well-shaft
         b. The water went down the drain

Figure 6.2 Proto-scene for *down*

The following are illustrative of *down* being used as a particle:

(6.10)   a. He stepped down
          b. He fell down

In contrast with *up*, we suggest that the functional element associated with *down* is that of negative value. It is negative in the sense that in (6.9a) the TR becomes invisible, in (6.9b) the TR is no longer accessible, in (6.10a), the TR is in a lower position, and, by implication, no longer in a position of command, or influence, and in (6.10b) the TR is no longer in a normative position, but a position of potential vulnerability. We experience positions described by *down* as being negative precisely because they correlate with limited access, or visibility, or loss of control or vulnerability. It is in this sense that the functional element associated with *down* is described as being a negative value.

The Quantity Cluster

As with the network for *up*, *down* has a Quantity Cluster, which is made up of three senses. One sense, the Less Sense, is the inverse of the More Sense found in the *up* Quantity Cluster. The other two senses, the Worse/Inferior Sense and Completion Sense, bear a somewhat different relationship to the Superior Sense and the Completion Sense associated with *up*. As we found with *up*'s Completion Senses, *down* also appears to have at least two Completion Senses which we hypothesize stem from different experiential correlates. We will make the point that while *down* constitutes, with *up*, a semantic contrast set, *up* and *down* do not form a 'simple' oppositional pairing. The fact that the Worse/Inferior Sense is not the inverse of the Superior Sense, and that the Completion Senses associated with *down* appear to have derived via different routes from the Completion Senses associated with *up*, supports the view that due to the distinct ways in which we interact with our environment in both upward and downward orientations, there will be some interactions salient in one configuration which are not salient in the other.

The Less Sense The Less Sense derives from the independently motivated correlation between quantity and vertical elevation. As *down* implicates smaller quantity, this implicature has come to be conventionally associated with the semantic network for *down*:

(6.11) The amount of water in the Potomac is down

In the example in (6.11), the use of *down* to prompt for a decreased quantity is derivable from context. This follows, since being physically *down* correlates with smaller quantity. However, we suggest that through the continued use of *down* in such contexts, the meaning element of less has become conventionally associated with *down* as a distinct sense.

In each of the following examples, we conventionally understand that there is less of the physical entity. This meaning does not appear to be derivable from context.

(6.12)   a. Lance has slimmed down
         b. The stock prices are down
         c. Turn the music down!
         d. The Pub on M Street always waters down the draught beer

In each of these sentences, *down* has a conventional reading of there being less of something, without being related to a physical decrease in vertical elevation. For instance, in (6.12a) the sentence does not suggest that 'Lance' has become shorter, but that his weight is less.

The Worse/Inferior Sense A consequence of having less of something is that often one is in a worse or inferior position. The meaning component of being worse off has come to be conventionally associated with *down*, as evidenced by the following:

(6.13a)   The old man is down on his luck
(6.13b)   Nobody knows you when you're down and out

The sentence in (6.13a) for instance, does not literally mean that the old man is somehow in a physically lower position than at other times in his life. Rather, owing to the conventionalized Worse/Inferior Sense associated with *down*, we understand that (6.13a) means that the old man is having bad luck. Similarly,

(6.14)   Oprah is down on fad diets[9]

is interpreted as Oprah holding an unfavourable opinion of fad diets, judging them to be inferior to other diets. Unless we had such an inferior component

---

[9] Sentences such as (6.14) are not acceptable in some dialects of English such as standard British English.

associated with *down* in our semantic network, there would be no way of predicting the meaning of this particular sentence.

The Completion Sense Like *up*, *down* has at least two Completion Senses associated with it. One of these seems to be connected to the Quantity Cluster and is illustrated in the following:

(6.15)   A: Is there any pizza left?
         B: No, the guys downed it last night

This usage seems to draw on the correlation between consuming and observing the amount of food visibly diminish. In many cases, when the act of eating and drinking is completed, the available food and drink are gone.[10] The argument that the Completion Sense has become an independent sense in the network is supported by sentences such as the following in which consumption of food and drink are no longer implicated:

(6.16)   Matt left the car lights on and now the battery's run down
(6.17)   We are down to the last moment of the game

Both these sentences depict situations involving depletion of a resource, the stored energy in the battery and the allotted time for the game. Notice that these uses are very similar to the Completion/depletion Sense associated with *up*. Here we see the interesting phenomenon that spatial particles whose TR–LM configurations are in an inverse relationship, and that have traditionally been represented as being 'opposites', have developed the same extended sense. In this case, the same basic human experience of consuming food and drink seems to figure plausibly in both extended senses, but the precise correlations differ. In the case of *up*, the correlation is between the specific act of lifting food (up) to one's lips and the amount of food concomitantly diminishing; in the case of *down*, the correlation is between a more general notion of consuming and the amount of food diminishing (going down). Although the basic spatial scene is the same, the elements that are highlighted differ.

As may have already become obvious from the discussion above, the Completion/depletion Sense associated with *up* does not derive from the Quantity Cluster, as the emphasis is on the upward motion associated with humans eating. In contrast, the Completion/depletion Sense associated with *down* does derive from the Quantity Cluster. Moreover, although both *up* and *down* have a Completion Sense that seems to derive from the general correlation between vertical elevation and quantity, the particular human experience giving rise to these senses differs. While the *up* Completion/container Sense (the first Completion

---

[10] This sense is also plausibly related to human anatomy and the physical experience of feeling food and drink move down the oesophagus.

Sense we discussed for *up*) derives from the correlation between vertical elevation and quantity, as it relates to the notion of filling a container to its capacity, this experiential motivation is paralleled by the Completion/depletion Sense associated with *down*, which relates to consumption and depletion. Hence, although the Completion/depletion Sense associated with *down* is similar in meaning to the Completion/depletion Sense associated with *up*, in terms of its derivation and motivation it has more in common with the Completion/container Sense of *up*.

The second source for a Completion Sense associated with *down* comes from the experience that entities which are maintaining a particular function are often standing erect or in an *up* position, while entities which have completed their usefulness or stopped functioning are often no longer erect (see Lakoff and Johnson, 1980 and Grady, 1997a for many examples). One of the salient ways a person or entity can be made to go from an erect, functioning position to a horizontal, non-functioning position is by being physically toppled or knocked down. When an object that was previously in an upright, erect position undergoes a downward orientation, it reaches a point where it cannot go any further. As the earth acts as a relatively stable surface to prevent further downward travel, once a TR is on the ground it cannot go any further. Hence, the downward trajectory is complete. Consequently, being *down* (on the ground), correlates with the end point of a trajectory, and the correlated motion or event being complete. As this sense interprets a location as the end point of a process, it utilizes an adprep (recall the discussion of the Completion Sense associated with *over* in chapter 4). Notice that in the following example, *down* could be paraphrased by *completed* or *finished*:

(6.18)   He has three term papers down and one to go

This Completion Sense appears to derive from a quite different route from either of the Completion Senses associated with *up*, supporting our contention that, due to varying ways in which we interact with particular spatial axes and spatial scenes, even contrast sets cannot be thought of as straightforwardly mediating oppositional pairs of meanings.

General orientation of the TR: *to* and *for*

In this section we examine the proto-scenes and several senses associated with *to* and *for*, two spatial particles which involve oriented TRs. These particles are particularly interesting for several reasons. As with *over* and *above*, in certain contexts, they seem to act as near synonyms, while appearing to be quite distinct in other contexts. Teasing out the precise differences and offering a descriptively adequate representation of the proto-scenes emphasizes the importance of the notions of construal and highlighting, as well as the importance of the functional element. Careful analysis of these two particles also demonstrates the embodied consequences of an oriented TR.

To versus *for*: primary versus oblique goal

We have seen that English spatial particles may in particular contexts appear to be near synonyms, while in other contexts they are clearly distinct, for example *over* versus *above* and *under* versus *below*. In certain contexts, *to* and *for* also seem to share a high degree of semantic overlap, as evidenced by the sentences in (6.19) and (6.20):

(6.19)   a. He ran to the hills
          b. He ran for the hills
(6.20)   a. She is hurrying to the ball
          b. She is hurrying for the ball

In these examples both *to* and *for* appear to prompt for an oriented TR directed towards a LM. In the sentences in (6.19) and (6.20), the TR appears to have a goal which involves reaching the LM. According to our model, we understand that the TR is in motion and hence following some trajectory because of the information coded by the verb. Sentences such as the following demonstrate that these particles can also occur in scenes which do not involve the TR moving towards the LM:

(6.21)   a. The timekeeper whistled/gestured/signalled/called to the referee
          b. The timekeeper whistled/gestured/signalled/called for the referee

While the scenes prompted for in the pairs in examples (6.19), (6.20) and (6.21) are very similar, subtle differences in interpretation exist. For instance, our intuitions are that the example in (6.19a) is more likely to be used in a context where reaching the hills is being emphasized, that is, *the hills* as a primary physical goal or objective. This might be the case, for instance, when reporting on a jogger's fitness regimen. In contrast, the sentence in (6.19b) is more likely to be employed when reaching the hills is a means to an end, rather than the end in itself. For example, in the case of warfare, where hills might afford cover or shelter from the enemy, then reaching the hills would serve the purpose of providing safety. This difference is emphasized in the following modified sentences:

(6.22)   a. He ran to the hills and back every day
          b. ?He ran for the hills and back every day

Thus, while *to* appears to profile a LM that constitutes a physical goal, what we will term the *primary goal*, *for* appears to relate the TR to an ulterior purpose, contingent upon reaching a particular LM. As the LM is not the primary focus in the sentences containing *for* we might accordingly describe it as the *oblique goal*. This sense of primariness versus obliqueness is highlighted in (6.21a) and (6.21b). The interpretation of (6.21a) is that the TR directs his or her whistle or signal at the referee, without the aid of any intermediary. In contrast, the sentence in (6.21b) allows for the interpretation that the referee is not in the immediate vicinity and might be contacted via an intermediary.

Interpreting a LM as an oblique goal that serves some ultimate purpose indicates a salient element of intentionality on the part of the TR. For instance, to head for the hills in order to avoid the enemy reflects a level of calculation and purposeful planning that goes beyond simply designating the hills as the end point of one's daily run. We hypothesize that intentionality is an important aspect of the functional element associated with *for* but not with *to*.

This hypothesis is supported by the sentences in (6.23) and (6.24) in which non-purposeful TRs, that is, ones that clearly lack intention, occur. In these sentences, *for* is semantically anomalous while *to* is acceptable:

(6.23)   a. #The ball rolled for the wall
         b. The ball rolled to the wall
(6.24)   a. #The balloon floated for the ceiling
         b. The balloon floated to the ceiling

In these sentences, we understand *the ball* and *the balloon* to be non-animate entities whose movements are controlled by physical forces such as gravity. Their rolling and floating cannot be construed as self-initiated or undertaken by these entities in order to achieve a particular purpose. It is in this sense that *for* requires a purposeful or intentional TR (and hence involves intentionality).

This analysis is further supported by the fact that while *to* can be used with a host of verbs denoting generalized motion, there is a subset of motion verbs with which *to* is ungrammatical as in (6.25), whereas *for* is acceptable:

(6.25)   a. *Mary set out/started/left to the store
         a.' Mary set out/started/left for the store
         b. *They departed to France
         b.' They departed for France
         c. *They set sail/out to Nova Scotia
         c.' They set sail/out for Nova Scotia

Each of the verbs in these sentences relates to the beginning phase of a journey. As such, each is related to the intentional processes of selecting a particular destination, choosing a mode of travel and, presumably consciously, selecting a certain course. Hence, we suggest that due to the salience of intentional components associated with these meaning elements, *for* is acceptable, while *to* is not.

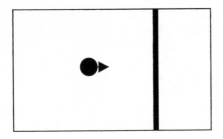

Figure 6.3 The proto-scene for *to*

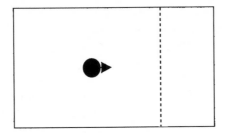

Figure 6.4 The proto-scene for *for*

The linguistic behaviour exhibited by *to* and *for* discussed above, suggests that *to* and *for* both designate TRs oriented with respect to LMs, but the status of the TR and LM associated with the respective spatial particles is distinct. A consequence of these differences in status of the TRs and LMs is a difference in the functional elements associated with each particle.

We propose that in the proto-scene for *to*, *to* denotes a spatial relation in which an oriented TR is directed towards a highlighted LM. Within this spatial configuration, the highlighted status of the LM makes it readily interpretable as a primary target or goal. Hence, the functional element associated with *to* is the LM as goal. Figure 6.3 represents the proto-scenes for *to*. The shaded sphere represents the TR. The arrow represents the orientation. The vertical line represents the LM. Note that the LM is in bold, indicating that the LM is profiled. The functional element associated with the proto-scene is that the LM constitutes the primary goal.

Figure 6.4 represents the proto-scene associated with *for*. The shaded sphere represents the TR. The arrow represents the orientation. The vertical line represents the LM. Note that the LM is represented with a dashed line, reflecting the view that it is not profiled. The functional component associated with the proto-scene in figure 6.4 is the oblique or secondary nature of the LM, that is, the notion that reaching or attaining the LM facilitates the primary purpose, which is contingent upon or facilitated by attaining the LM.

Before concluding this discussion of the proto-scene associated with *for*, we must briefly consider the etymology of this spatial particle. In Old English *for* was used interchangeably with *fore*, both of which derived from the same Old Teutonic root meaning 'in front of'. By Middle English *for* and *fore* had developed distinct meanings with the two forms no longer being interchangeable. While *fore* retained the In Front Of meaning (cf. *forehead*, etc.), this meaning had become obsolete with *for*. Hence, unlike the majority of the other spatial particles we have investigated in this book, one of the key criteria proposed in chapter 3 in order to ascertain the primary sense of *for* is inappropriate. Recall that we posited that one of the lines of evidence for identifying the sense which counts as primary in the synchronic network is the sense with the historically earliest antecedent. As the In Front Of Sense, the historically earliest meaning, is no longer associated with the synchronic network of *for*, then this sense cannot be considered to be the primary sense in the synchronic network. The largest number of senses in the semantic network of *for* relate to the notion of purpose; as predictability and preponderance of senses are two key criteria for determining the synchronic primary sense, the proto-scene (recall the discussion in chapter 3), we have taken the functional element of purpose as a key element of the proto-scene of *for*. This coheres with the foregoing discussion concerning the notion of intentionality associated with uses of *for*.

The semantics of 'to'

We noted above that the proto-scene for *to* designates a relation in which the TR is oriented with respect to a highlighted LM. This configuration often seems to give rise to the inference of motion of the TR directed towards the LM. Indeed, many previous analyses have assumed that path is an inherent part of the basic meaning associated with *to*. However, a path – in the sense of a series of spatially contiguous locations mediating a starting point and an end point – is not explicitly coded by *to*, as illustrated by the following in which only orientation is apparent:

(6.26)   a. The clock tower faces to the east
         b. She looked to her left / the distant hills
         c. He is pointing to the clump of grass

Based on our definition, a path is distinct from orientation (or directionality) as it additionally involves a means of passage. Notwithstanding, since orientation often does correlate both with path and indeed with motion (hence a trajectory – which is to say motion of a TR along a path) – given that we are typically oriented with respect to our goal when we undergo motion along a path towards our goal, as in the daily drive to work, for instance – it is perhaps not surprising that previous analyses have conflated these distinct notions and associated path with *to*. Nevertheless, we argue that both path and motion, as we have defined them, are the result of conceptual integration of linguistic prompts, and are not primarily coded by *to*, as reflected by the proto-scene designated above.

Accordingly, we now turn to a brief examination of a subset of senses associated with *to*. Our goal is to highlight the meaningful consequences of a spatial scene that involves an oriented TR. Owing to space constraints, we have attempted to keep our argumentation to a minimum. However, in carrying out the analysis, we have followed methodology laid out in chapter 3.

The Locational Sense In this sense *to* denotes a relation in which the TR is located with respect to the LM, but the TR is not oriented towards the LM:

(6.27)   a. In this picture, Diana is standing to my left
         b. The boarders lived in the rooms to the back of the house
         c. Please take the seats to the front of the auditorium

Notice that these uses of *to* do not involve the TR being oriented in the direction of the LM. For instance, in (6.27a), there is no sense that the TR, *Diana*, is oriented toward (or is facing) the speaker's left side from the perspective of the vantage point. Rather, the conventional interpretation is that of the TR being generally located in the vicinity of the speaker's left side. This lack of orientation of the TR is underscored by the fact that this sentence can be paraphrased as follows:

(6.28)   In this picture, Diana is standing **on** my left[11]

Again, this paraphrase does not involve any notion of the TR being oriented towards the speaker.

The development of a Location Sense in which orientation of the TR is not involved is consistent with the proto-scene we have posited for *to*. In our canonical representation of the TR–LM relation, the TR is the element in focus; the role of the LM is to locate the TR. However, in our proto-scene for *to*, the LM is given an unusual degree of saliency due to the TR being oriented toward the LM. It follows from this that in some contexts the role of the LM, being largely to locate the TR, might come to predominate in the relationship being denoted. In such instances, the LM would act as a particularly salient reference point with respect to the location of the TR, facilitating the development of a distinct Locational Sense.[12]

---

[11] The TR–LM relationship in sentences (6.27) and (6.28) can be paraphrased by *at*. Both *on* and *at* involve proto-scenes in which the TR and the LM are adjacent or co-located; neither involves orientation of the TR.

[12] Grady (personal communication) has suggested that this sense of *to* might represent a step in the grammaticalization process in which *to* is no longer acting as a spatial particle, but rather has taken on the role of a functional marker which indicates the speaker is about to describe the spatial scene.

The Contact Sense In this sense, *to* denotes contact between the TR and LM as illustrated by the following:

(6.29)   a. The poster portrayed a young woman with her finger to her lips
         b. Apply the soap directly to the stain for best results
         c. Cheek to cheek, hand to hand, toe to toe

We suggest that this sense arose as a result of the experiential correlation between the achievement of a particular goal and contact (or very near contact as in *face to face*) between the TR and the LM. Put another way, when we achieve or realize a goal, such as, for instance, arriving at the office, we are simultaneously located and hence in physical contact with the office premises. Hence, in many scenarios involving a TR oriented towards a LM that is construed as a goal, the TR is likely to undergo motion, thereby reaching the LM. So in situations such as:

(6.30)   Jane's hoping to get **to** London this weekend

the goal being expressed is for Jane to physically relocate herself from her present location to that designated by *London*. In this context, reaching London entails contact with some part of London.

The Contact Sense meets the criteria of being a distinct sense, as without knowing that *to* explicitly codes contact, context alone would not account for the interpretation that an expression such as *finger to lips* means 'finger touching lips', rather than, for instance, a finger pointing in the direction of one's lips.

The Attachment Sense A sense closely related to the Contact Sense is the Attachment Sense. In this sense, *to* denotes a relation, in which the TR is attached or joined to the LM such that it forms a part of or is contiguous with the LM.[13] Consider the following:

(6.31)   a. He added a fence to the garden
         b. The vestibule to the House of Commons
         c. Chris and Katherine are married to each other

This sense most likely arose due to the oriented TR reaching its goal, and hence coming into contact with the LM. The notion of physical attachment entails one entity being physically fixed or joined with another in a (quasi)-permanent way. In many cases, the attachment correlates with the TR having first been oriented with respect to the LM and subsequently undergoing contact, as in for instance (6.31a). As an addition such as adding a fence implicates a permanent

---

[13] Interestingly, this is one of the oldest attested extended meanings associated with *to*. Reflexes of this meaning are found in forms such as *together*.

situation, the notion of attachment, through pragmatic strengthening, has come to be associated with *to*, as evidenced even by a socio-legal relationship rather than a purely spatial one, as in (6.31c).

The Comparison Sense In this sense *to* denotes a relation in which the TR is compared with the LM:

(6.32)   a. The design of this sweater is inferior to that one
         b. The motion was carried by 50 votes to 29

Here, *to* denotes a relation between the TR and the LM such that a comparison is facilitated. This sense probably arose as the act of comparison correlates with bringing one object to another so that they can more easily be examined and compared. Owing to pragmatic strengthening, this aspect of context has become conventionally associated with *to*.

The Event Sense In this sense, *to* denotes a relation between a particular TR and an event brought about by the TR. The event facilitated or undertaken by the TR is coded by the LM. Consider some examples which are illustrative of this sense:

(6.33)   a. The captain went to the boaters' rescue
         b. The financier came to the company's aid
         c. We went to lunch

We hypothesize that this sense derived from the tight correlation in experience between a place/LM (which is understood as the primary goal of the TR's actions) and the event which occurs at the particular location. Put another way, events take place at specific locations, and thus there is a tight experiential correlation between events and locations. For instance, in (6.33a), the TR, *the captain*, facilitates *the boaters' rescue* by undergoing motion in order to be in the location where the rescue is required. In these sentences, in which there is such a close connection between place and the event which occurs at the location, one might argue that the result meaning is supplied by context. However, evidence that the Event Sense is a distinct sense is provided by contexts where motion is not apparent, and thus the experiential correlation between movement to a location/LM and the event is not overt. Consider the following examples:

(6.34)   a. He was sentenced to twenty years of hard labour
         b. This is a means to an end
         c. She sang the child to sleep

In all these sentences, an Event Sense is evident in the absence of physical motion towards a location/LM. Without an Event Sense being associated with *to*, we cannot account for the conventional meaning associated with *to* typically assigned by native speakers. Although it is beyond the scope of this book to explore the role of *to* in complements, we hypothesize that the role of *to* as an infinitival subordinator in complementation may be ultimately derived from this particular sense (see Wierzbicka, 1988, and references therein).

The semantics of 'for'

Now let's turn to a brief consideration of the semantics of *for*. In contrast to the semantics of *to* – where a number of senses were related to direction, attaining a particular target or goal, and contact – the preponderance of senses associated with *for* are primarily concerned with motives, intentions and purposes, reflecting the more intentional character of the functional element associated with the proto-scene. The senses we have selected for presentation here are illustrative of this difference.

The Purpose Sense In this sense, the LM, which is closely related to the TR's purpose or the entity sought, is in focus. This represents a change in construal from the proto-scene in which the LM is explicitly not in focus. As we have seen previously, a change in construal often results in a new sense. In this sense *for* denotes a relation in which an action by the TR is associated with a particular purpose. Consider some examples:

(6.35)   a. He arrived at 7.30 for dinner
         b. She returned for the prize
         c. She held on for dear life
         d. She prayed for a miracle

In each of these examples the TR performs a particular activity in order to achieve some purpose. For instance, in (6.35a) the arrival at 7.30 is motivated by a dinner engagement. In (6.35b) the return is due to a prize. In (6.35c) the act of 'holding on' is for reasons of survival, while the purpose of the TR's actions in (6.35d), engaging in prayer, is to achieve a miracle.

We hypothesize that this sense originated by virtue of the TR undergoing motion and reaching a particular location which concomitantly served an ulterior purpose. For instance, returning to our example of *He ran for the hills*, the act of running serves to achieve a particular purpose, namely reaching safety. As such, the act of running for the hills correlates with the ulterior purpose. Once the implicature of purpose associated with motion has been strengthened, this meaning is free to be generalized to activities that have an ulterior purpose, irrespective of whether they involve motion. The Purpose Sense, then, derived from the correlation between motion undergone by the TR and the achievement of an ulterior purpose.

The Intended Recipient Sense In this sense *for* introduces the intended recipient of a particular action. Hence, the recipient motivates the particular action designated. Consider some examples:

(6.36)   Susan bought the gown for Carol
(6.37)   Moosa prepared the curry for Donna

As actions such as buying gowns and preparing curries are motivated in part by the purpose for which they are intended (in this case to give to a particular recipient), there is a correlation between a particular recipient and the purpose of the action. For instance, in (6.36) the purpose of buying the gown is to give it to Carol. Hence, the recipient correlates with the purpose. In consequence, due to pragmatic strengthening, *for* has developed an Intended Recipient Sense in which it can denote a particular action such as buying a gown expressly with a recipient in mind, here Carol.

The Benefactive Sense In this sense, *for* denotes a relation between an action and a beneficiary:

(6.38)   a. She raised money for charity
          b. He scored for United
          c. They sang for each other

Clearly, this sense appears to be closely related to the Intended Recipient Sense. The difference is that while in the Intended Recipient Sense receipt is not entailed – the sentence in (6.37) is still felicitous even if Moosa were involved in a car-crash while en route and hence failed to deliver the curry – in the Benefactive Sense the recipient does actually take receipt of the intended benefit. Hence, in this sense a particular action directly benefits a particular entity. Given that intended recipients as in (6.38) are beneficiaries, then one motivation for the Benefactive Sense may be due to the correlation between being an intended recipient and receipt of an entity or an action. An alternative motivation may be that the purpose for performing a certain action, such as, for instance, raising money, may be to benefit charity. Either of these motivations may, separately or in tandem, have served the conventional association of the Benefactive Sense with *for*.

As with our analysis of *to*, the discussion illustrates that a preposition such as *for*, ultimately grounded in spatio-physical experience, systematically gives rise to non-spatial senses.

Orientation of the LM: *in front of, before, behind* and *after*

Having considered spatial particles that involve an oriented TR, we now turn to a consideration of particles that relate to an oriented LM. Most previous accounts of these four spatial particles *in front of, before, behind,* and *after* have not attempted to distinguish between the seemingly near synonyms *before* versus *in front of* and *behind* versus *after*. For instance, Celce-Murcia and Larsen-Freeman (1999) define *before* as '*in front of*' (410). However, careful analysis of the linguistic evidence shows that there are definite differences.

When an attempt has been made to distinguish *before* versus *in front of* or *behind* versus *after*, the analysis has tended to go no further than noting that while *in front of* and *behind* primarily designate spatial/locational meanings, *before* and *after* are largely used to express temporal relations (e.g., Langacker, 1987). For instance, Lindstromberg (1998) notes that *in front of* is used to indicate location while *before* primarily indicates sequence, and as such is often employed with 'LMs of time' (p. 108). However, he offers no explanation for this divergence in meaning. Lindstromberg also notes that the semantics of *before* overlap with *in front of* in very limited situations, which relate to a 'locational' (ibid.) sense, suggesting that: '*Before* is sometimes used in the sense of "in front of" to emphasize that the [TR] (virtually always human) is less important or less grand than the LM' (ibid.), as in sentences such as: *He knelt before the Queen.* Again, there has been no attempt to account for such a distribution of meaning.

We will argue that in the synchronic proto-scene, which involves a horizontal axis rather than a vertical one, *in front of* and *behind* are each associated with a LM that is conceptualized as asymmetric on the front/back axis and an un-oriented TR. Our conceptualization of front versus back crucially references the human body in which the primary organs of perception are located in the front of the head. A consequence of having an oriented LM partitioned into front and back and an un-oriented, non-partitioned TR is that the LM has a privileged vantage point which the TR does not have. The functional result of this spatial configuration involves perceptual accessibility of the TR to the LM. Thus, we posit a functional element of positive (or presence of) perceptual accessibility for *in front of* and negative (or lack of) perceptual accessibility for *behind*. Positive perceptual accessibility entails surety of the location of the TR on the part of a sentient LM.

As for *before* and *after*, the proto-scene characterized for each is also one in which a front/back axis is attributed to the LM. In contrast to *in front of* and *behind*, both *before* and *after* specify that the TR is also oriented. The result is that both the TR and the LM have vantage points on the scene. Since the TR is the default focal element, the TR's vantage point is privileged, rather than the LM's vantage point as was the case in the scene denoted by *in front of*. A result of seeing this spatial configuration through the eyes of the TR is that the functional element associated with *before* is 'in advance of' or leading. In other words, the TR is construed as leading the LM. A result of seeing the spatial scene denoted by *after* through the eyes of the TR (which is oriented to the back of the LM) is that the TR is construed as following the LM. The functional element associated with *after* is that of following or pursuit. Both of these functional elements involve the notion of sequence. These functional elements limit the spatial relation associated with the proto-scenes for *before* and *after* to contexts involving what we will term, following Hill (1978), an *in tandem* alignment between the TR and LM.

We will also argue that in the case of *before*, its historically broad semantic territory has been partially taken over by *in front of*, a more recent arrival into English. A consequence is that the sense associated with *before* has become more specialized (used in more restricted contexts) than it was historically; concomitantly, the sequential/temporal meaning has become the clearly predominant use. This analysis allows us to account for Lindstromberg's observation concerning the rather unusual restrictions on what he terms the 'locational' use of *before*. In addition, while *before* and *after* have primarily come to denote a Sequential Sense, *in front of* and *behind* have not developed a Sequential Sense.

It is worth pointing out that, unlike spatial particles such as *to* and *for*, for instance, *in front of, before* and *behind* have not developed goal or purpose-related senses. *To* and *for* involve orientation of the TR towards the LM. However, in the case of *before, in front of* and *behind*, the TR is not oriented towards the LM.[14] As the LM constitutes what we have termed the locator, the entity which is typically less likely to move, and hence the entity which serves to locate the TR (recall the discussion in chapter 3), it follows that these spatial particles are highly unlikely to develop goal-type senses. Consistent with this analysis, *after*, whose proto-scene we represent as involving a TR that is oriented in the direction of a LM (as well as an oriented LM), has developed a goal sense, as in *Lou went after some ice cream.*

The etymology of *before* and *in front of*

As we are suggesting that *in front of* has taken over a substantial part of the semantic territory at one time associated with *before*, it is particularly appropriate to begin our analysis of these forms by briefly summarizing the historical antecedents of the proto-scenes for *in front of* and *before*. As the lexeme *front* – derived from Old French – supplanted the indigenous *before*, we will begin with the historically earlier *before*.

The etymology of 'before'

The spatial particle *before* relates historically to Old English *beforen/biforan*, Old Saxon *biforan*, Old High German *bifora* glossed as 'be front' or 'ahead'

---

[14] In fact, in the case of the proto-scene associated with *before*, the TR is oriented away from the LM.

(Barnhart, 1988), as well as to *be* + *fore*. *Fore* was a separate preposition in Old English (it appears in *Beowulf*, as does *bi* + *foran*) and meant 'located at the front of'. *Fore* is related to Sanskrit *puras* which is glossed as 'at first, in advance' and the related preposition *puristat* which is glossed as 'before' (temporal and sequential) and 'in the presence of'.

Beforen appeared as early as 725, in *Beowulf*, in which it evidenced two senses – In Advance Of and Located At The Front Of or In The Presence Of An Animate Being; several variations of *before* appear in the Concordances of the *Chester Mystery Plays* dating to around 1100. Of the 104 citations in the *Chester Mystery Plays*, 34 are clearly non-sequential in interpretation. Of these only one potentially refers to a non-animate LM. In all the rest, the LM is either human or divine (God, Jesus, Passion, etc); in fact, in 14 of the citations, the equivalent of the phrase *before your/his/my face* or *sight* occurs.[15] The remainder, 75 per cent of the instances, have sequential or temporal interpretations.

In terms of a locational interpretation, although not listed in earlier concordances, attested sentences such as the following: *Had he his hurts before? Ay, on the front* (Shakespeare) demonstrate that the interpretation 'located on the front side' was also historically associated with *before*. This locational use of *before* is no longer part of the particle's synchronic semantic network.

The etymology of 'in front of'

The etymology of *in front of* is distinct from *before*. *Front* entered the English language from Old French *frons*, which is glossed as 'forehead', sometime around 1300 (Barnhart, 1988). The root is related to Sanskrit *bhala*, which is glossed as 'face' (Lanman, 1884). The collocation *in front of* appears to have always been associated with a non-sequential, Locational Sense 'located at the front of X'. In this sense, the early uses of *in front of* appear to be very similar to the early locational uses of *before*. Based on historical evidence, it appears that sometime in the fourteenth century *front* was also used to mean '*foremost part*', no longer strictly referring to the human anatomy. As such, the range of contexts in which it could occur, and the LMs to which it could be applied, began to broaden. Synchronically, *in front of* appears largely to retain this proto-scene (as explicated in the next section).

We speculate that the introduction of *front* and *in front of* into English created a situation in which the contexts where *before* retained a locative reading of

---

[15] The following are representative of the 'location' uses found in the Chester Mystery Plays:

but sitt righte here before his face
sonne, I will tell you before your face
That sight that before me I see
his child was slayne before my eye
    (Pfleider and Preston, 1981: 56–57)

'in front of' became highly restricted, almost exclusively limited to scenes involving animate LMs, as we shall see. Hence, many of the locative uses formerly associated with *before* have become archaic, as in *I spent two years before the mast*.

The semantics of 'in front of': the proto-scene

In the proto-scene for *in front of*, the LM is oriented, due either to possessing inherent front/back asymmetry or to being conceptualized such that it has front/back asymmetry. The TR, however, is not oriented. In the proto-scene for *in front of*, the TR is located at the 'front' of the LM, that is, the LM is oriented towards the TR. In terms of human experience, if the LM is human, a consequence of the LM being oriented with respect to the TR is that the TR is often perceptually accessible and located with surety. This is illustrated in such everyday experiences as:

(6.39)   Jean looked everywhere for her glasses and suddenly realized they were on the counter, right in front of her all the time

In this sentence, when the TR, *the glasses*, are recognized as being in an 'in front of' position in relation to the LM, *Jean*, they are perceptually accessible to the LM and, as a result, their location is confirmed. As such, we posit that the functional element associated with *in front of* is that of perceptual accessibility. Consider another example that evidences the proto-scene:

(6.40)   Child: I want some ice cream
          Mother: Eat the food in front of you. Maybe you can have ice cream when you're finished.

In the example in (6.40), the LM, *you*, is intrinsically oriented towards an unoriented TR. The TR, *food*, is located at the front of the oriented LM and accessible to the LM.

The example in (6.41) also illustrates the proto-scene associated with *in front of*. In interpreting the following sentence:

(6.41)   The teacher stood in front of the class as he explained the day's lesson

the default interpretation seems to be that the TR, *the teacher*, is facing the LM, *the class*, or what we will term, following Hill (1978), a *mirror-image* alignment. This interpretation is largely due to our understanding that participants in non-electronically mediated oral communication canonically adopt the mirror-image alignment. However, as illustrated by the following sentence, a mirror-image reading is not inevitable when employing *in front of*:

(6.42)   The teacher was difficult to hear when he was in front of the class because he often spoke as he wrote on the blackboard

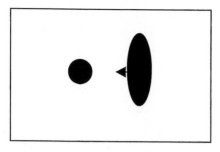

Figure 6.5 Proto-scene for *in front of*

In this instance, the TR, which happens to be inherently oriented, and the LM are actually in what Hill (1978) terms an *in tandem* alignment in which both are facing in the same direction; hence, the students are facing the teacher's back. We discuss this alignment at length below. For now what is important to note is that, even though both the TR (the teacher) and the LM (the students) have a vantage point (Langacker, personal communication, argues that any animate being in a scene will have a vantage point), it is the LM's vantage point that is privileged. The scene refers to what the students see and hear, not what the teacher sees (and hears).

We see this same privileging of the LM's vantage point in the following:

(6.43)   The rabbi performed the ritual in front of the congregation
(6.44)   The murder took place in front of several witnesses[16]

The key to all the sentences in (6.40) through (6.45) seems to be that the TR is located at the front of the LM, irrespective of whether the TR is inherently oriented, or, if it is inherently oriented, irrespective of which direction it is facing with respect to the LM. By virtue of being located at the front of the oriented LM (whose vantage point is privileged), the TR is perceptually accessible to the LM.

The proto-scene for *in front of* is given in figure 6.5. The TR is denoted by the small shaded sphere. The LM is designated by the elongated sphere, with orientation denoted by the direction of the arrow emerging from the LM.

Functional orientation

Thus far in our discussion of the proto-scene for *in front of*, we have considered only animate LMs, which have inherent front/back orientation. However, the

---

[16] We have not been able to find any context-independent uses of *in front of* which involve the interpretation of perceptual accessibility. Therefore, we conclude that this is not a separate sense in the network.

proto-scene for *in front of* can also be used with inanimate LMs, which are what we will term *functionally oriented*. The following are illustrative:

(6.45)   a. On winter evenings, they often talked for hours in front of a roaring fire in the hearth/fireplace
         b. John stood in front of the oncoming car
         c. John ran in front of the car as it rolled down the hill

In these sentences, the orientation of the LM is determined by our understanding of either its accessibility and typical use or actual movement. Thus, in (6.45a) what counts as the front of the LM is that part which affords accessibility, or typical use and movement (6.45b) or actual movement (6.45c). In other words, the way in which we interact with the LM, and thus its function, provides a front/back asymmetry. In (6.45b), the interpretation is that John is located proximal to the hood of the car, that part generally understood to be the car's front, by virtue of canonical motion associated with cars. In (6.24c), the front of the car is determined by its leading edge. As Svorou (1994) has pointed out, sentences like (6.45c) are equally acceptable if the car is rolling down the hill such that either its trunk or its hood is the leading edge. What is crucial is that the TR is located proximal to what is conceived to be the front of the LM in that particular context, as defined by direction of travel, which typically (but not inevitably) correlates with inherent front/back organization.

As is evident from the linguistic examples considered in this section, with the meaning of *in front of*, the orientation of the LM is crucial; the TR must be located at the front of the oriented LM. Moreover, the LM can be either animate or non-animate. In the case of non-animate entities, the orientation of the LM is determined by that part of the LM which counts as the leading edge for motion. Since such LMs are thus oriented, it follows that by virtue of interacting with oriented LMs, a TR is thereby accessible to the LM. Accordingly, the functional element associated with *in front of* is that of (perceptual) accessibility.

The inherently unoriented LM

Special case I: mirror-image alignment In some of the examples involving inanimate LMs, as in (6.45a) above, the LM is construed as having a front/back orientation because of the way in which such LMs are typically accessed. LMs of this kind are not inherently oriented, but are what we described as being functionally oriented. They are oriented by virtue of how TRs typically interact with them, and hence by virtue of the function they serve. However, some LMs can be accessed from any direction. For instance, a bush or a tree can be accessed irrespective of which side of the LM the TR is located. Consequently, such LMs cannot be construed as being either inherently or

Figure 6.6 Mirror image alignment in a closed scene

functionally oriented. Yet, even with such examples, *in front of* can still be employed:

(6.46)   Sarah stood in front of the bush/tree

The difficulty, then, with such an example is to be able to explain why *in front of* can be used and intuitively 'feels' so natural, in spite of the LM's lack of orientation.

H. Clark (1973) observed that many of our daily interactions involve what he termed the *canonical encounter*, entailing a face-to-face interaction between us and others. The canonical encounter gives rise to what we will label, borrowing terminology from Hill (1978), a *mirror-image* alignment, which is diagrammed in figure 6.6.

Mirror-image alignment is extremely prevalent in our everyday interactions. It particularly occurs in what Hill terms *closed scenes*, that is, a spatial scene involving just two entities (in contrast with *open scenes* which involve more than two entities, as in a foot race between three or more participants). Now let us consider how the notion of the canonical encounter and mirror-image alignment can assist in accounting for the use of *in front of* with inherently non-oriented LMs.

In the spatial scene designated by the example in (6.46), there are two entities, Sarah and the LM, *the tree*; as such, this constitutes a closed scene. In closed scenes involving animate entities the mirror-image model is tightly correlated. That is, while it is not inevitable that by virtue of two animate entities being related in a spatial scene they will assume a mirror-image alignment, it is typical for such spatial scenes to involve a mirror-image interaction. This follows as in our everyday lives when we interact with a second person (or other animate entity such as, for instance a pet cat or dog), we do so primarily in a mirror-image way. After all, we do not usually address other people's backs, as when others are facing away from us.

We suggest that when a closed scene is designated, it is natural to construe the TR as **the vantage point**. Moreover, in an example such as (6.46), a closed scene involving an animate TR and an inanimate LM, it is common to project a front/back axis onto the LM, which objectively is non-oriented (see Hill, 1978; Vandeloise, 1991).[17] In English, and in many other languages, a mirror-image

---

[17] This is a language-specific trait.

alignment is projected, such that from the perspective of the animate TR, the LM is 'facing' the TR. From this perspective, the TR, *Sarah*, can be felicitously described as being located *in front of the tree*.

Special case II: the orientation frame   In our final set of examples relating to the proto-scene for *in front of*, we turn to a second subset of sentences involving inherently unoriented entities. Examples of this kind cannot be explained in terms of the projection of a front/back orientation onto the LM by virtue of mirror-image alignment. By way of illustration consider the following:

(6.47)   On the conveyor-belt that moves bottles to the washing machine, smaller bottles are always placed in front of larger bottles

In the case of unlabelled bottles, which cannot be construed as having front/back asymmetry, on first inspection it is perplexing that they can be denoted by *in front of*, as it is not immediately obvious what the vantage point might be from which such a scene is construed. Clearly, for mirror-image alignment to be construed, an on-stage vantage point is required. Since all the entities involved are non-oriented, it is difficult to attribute a vantage point to one of them. A second difficulty in accounting for this sentence in terms of mirror-image alignment is that the scene described is not a closed scene, since several entities are related to each other in the scene in (6.47).

Talmy (2000) has observed that in certain contexts, a *secondary reference object* serves to impose what we will term an *orientation frame* on entities, which may otherwise have different orientations. In (6.47) the conveyor-belt (the secondary reference object), by serving to cause the bottles to be moving in the same direction, imposes an orientation frame. As such, smaller bottles can be construed as being in front of larger bottles by virtue of the orientation frame, even though the bottles themselves lack inherent orientation.[18]

The Priority Sense

Having considered the proto-scene for *in front of*, we will consider one other sense associated with this spatial particle. The purpose of doing so is to make the point that experiential correlation and pragmatic strengthening represent

---

[18]   Consider the sentence *When I entered the kitchen, I saw that the cereal box was in front of the bowl*. This sentence also represents an open scene, involving entities, the box and the bowl, which are not inherently oriented, and a third entity, *I*, which is clearly the construer and the on-stage vantage point. This scene seems potentially to involve both mirror-image alignment and a secondary reference object. Here, the on-stage construer acts as the secondary reference object which imposes an orientation frame on the two unoriented entities such that the entity most proximal to the vantage point is construed as the focal element or TR. Moreover, the on-stage construer appears to project a mirror-image alignment such that the unoriented LM is construed as having a front/back axis, licensing the use of *in front of* to denote a spatial relation between them vis-à-vis the third-entity vantage point.

powerful phenomena in the development of additional, non-spatial senses becoming associated with a particular form.

In this sense, a relation is designated such that the TR is conceptualized as being more privileged, more important than, or superior to the LM in some way. As is clear from the examples below, these sentences do not necessarily relate to spatial scenes (as they are non-spatial in nature), but as we shall see, derive from a particular spatial configuration:

(6.48)   In the opening of Parliament, the Prime Minister has put reform of the National Health Service in front of outlawing cigarette advertising

In this example *in front of* denotes a non-spatial relation between a TR and a LM. Moreover, the conventional reading is that the TR is in some sense more important or more privileged than the LM. In (6.48) the TR, *the Prime Minister*, privileges one aspect of the legislative programme, reform of the National Health Service, over another, a ban on cigarette advertising.

The Priority Sense is distinct from the proto-scene, as there is an additional meaning component apparent, and the TRs and LMs employed are wholly non-spatial. After all, the sentence above does not give rise to the interpretation that health reform is an entity physically located in front of a cigarette advertising ban.

In order to see how the Priority Sense may have derived, consider the following:

(6.49)   The marathon was just in the beginning stages, but Steve was already over a mile in front of the other runners

The example in (6.49) is compatible with the proto-scene in so far as the TR, *Steve*, is physically located in front with respect to *the other runners*, the LM. Although the entities depicted in the sentence are human, our knowledge of races tells us that they are not in a mirror-image alignment. After all, runners in a race are typically facing in the same direction, the direction of the finish line, rather than facing each other. This is essentially the same configuration depicted in (6.42), *The teacher was difficult to hear when he was in front of the class because he often spoke as he wrote on the blackboard*, in which the oriented TR, *the teacher*, is facing the blackboard and the oriented LM, *the class*, is also facing the blackboard. As such, these scenes involve what, following Hill (1978), we term *in tandem* alignment. In tandem alignment of entities is diagrammed in figure 6.7. The spatial configuration between the two entities in the scene is essentially the same as the proto-scene; the important change is that the TR, the figure on the right, as well as the LM, the figure on the left, happen to be oriented.

In many of our daily experiences ranging from the almost inevitable traffic jam to work, to waiting in line to be served in the bank, to foot races, as described by (6.49), we encounter in tandem alignment. These are often, but not inevitably

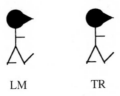

LM   TR

Figure 6.7 In tandem alignment

open scenes. A consequence of in tandem alignment is that the entity *in front of* another entity is further ahead, and thus closer to achieving the particular objective in question, such as reaching a particular destination (such as a place of work), or realizing a desired objective (such as winning a race, standing in line to buy tickets, deposit money into a bank account, etc.). Hence, as far as in tandem interactions are concerned, being in front correlates with achieving the ultimate objective associated with the activity engaged in; thus, the entity in front is thereby more privileged and enjoys a greater priority. For this reason, we suggest, *in front of* has derived a Priority Sense, distinct from the proto-scene for *in front of*, as evidenced by the example in (6.48).

The semantics of *before*: the proto-scene

As we have just seen in our discussion of *in front of*, the Priority Sense and the proto-scene involve essentially the same relationship between the TR and LM. In both senses, the LM is oriented towards the TR. The salient difference is that the in tandem alignment of the Priority Sense also involves the TR being oriented in the same direction as the LM. This can occur in our real-world experience when an 'in front of' relation involves a human TR that is directed away from the oriented LM. As we have just seen, *in front of*, whose proto-scene designates a 'located at the front of' meaning, appears to have developed a sense involving an in tandem alignment. Conversely, it would not be surprising to find a spatial particle whose proto-scene involves an in tandem configuration also developing a 'located at the front of' meaning. *Before* seems to be just such a particle.

It will be recalled from chapter 3 that one of our criteria for determining which sense should be considered the proto-scene is the synchronic sense most closely related to the historically earliest sense. However, as we saw in the discussion of the etymology of *before*, even in Sanskrit and Old English, we find evidence for two competing senses, the Location Sense (involving a TR and an oriented LM) and the In Advance Of Sense (involving an in tandem configuration). Thus, the criterion of earliest historical use does not distinguish between the two possible proto-scenes.

The criterion of use in composite forms does suggest a distinction. All the composite forms listed in *Webster's New International Dictionary, Unabridged*

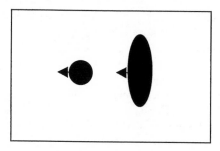

Figure 6.8 Proto-scene for *before*

involve an In Advance Of Sense. The following are representative: *before-cited, beforehand, before-mentioned, before-named*, and *beforetime*.

Additionally, predominance in the semantic network gives a slight edge to the In Tandem or In Advance Sense being the better candidate for the proto-scene. This follows as four (those in bold) out of six (**Preceding, Temporal, Priority, Sooner/Rather Than**, Location, Access To) senses seem to derive from this sense.[19]

On the basis of our established criteria, we posit the following proto-scene for *before*. Both the TR and the LM are oriented. The elongated sphere in figure 6.8 represents the LM; the smaller sphere represents the TR. The functional element, as we will discuss below, is that of leading, which in turn implicates sequence.

The following exemplify the proto-scene:

(6.50) a. The bay reached the finish line before the grey filly
        b. Hilary arrived home just before Matt
        c. Barring a flanking assault, the soldiers in the front lines encounter the enemy before the soldiers in the rear lines

A recurring consequence of two animate, oriented entities being in an in tandem alignment and in motion is that the one in the advance position will encounter other entities first. An unavoidable consequence of the TR and LM being so aligned is that the TR and the LM will encounter other entities sequentially. For instance, consider the scenario of a race, with three runners, A, B and C. Runner A finishes first, runner B second and runner C third. In such a scenario, by virtue of A being located in front of runners B and C, A is sequenced prior to both B and C, and arrives at (or encounters) the finish line

---

[19] The following illustrate each of these six senses:
Preceding: *The scouts fanned out before the main body of the army*
Temporal: *Alice arrived before Bill*
Priority: *We've decided to put public safety before everything else*
Rather Than: *I'd throw out those ratty clothes before I'd wear them*
Location: *The hot steaming soup was placed on the table before him*
Access To: *The world was all before them where to choose* (Milton)

prior to, or in advance of, B and C. The tight correlation between location and sequence in scenes involving an in tandem alignment has resulted in the strong implicature of sequentiality becoming associated with *before*.

Similarly, a recurring consequence of two static entities being in an in tandem alignment is that a person approaching the static entities would encounter them sequentially. So, if three people, Gary, Nicole and Eric, are standing in line, one behind the other, and a fourth person, Donna, approaches from the front of the line, Donna will encounter the three in sequential order.

Moreover, a ubiquitous aspect of human experience is that when we are in motion, we encounter static entities which are aligned but not necessarily inherently oriented. However, as we approach these objects, we often perceive the side nearest to us as most salient and thus assign the near side a functional orientation of front. Thus, we experience two aligned but unoriented objects, such as lamp posts, as being in an in tandem alignment as we encounter them. It is inevitable that we encounter such aligned objects in sequence. Under such a construal, *before* is licensed. We hypothesize that with use the implicature of sequence associated with *before* (and its 'in advance of' or leading functional element) has gained in salience such that *before* can be used to denote any set of ordered entities, as in the following:

(6.51)   a. A is before B in the alphabet
         b. Your name is before his on the list of people to be admitted to the programme
         c. In your official signature in English, your given name is always before your family name
         d. Monday is always before Tuesday

It is worth highlighting the fact that sequences are temporally framed relations, either because the event itself correlates with the passage of time, such as a foot race, or because the processing required to relate two discrete units in a sequence, as in two letters in the alphabet, correlates with the passage of time. Hence, a sequence is necessarily a temporal concept, and as such a Sequence Sense is thereby a Temporal Sense (see Evans, 2000, for a discussion of the relationship between before and after relations as they relate to other temporal concepts). Thus, our proto-scene is consistent with the observations by Langacker (1987), Lindstromberg (1998), Talmy (2000) and others that *before* is largely associated with temporality while its origins are spatial in nature.

The Location Sense

Some sentences employing *before* do not necessarily involve an in tandem alignment and do not have a sequential interpretation. These uses of *before* appear to be (nearly) synonymous in interpretation with the proto-scene associated with *in front of*:

(6.52)   The rabbi performed the ritual before the congregation
         (Cf. The rabbi performed the ritual in front of the congregation)
(6.53)   When deserving citizens are knighted, they kneel before the queen
         (Cf. When deserving citizens are knighted they kneel in front of the
         queen)
(6.54)   John was summoned before the principal
         (Cf. John was summoned in front of the principal)

Crucially, in these spatial scenes the vantage point of the LM is privileged. In contexts such as these, in which the LM is human – *the congregation, the queen* and *the principal* – and the perspective of the LM is privileged, *before* denotes a Location Sense, virtually indistinguishable from the proto-scene of *in front of*. By virtue of being positioned at the front of an animate, oriented LM, the TR is perceptually accessible to the LM. The TR is thus in a position to be scrutinized by the LM.

It is important to emphasize that this sense is restricted and in many contexts appears to have been superseded by *in front of*. In most scenes in which the LM is inanimate, *before* is not acceptable, or at best sounds archaic:

(6.55)   ?Look, Chris is standing before his new truck in this picture.
         (Cf. Look, Chris is standing in front of his new truck in this picture)

Some native speakers even find the use of *before* to relate a TR to non-human LMs semantically anomalous or archaic:

(6.56)   ?She placed the bowl of milk before the cat
         (Cf. She placed the bowl of milk in front of the cat)

This suggests that *before* has primarily retained its historical 'located at the front of' meaning in specific contexts, which involve human LMs, as evidenced in the examples in (6.52) through (6.54). This 'location' use appears to have been retained, at least partially, through anecdotal sayings, children's verse and events, and language governed by historical precedent such as knighting ceremonies.[20] The spatial scene associated with the Location Sense for *before* is diagrammed in figure 6.9.

In terms of the spatial relation designated by this sense, *before* looks very like the proto-scene for *in front of*, except for the partial shading of the LM which is meant to represent an eye. The eye indicates that the LM must be animate and have perceptual access to the LM.

---

[20] It may be that this preservation has occurred, at least in part, through English literary heritage. For instance, this use of *before* occurs in nursery rhymes and wise sayings, which children hear repeated many times at an early age:
Wasn't that a dainty dish to place before the king?

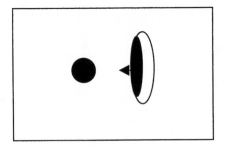

Figure 6.9 Locational scene of before

One reason why *before* may have retained its historically more productive Location Sense in just those contexts in which the TR is in the presence of an 'exalted' entity, as noted by Lindstromberg, may be because as humans we naturally tend to take note of other humans, and particularly those who can potentially affect us. Clearly, this is grounded in our socio-physical experience with the world. As infants, it is our human caretakers who feed us, hold us and talk to us, not our family pets (no matter how beloved), or inanimate beings (no matter how fascinating all the blinking lights and beeping noises of the most sophisticated toys might be). Moreover, designating the LM as an animate entity, in effect highlights the LM's viewpoint or perspective. This emphasis on the vantage point of the human LM also seems to account for the intuition that *before* seems slightly more natural than *in front of* in certain 'location' uses, for example *The ultimate sanction for the misbehaving schoolboy is to be summoned before the headmaster*.

The view that *in front of* has superseded some of *before*'s earlier semantic territory is confirmed by the unacceptability of *before* in contexts involving inanimate LMs even when they are inherently oriented, and the unacceptability of *before* in LMs that are not inherently oriented, but receive a relative orientation by virtue of, for instance, an orientation frame.[21] Attested cases of earlier

---

[21] Indeed, the unacceptability (or at best archaic quality) of *before* with a non-sequential reading contrasts with the acceptability of *in front of*, as evidenced by the following:
Inanimate LM oriented by virtue of its leading edge

    A. *John stood before the oncoming car
       (Cf. John stood in front of the oncoming car)

Inanimate LM oriented by virtue of its leading edge

    B. *John ran before the car as it rolled down the hill
       (Cf. John ran in front of the car as it rolled down the hill)

Inanimate LM oriented by virtue of projection of mirror-image alignment

    C. *Kathy stood before the tree/bush
       (Cf. Kathy stood in front of the tree/bush)

uses of *before* with a Location Sense now sound archaic: *The battle was before and behind* (2 Chronicles, xiii, 14. King James Version).

The Priority Sense

Like *in front of*, *before* has a Priority Sense associated with it. In this sense *before* denotes a non-spatial relation between two entities in which the notion of being more privileged or more important in some way is signalled. Consider some examples:

(6.57)   a. My father tried never to place one of his children before another
          b. This airline makes a virtue out of placing safety before all else

In these examples the TR is afforded a higher priority than the LM. This relation is designated by *before*. Clearly, this sense is distinct from the proto-scene associated with *before* as it involves an additional, non-spatial relation.

As we observed above, a consequence of being physically located in an *in front of* location during an in tandem alignment is that this results in being more privileged or receiving greater priority. After all, being first in line or coming first in a foot race (experiences which involve an in tandem alignment) correlate with advantages or privileges. Given that the proto-scene associated with *before* involves just such an in tandem alignment, it is natural that *before* should have also developed a Priority Sense.

Behind and *after*

Synchronically, *behind* and *after* work, in general, in analogous ways to *in front of* and *before*. As with *in front of*, we hypothesize that the proto-scene associated with *behind* designates a LM with front/back orientation. Given that the sensory organs in humans are located primarily in the front of the face, the back of the human is associated with lack of perceptual accessibility. The interactive consequence of a TR located at the back of a front/back oriented LM is that the LM does not have perceptual access to the TR. Thus, the functional element denoted by *behind* relates to lack of perceptual access and lack of surety about the location of the TR. Similarly, we hypothesize that the proto-scene associated with *after* is analogous to the proto-scene associated with *before*, which designates a spatial relation in which both the TR and the LM are inherently oriented, and are related by virtue of an in tandem alignment.

Inanimate TR/LM oriented by virtue of an orientation frame

D. *On the conveyor-belt that moves bottles to the washing machine, smaller bottles are always placed before larger bottles [location reading]
(Cf. On the conveyor-belt that moves bottles to the washing machine, smaller bottles are placed in front of larger bottles)

A consequence of this configuration is that the functional element associated with *after* is one in which the TR is following or pursuing the LM. Although *in front of* and *behind*, on one hand, and *before* and *after*, on the other, constitute contrast sets, as we observed with *up* and *down*, it is overly simplistic to suggest that a straightforward opposition exists between these pairs of spatial particles.

The semantics of *behind:* the proto-scene

The etymology of this particle is *be + hind*. *Hind* is clearly associated with an anthropomorphic/zoomorphic model, as in 'hind end' or 'hind quarters' of a person or animal. Thus, *behind* originally meant roughly 'located at the back'.

The proto-scene we propose for *behind* locates the TR at the back of the LM, that is, the TR is understood to be located such that the front of the LM is directed away from the TR. Consider the following sentence by way of illustration:

(6.58)   The student stood behind the teacher

In this sentence, the TR is located with respect to the teacher's back. Hence, the LM must have front/back orientation, such that the front is directed away from the TR. The student can be either looking at the teacher's back or turned away, with his or her back towards the teacher. The orientation of the TR is not crucial. In fact, many TRs which participate in constructions with *behind* do not have inherent front/back orientation, as evidenced by the following:

(6.59)   Behind the married couple, there is a large table covered with presents

The proto-scene for *behind* is diagrammed in figure 6.10. As with the proto-scene posited for *in front of* and *before*, the small shaded sphere represents the TR. The larger elongated sphere represents the LM. The arrow indicates the orientation of the LM, such that the TR is situated at the back of the LM,

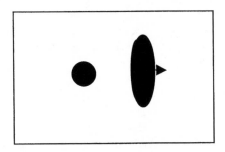

Figure 6.10 Proto-scene for *behind*

and hence is positioned *behind* with respect to the LM. The functional element denoted by *behind* relates to lack of perceptual access and lack of surety about the location of the TR.

Functionally oriented LMs

As with *in front of*, non-animate entities can also serve as LMs if, by virtue of the way in which we interact with them, we normally construe them as having front/back orientation:

(6.60)   The road is behind the house

In an example such as (6.60), as houses normally have a designated main access, houses are construed as having asymmetric structure and hence access. As such, the side that provides primary access is construed as the front (Langacker, 1987). In (6.60), the TR, *the road*, is located nearest the side opposite to the front, that is, the back of the house. As noted in our discussion of *in front of*, while a LM such as *the house* does not necessarily have inherent orientation it does have what we termed functional orientation.

Inherently non-oriented LMs

Special case I: mirror-image alignment Analogous to *in front of*, the proto-scene associated with *behind* can also denote a spatial relation between a TR and an inherently non-oriented entity by projecting a front/back orientation onto such LMs. Recall that one way for this to occur is when a mirror-image alignment holds between two entities. In such spatial scenes the vantage point is on-stage; it is with respect to the on-stage vantage point that a mirror-image alignment occurs. Consider the following:

(6.61)   Sarah stood behind the bush/tree

In this sentence the vantage point is on-stage and constitutes the position from which the scene is viewed. For instance, in (6.61), for the TR, *Sarah*, to be construed as being behind the inherently non-oriented LM, the scene must be being viewed from a vantage point in which the tree intervenes between the TR and the vantage point. As such, while the front/back orientation is the result of a mirror-image alignment between the vantage point and the LM, the relation designated is that between the TR and the LM.

Special case II: orientation frames In spatial scenes in which the vantage point is not on-stage, and in which the TR and LM are inherently non-oriented, a secondary reference object (recall the discussion earlier) can serve to impose an orientation frame. As such, this provides relative orientation which serves to relate the otherwise non-oriented TR and LM. Consider the following example:

(6.62)   On the conveyor-belt that moves bottles to the washing machine, smaller bottles are always placed behind larger bottles

In this example, by virtue of an orientation frame being imposed by the directionality of the secondary reference object, the conveyor-belt, unlabelled bottles, which are otherwise non-oriented, can be related by virtue of the proto-scene for *behind*.

The Lack of Priority Sense

Like *in front of*, *behind* also has a sense that relates to priority. As *behind* forms a contrast pair with *in front of*, this sense relates to a lack of priority, and hence a concomitant lack of importance or being privileged. Consider an illustrative example:

(6.63)   The president placed environmental welfare behind all other items in his legislative programme

In this sentence a non-spatial relation is designated in which the TR, *environmental welfare*, is less privileged or lacks importance vis-à-vis other items on the legislative agenda. We suggest that, just as with *in front of*, this sense has derived from the proto-scene associated with *behind*, in which an in tandem alignment between TR and LM occurred. Consider some examples:

(6.64)   a. The marathon was just in the beginning stages, but Lissa was already over a mile behind the other runners
          b. Gary was behind Jim in the ticket line

Examples such as those in (6.64) are compatible with the proto-scene. However, here, there is an in tandem alignment between the TR and LM. As being located behind another entity correlates with being less likely to achieve a desired objective or outcome (e.g., winning the race, gaining a prize, obtaining tickets which might sell out, etc.), there is a concomitant correlation with being less privileged. As such, being *behind* in a spatial scene involving an in tandem alignment correlates with a lack of being privileged or a lack of relative importance. Due to this correlation, *behind* can, in such contexts, implicate a lack of priority. Through pragmatic strengthening we suggest that *behind* has developed a Lack of Priority Sense, as evidenced by the example in (6.63).

The semantics of *after:* The proto-scene

After shares semantic space with *behind*, but the etymological origins of the two particles are very different and continue to constrain their use. *After* derives from a comparative form of *af*, which was apparent in Old English and meant 'off' or 'away'. Hence, the comparative 'af + ter' meant 'farther off' or 'farther away'. Unlike its contrast partner *before*, which has a Location Sense as part of its polysemy network, *after* appears not to have a Location Sense along the lines of 'located at the back of the LM', as evidenced by the following:

(6.65)   *He knelt after the King [intended reading: behind the King]
(Cf. He knelt before the King)

Nevertheless, *after* does have a spatial sense associated with it, which parallels some of the in tandem uses of the proto-scene for *behind*. Consider some examples by way of illustration:

(6.66)   A bear was moving briskly through the wood with a cub trailing after her
(Cf. A bear was moving briskly through the wood with a cub trailing behind her)

(6.67)   An extremely tall man was striding through the crowd with a boy scurrying after him
(Cf. An extremely tall man was striding through the crowd with a boy scurrying behind him)

In examples such as these, in which an in tandem alignment is evident, *after* can felicitously prompt for a spatial relation in which the TR is located at the back of an oriented LM, which is oriented in the same direction as the LM. This suggests that *after* specifies a relation in which both the TR and the LM are oriented, and moreover, share an in tandem alignment.

However, in many contexts involving an in tandem alignment, *after* cannot be felicitously used:

(6.68)   *Steve was a mile after the other runners
(Cf. Steve was a mile behind the other runners)

(6.69)   *Jim stood after Gary in the ticket line
(Cf. Jim stood behind Gary in the ticket line)

Similarly, in contexts involving LMs with functional orientation, mirror-image alignment or orientation frames, *after*, unlike *behind*, also appears to be unacceptable with a spatial reading:

(6.70)   * The road is after the house [functionally oriented LM]
          (Cf. The road is behind the house)
(6.71)   *Sarah is after the tree [projected front/back orientation due to mirror-
          image alignment]
          (Cf. Sarah is behind the tree)
(6.72)   ?On the conveyor-belt that moves bottles to the washing machine,
          smaller bottles are always placed after larger bottles [orientation due
          to orientation frame][22]
          (Cf. On the conveyor-belt that moves bottles to the washing machine,
          smaller bottles are always placed behind larger bottles)

The question then is, why can *after* be employed in (6.66) and (6.67) with a
spatial reading which overlaps with *behind*, and yet not be acceptable in the other
examples considered? One reason is that, unlike *behind, after* can be employed
only with an in tandem alignment, suggesting that it designates an oriented
TR as well as an oriented LM. This configuration, therefore, is also distinct
from *in front of*, whose proto-scene designates only an oriented LM. Moreover,
as the proto-scene for *after* relates exclusively to an in tandem sequence, the
functional element associated with *after* in its spatial reading is that of following
or pursuing, and hence involves intentionality and purpose rather than location
per se. For instance, in (6.68), the distance between Steve and the other runners
is being emphasized. As such, the relative location of Steve vis-à-vis the other
competitors is being profiled. As such, *after* is infelicitous in this sentence.
However, if we profile *Steve*'s competing with the other runners (and hence
attempting to catch them up), rather than the relative distance between Steve
and the other runners, the use of *after* becomes acceptable:

(6.73)   Although a mile back, Steve ran after the other competitors with re-
          newed vigour

In this sentence, *after* does designate a spatial relation. Yet, rather than being
primarily concerned with location, the functional component associated with
after is that of the TR following or being in pursuit, as is clearly attested by the
sentence below:

(6.74)   The police chased/came after the robbers

Here, the notion of pursuit is evident. As we are positing that *behind* has a
functional element of lack of perceptual accessibility related to location rather
than pursuit associated with the proto-scene we would expect that in such a

---

[22] Grady (personal communication) suggests that this sentence sounds more acceptable than the
previous examples because movement is involved.

sentence *behind* would be at the very least unnatural, if not infelicitous, which is exactly what we find:

(6.75)   ?The police chased/came behind the robbers

It will be recalled that in our discussion of *in front of* versus *before*, we suggested that as *front* entered the language from Old French, the overlap in the Location Senses between *in front of* and *before* is accounted for by the more recent form *in front of* encroaching on the semantic territory formerly belonging to *before*. The situation between *behind* and *after* is somewhat different as *behind* and *after* are indigenous forms, both of which occurred in Old English. The difference in the spatial and functional components associated with the proto-scenes, can, we suggest, be explained in terms of the historically earlier meanings associated with these forms.

We noted above that the original meaning associated with *after*, apparent in Old English, was a comparative form of *af*, *af-ter*, which meant 'further off'. In certain situations in which an object was perceived as having a front and a back, *af* or *aft* became associated with the part of the object which was perceived to follow, as in the *aft* of a ship or the *afterdecks*. Given this earlier meaning and its association with parts that 'trail' the front of an object, such as a ship, it seems plausible that the functional element of following or pursuing should have become associated with the synchronic proto-scene (thereby distinguishing *after* from *behind*). Moreover, in many in tandem alignments, such as when trying to keep up with another entity, such as a fast-walking parent in a crowd, other competitors in a foot race, or, for instance, when chasing or hunting, there are times in the pursuit when the pursued may not be visible, and hence may be 'farther off'.

However, in scenarios in which the TR is distant from the LM, where the distance can be quantified and the relative locations established, *behind* also seems acceptable, as in sentences such as: *Steve is a mile behind the others*. In sum, the proto-scenes associated with *behind* and *after* are in part motivated by their historical semantic antecedents. Accordingly, the proto-scene for *after* is presented in figure 6.11. The larger, oriented element represents the LM; the smaller element represents the TR.

The Sequential Sense

Owing to its proto-scene with a functional element of following or pursuing, *after* is well placed to develop a Sequential Sense. In this it forms a contrast set with the Sequential Sense associated with *before*. In the examples given below, two entities in a sequence are denoted. As we observed in our discussion of *before*, sequences are inherently temporal, as they involve processing and/or

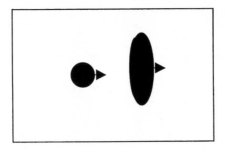

Figure 6.11 Proto-scene for *after*

experiencing discrete, temporally located events, which often become routinized as part of a sequence routine (e.g., reciting the alphabet):

(6.76)   a. O is after A in the alphabet
          b. Wave after wave crashed into the cliff
          c. Dessert always comes after the main course
          d. Tuesday is after Monday
          e. Joan sang after Mary

As noted in our discussion of *before*, sequences correlate with scenes involving an in tandem alignment of entities in motion. In a foot race for instance, the winner, the runner spatially in advance of the other runners, crosses the finish line first. Hence, being located ahead, correlates with the event of arriving first. Arrival constitutes an event in a sequence which correlates with a particular location, the point of arrival (e.g., the finish line in a race). As the proto-scene for *after* is so closely associated with in tandem alignment, it is perhaps inevitable that, due to the tight correlation in experience between motion of this kind and the sequence of events such as arrival and departure etc., *after* should have developed a sequential meaning component. In its Sequential Sense, *after* designates a relation between the TR and the LM, the TR being sequenced subsequent to the LM, as evidenced by the examples above.

Conclusion

In this chapter we have analysed a range of spatial particles (and the spatial scenes with which they are related) pertaining to orientation. While *up, down, to* and *for* relate to orientation of the TR, *in front of, behind, before* and *after* all involve orientation of the LM. The particles *before* and *after* add the additional element of the TR, as well as the LM, being oriented. In general terms, the analysis presented here supports the perspective of the principled polysemy approach developed in the preceding chapters. In particular, the conclusions support the general view adduced that non-spatial meaning is often derived from spatial experience, which is meaningful due to the way in which we interact with the world around us. For instance, following Hill (1978), we have argued that recurrent, face-to-face interaction with other humans has given rise to the tendency to project a mirror-image alignment in closed scenes involving non-oriented entities. Additionally, human interaction with inanimate objects often results in construals of orientation based on function, such as assigning a house a front/back orientation based on typical access or aligned lamp-posts a front/back orientation based on the side which is visible to a human as he or she approaches the lamp-posts.

7   Bounded landmarks

A number of spatial particles appear to mediate relations in which the dimensions of the LM are essentially irrelevant. As we saw in our discussions of *over*, the extendedness or dimensionality of the LM appears to have no particular bearing on the relationship mediated by *over*. In contrast, in this chapter we will explore a set of spatial particles, *in, into, out, out of* and *through*, which are sensitive to certain dimensions of the LM, namely the dimensions which collectively give rise to the notion of boundedness.

We define a bounded LM as one that possesses an interior, a boundary and an exterior. Canonically, we think of bounded LMs as three-dimensional objects, such as boxes or rooms. Entities that are typically thought of as having a one-dimensional or two-dimensional structure are not typically conceptualized as a bounded LM; for instance, they are not typically thought of as possessing an interior. However, as we have seen in our previous discussions, humans have the capacity for construing spatial scenes from a variety of perspectives; this ability appears to extend to how the dimensionality of any given entity is construed for the purposes at hand. The linguistic evidence shows that the conceptualization of a particular LM as bounded is determined not in absolute terms by its geometry (although clearly this does play some part), but rather by virtue of the way in which humans experience and interact with the LM in question.

By way of example, consider the following:

(7.1)   a. Turn right **at** George Street[1] and go three blocks[2]

---

[1] This use of *George Street* may be a metonymy representing the intersection of 'George Street' and another street. We can imagine an alternative scenario along the lines of: *Walk straight across this field. The first street you will come to is George Street. At George Street, then turn left.* In this case, there may be a conceptual intersection between the walker's trajectory and George Street. However, it also seems plausible to argue that the conceptualization is the point at which the walker is first co-located with George Street, representing the spot at which the walker should turn.

[2] We do not offer a formal analysis of *at* in this book, but our investigations suggest, along with many previous analyses, that *at* indicates co-location between a TR and a LM, in which the location is conceptualized as a point.

b. There is a lot of traffic **on** this street[3]

c. There are several potholes **in** the street in front of my house

All three of these examples involve essentially the same physical entity, a *street,* which constitutes the LM. However, in each spatial scene, the construer is interacting with and conceptualizing the LM in a different way. In sentence (7.1a), *the street* is construed as a one-dimensional point; it is simply serving as a reference location within the speech event of giving directions. In sentence (7.1b), *the street* is being construed as a two-dimensional, planar surface; the interpretation is that it is serving its common function as a passageway that provides solid support for the vehicles that travel along it. In the example (7.1c), *the street* is being construed as a three-dimensional LM, which is understood as having internal structure as revealed by *the potholes;* the potholes are not simply situated on the road's normal boundary, its uniform planar surface, but are situated interior to the normal surface such that they reveal the depth and internal structure of the street. Thus, the street is conceptualized as crucially having an interior and the potholes can felicitously be described as *in* the street.

Consistent with the view of embodied experience articulated throughout this book, the way in which humans experience and interact with bounded LMs has functional consequences. These consequences are reflected in the meanings typically associated with the spatial particles *in, into, out, out of* and *through.* One consequence of our interaction with certain kinds of bounded LMs is that we experience them in terms of containment.[4] Containment itself is a complex relation, involving numerous functional consequences. In the guise of containers, bounded LMs constrain and delimit movement of their TRs, as in a coffee cup which constrains the coffee it contains to a specific location, or a prison cell, which restricts the movements of a convict. In certain circumstances, constraining movement can be understood as providing support, thus a cut flower can be held in an upright position as a result of being placed in a vase. If the boundaries of the container are opaque, they prevent us from seeing beyond them, or the interior area from being seen by entities outside, as in a walled

---

[3] We do not offer a formal analysis of *on,* but we suggest, much in keeping with previous research, that *on* mediates a relation of contact between a TR and a LM, which is a two-dimensional planar surface.

[4] A common confusion in some previous semantic analyses has been to equate the functional component with the spatial configuration, even in work by cognitive linguists. For instance, Lakoff (1987) characterizes what he terms the *containment schema* in terms of three structural properties: *interior, boundary* and *exterior.* This view appears to suggest that a containment relation is defined by virtue of these structural (i.e., spatial) elements. While we agree that containment is related to these structural properties, it does not follow from this that the structural properties described can be equated with containment. After all, containment is also related to the notions of delimitation, opacity, safety and support, etc, commonly associated with certain types of LMs as we interact with them. Hence, it is worth reminding ourselves that the concept of containment is a consequence of the nature of our interaction with structural properties of this kind, and not due simply to the structural properties themselves.

garden or a windowless room. Containers can also provide protection, as with a jeweller's safe. For the elements within a container, the container surrounds and largely determines the environment in which those entities exist. Different aspects of the experience of containment are profiled by the various uses of the spatial particles *in* and *out*, as we shall see. A second consequence of our interaction with bounded LMs is that they can serve as goals. For instance, after leaving work, for many people the goal is to arrive at home in order to interact with family, relax, etc. The *salient space* in which these anticipated activities take place is a bounded LM, the living quarters; thus, being in the salient space, the bounded LM, is closely related to achieving goals. A third way in which we interact with bounded LMs is that we emerge from them, as when we leave home each morning. Equally, we draw other entities from bounded LMs, as when a jeweller withdraws a diamond brooch from a safe. In this way, bounded LMs have source properties, as lexicalized by *out of*. A fourth way in which we interact with bounded LMs is when we pass from one side to another, as when walking from room to room in a building. Thus, we can experience bounded LMs as segments of a path or a passageway. This relation is captured by *through*.

Spatial structure versus the functional element for *in*

With respect to the spatial particle *in*, Vandeloise's (1991, 1994) discussion of the functional aspects of containment provides an elegant demonstration that spatial components cannot be equated solely with spatial elements. The diagram provided in figure 7.1 is inspired by Vandeloise.

He observes that an image such as that depicted in figure 7.1 could be construed as being either a bottle or a light bulb. However, while we can felicitously describe the relation between the light bulb, the TR, and its LM, the socket, as in (7.2):

(7.2)   The bulb is in the socket

we cannot felicitously describe the relation between a bottle and its LM in terms of the spatial relation designated by *in*:

(7.3)   ??The bottle is in the cap

Figure 7.1 After Vandeloise, 1994: 172

Vandeloise points out that as the spatial relation holding between the TR and LM in each of these sentences is identical, a spatial-geometric configuration alone cannot account for the relation described by *in*, or any other spatial particle. He argues that the relevant factor accounting for the contrast in acceptability between sentences (7.2) and (7.3) is functional: '[W]hile the socket exerts a force on the bulb and determines its position, the opposite occurs with the cap and the bottle' (1994: 173). Put another way, not only is the position and hence successful functioning of the bulb contingent on being *in* (i.e., contained by) the socket, but the socket also prevents the bulb from falling to the ground and thus provides a constraining or supportive element. In contrast, the position and successful functioning of the bottle is not contingent on being *in* the cap.

Herskovits (1986, 1988) has also emphasized that geometric-spatial relations are not sufficient to explain the complete range of spatial uses commonly associated with spatial particles. For instance, she noted that *in* applies to a wide range of spatial scenes, many of which do not require that the TR be enclosed by the LM. For example, *in* can be employed in the sentence *The pear is in the bowl* to describe a spatial scene in which the bowl holds so many pieces of fruit beneath the pear that it is physically higher than the rim of the bowl, and hence not strictly enclosed within the LM. She argued that the fact that native speakers of English can use *in* to describe spatial scenes of this kind indicates that principles beyond spatial-geometric relations must be involved. Although her particular solution of positing multiple levels of abstractness and a special set of pragmatic principles differs in certain ways from Vandeloise's notion of a functional element, her recognition that a crucial component of the spatial meaning associated with spatial particles relates to how we interact with spatial configurations – what we call *spatial scenes* – is consonant with the spirit of Vandeloise's work, and indeed with our own.

The observation that the lexeme *in* is associated with a functional relation (in additional to purely spatial properties) has also been noted by Sinha and Jensen de López (2000), as well as researchers involved in language acquisition (Bowerman, 1996) and psycholinguistic experimentation. Sinha and Jensen de López (2000) make the following observation: 'Move a cup of coffee, and the coffee goes with the cup. This property of containment is fundamental to the basic human usage of containers, which not only . . . enclose, but also constrain the movements of their contents. We can call this a functional, as opposed to logical, property of containment' (pp. 30–31). Garrod, Ferrier and Campbell (1999) specifically tested spatial-geometrical versus functional aspects associated with the particles *in* and *on* in terms of native speakers' judgements concerning which spatial particle most appropriately described 'spatially indeterminate' scenes, along the lines of figure 7.1. They conclude that an account of spatial particles that includes both spatio-configurational and functional components is necessary to account for their results. A consequence of this for future research, particularly for cross-linguistic studies, is that analyses of 'equivalent' spatial particles in related languages, for example the spatial particle *in*, in English, Dutch and German, will need to consider not only the spatio-configurational properties associated with spatial particles, but also similarities and potential differences in functional elements.

Partial inclusion

One recurring question concerning containment has been how fully the TR must be enclosed by the LM in order to be construed as contained (e.g., Herskovits, 1988; Vandeloise, 1994, etc.). This issue relates to how it is that *in* can mediate a relation in which the TR is completely surrounded by the LM, as in: *The sweater was in a beautifully wrapped box*, as well as a relation in which only a small portion of the TR is enclosed by the LM, as in: *The light bulb is in the socket*. Again, we argue that recognition of the functional aspect associated with a spatial particle, as well as the flexibility in human construal of the pertinent properties of any physical entity, is crucial to understanding the use of spatial particles that mediate relations with bounded LMs.

One common use of the proto-scene associated with *in* and involving partial inclusion concerns wearing items of apparel. Items of apparel are commonly experienced, and hence conceptualized, as having an interior, a boundary and an exterior, and as functionally involving certain aspects of containment such as protecting, surrounding and obscuring visual access to the elements being contained. Thus, the use of *in* to describe the relationship between the wearer and the piece of clothing is one licensed by the proto-scene.[5]

(7.4)   a. The rock singer in the tight leather pants
          b. The construction worker in the hard hat

It is particularly striking that in most instances, the TR, the human wearing the clothing, will be only partially enclosed by the LM.

Similarly, in examples such as (7.5), while there is a spatial relation holding between the TR and LM in which the elements interior, boundary and exterior are involved, the TR is only partially enclosed by the LM, as illustrated in figure 7.2.

(7.5)   The flower is in the vase

---

[5] Of course, clothing and the wearing of clothing can be conceptualized differently. One alternative conceptualization is to construe the body part as supporting the item of clothing. Under this construal, *on* would be the English spatial particle of choice. Thus we find expressions such as:

Delta Dawn, what's that dress that you have on?
Truman had on a silk ascot the last time I saw him.

Figure 7.2 *The flower is in the vase*

This spatial scene can be mediated by *in* precisely because this partial enclosure provides the contingent support or constraint for the flower, which is a key aspect of the containment function. In sum, sentences (7.2) through (7.5) demonstrate that *in* can mediate a TR–LM configuration involving partial inclusion, as long as functional elements of containment are also saliently involved.

The semantics for *in*

This chapter focuses on a range of spatial particles which relate to bounded LMs. We will begin with the semantics of *in*. As this spatial particle is associated with a particularly extensive and complex network of senses, we will restrict our discussion to a limited set of senses that exemplify the way in which human interaction with bounded LMs motivates a range of contrasting senses.

In and its Indo-European cognates (particularly in French, Dutch and German) have been extensively studied (see Dirven, 1993; Hawkins, 1988; Herskovits, 1986, 1988; Hottenroth, 1993; Lindstromberg, 1998; Miller and Johnson-Laird, 1976; Quirk *et al.*, 1985; Vandeloise, 1991, 1994). Despite having been so well studied, the present analysis represents, we suggest, the first that provides a methodologically motivated account for the range of polysemy associated with *in*. Moreover, the analysis of *in* will constitute a useful first step in understanding the semantics associated with other spatial particles associated with bounded LMs.

The proto-scene for 'in'

As already noted, the proto-scene for *in* constitutes a spatial relation in which a TR is located within a LM which has three salient structural elements – an interior, a boundary and an exterior. In addition to the spatial relation designated, the proto-scene for *in* is associated with the functional element of containment. The proto-scene for *in* is given in figure 7.3. The LM is designated by the bold lines while the TR is designated by the shaded sphere.

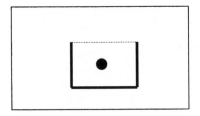

Figure 7.3 Proto-scene for *in*

Non-canonical bounded LMs As we noted above, because of the flexibility of human conceptualization, the requisite spatial and functional components can be understood to exist with spatial scenes that do not involve canonical three-dimensional LMs. For instance, in the following examples the LM is conceptualized as being physically planar, and hence two-dimensional. By virtue of such LMs being construed as possessing an interior (and thereby a boundary and an exterior), these LMs are conceptualized as bounded, licensing the use of the proto-scene for *in*:

(7.6)   a. The cow munched grass in the field
         b. The tiny oasis flourished in the desert

In (7.6a) we conceptualize *the cow* as being 'contained' by the field. Yet, the field is not a canonical three-dimensional LM. By virtue of a field having an interior (that part which constitutes the field), a boundary such as a track, road, fence or hedge which marks the perimeter, and an exterior (that part which is not the field), this particular spatial scene can be construed as involving a bounded LM and hence a containment relationship. It might be objected that fields containing cows and other livestock are often bounded with barriers such as gates, fences or hedgerows which specifically constrain movement and thus this spatial scene does involve a canonical, three-dimensional LM. Notice, however, that the LM appears to be conceptualized as bounded even in examples in which there is no physical impediment delimiting movement, as evidenced in (7.6b). That is, by virtue of there being a LM that can be conceptualized as having an interior which contrasts with an exterior, a boundary is entailed and a concomitant designation of containment arises. Hence, in (7.6b), *the oasis*, the TR, is conceptualized as being 'contained' by *the desert*, the LM, even though there are no physical barriers such as fences bounding the desert.

Analogously, *in* mediates the spatio-functional relation in spatial scenes involving continents, seas, countries, regions, provinces and other geo-physical divisions, such as cities, etc.

(7.7)   a. China is in Asia
         b. London is the largest city in the United Kingdom
         c. She lives in New York City

In also denotes spatial scenes in which a prevailing atmospheric condition is conceptualized as enveloping the TR:

(7.8)   a. The flag flapped in the wind
          b. The child shivered in the cold
          c. The rabbit froze in the glare of the car's headlights

Other spatial scenes involving the proto-scene for *in* include examples such as the following in which a collective of individuals is conceptualized as a single mass. Consider some examples:

(7.9)   a. The child couldn't be seen in the crowd
          b. The old cottage was located in the wood

Examples such as those in (7.9) relate to what Lakoff (1987) termed a multiplex-mass transformation, which relates two distinct construals of the same entity. Lakoff illustrated this as follows: 'Imagine a large herd of cows up close – close enough to pick out the individual cows. Now imagine yourself moving back until you can no longer pick out the individual cows. There is a point at which you cease making out individuals and start perceiving a mass. It is this perceptual experience upon which the relationship between multiplex entities and masses rests' (1987: 428). Owing to this perceptual phenomenon, collective entities such as people can be perceived and hence conceptualized as a single mass entity, a crowd. Once this has occurred, the LM, *the crowd*, can be construed as occupying a bounded space. Thus, such a single mass entity can be conceptualized as a bounded LM, possessing not only a boundary but also an interior and an exterior.[6] Moreover, our experience of being part of a crowd often involves a number of the functional aspects of containment such as the sense of having our movements constrained, of being surrounded, of our view being obstructed, etc. Thus, the use of *in* is licensed in such situations.

Beyond the proto-scene

Due to the ubiquity of bounded LMs in our everyday experience, and the range and differences in such LMs, it is hardly surprising that we interact with bounded LMs in many different ways. This is reflected by the complexity of the polysemy network associated with *in*, and the range of senses associated with it. We have identified at least twenty-seven distinct senses, subsumed by six clusters of senses. Rather than attempting to provide a detailed overview of the entire

---

[6] It is worth noting that the notions of mass entities and boundedness are in principle distinct. That is, mass entities are not inevitably bounded. For instance, Talmy (2000) argues that while concepts such as *timber* and *furniture* relate to mass conceptions (he uses the term *multiplex*), these notions are inherently unbounded in conceptual terms. This situation contrasts with notions such as *family*, which describes a mass entity that is necessarily bounded.

network (as we did in our analysis of *over* in chapter 4), and as our purpose is to illustrate the nature and range of senses that boundedness can give rise to, we will here provide a brief overview of a limited range of the senses associated with each cluster. The six clusters of senses derived from the proto-scene reflect the different configurational and functional elements associated with a bounded LM whose functional element is containment.

The Location Cluster

We observed above that one aspect of the notion of containment relates to the movement or action of an entity being constrained, by virtue of being enclosed by a bounded LM. Johnson (1987) has argued that a consequence of this imposition is that the location of a contained TR is determined by the location of the bounded LM. In other words, the bounded LM necessarily serves to locate the contained TR with surety. Take the example of an infant in a playpen – move the playpen and the infant thereby follows suit. Indeed, the contained TR is located with surety even if the TR is not perceptually accessible. For example, the location of the infant in the playpen is known, even if the infant is not immediately within sight, as when the parent steps out of the room. Thus, there is a strong experiential correlation between a TR being contained and being located with surety.

Experimental work in child language acquisition (E. Clark, 1973) also suggests a strong conceptual relationship between location and containment, and that young children perceive containers as default locations. In the first step of an experiment (E. Clark, 1973), the experimenter asked eighteen-month-olds to 'Do this' as a block was placed in a crib. The children mimicked the experimenter's placement of the block perfectly. In following steps, the experimenter again said 'Do this' but placed the block beside the crib, then under the crib. In these conditions, the children still placed the block *in* the crib. In other words, given a movable object (a TR), a container (a LM) and the task of locating or placing the object, these young children seemed to construe containers as natural locators.

In the Location Cluster of senses, the notion that a bounded LM serves to pick out the salient space which contains the TR is privileged and gives rise to a range of closely related senses. We will briefly survey four of these: the In Situ Sense, the State Sense, the Activity Sense and the Means Sense.

The In Situ Sense An experiential correlate of being located with surety is that the TR crucially **remains** in a particular location. The conventional interpretation that the TR remains co-located with the salient space designated by the LM for an extended period provides additional meaning not apparent in the proto-scene. Moreover, this designation suggests an attendant purpose for being so located. This sense is illustrated by the following examples:

(7.10) a. What are you in for? [asked in a hospital = 'What's wrong with you?' or a prison = 'What were you convicted of?']
        b. He stayed in for the evening
        c. The workers staged a sit-in

In (7.10a) the TR is located at the LM (the hospital or the prison) for an extended period of time and for a particular purpose. Notice that this question would not be felicitous if the addressee were clearly at the hospital or prison for a brief visit, even though the addressee were physically located within the building, clearly a bounded LM.[7]

In the sentence in (7.10b), the TR, *he*, remains located at home,[8] rather than, for instance, going to a nightclub or some other location. In (7.10c) the TR, *the workers*, remain at their place of work, refusing to leave, in order to protest. In each of these examples, the TR remains located for an extended period, for a particular purpose and/or due to a volitional act or event. In sum, a commonly occurring consequence of a TR being located within a bounded LM is that the TR is located with surety. Additionally, in many cases, the TR remains located within the LM for an extended period of time. As a result, an In Situ Sense has become associated with *in*.

The State Sense Grady (1997a) and Lakoff and Johnson (1999) have argued that a primary metaphor, one which is based on a common correlation in experience, involves a particular location (LM) and the state experienced by the entity (TR), or the particular situation that the TR happens to be experiencing. For instance, the infant (TR) sitting on the parent's lap, enclosed in the parent's arms (LM), will often experience a sense of security and love. Some young children experience a sense of isolation and fear when left alone in a dark room at night. Through recurring instances of a particular emotional state being experienced in a specific locale, the correlation between location and emotional and/or physical state becomes established. This correlation gives rise to conceptual associations such that we conceptualize and hence lexicalize states in terms of location.[9]

---

[7] The appropriate question for the short-term visitor is something like *What/Who have you come in for?* placing emphasis on the act of coming, rather than the state of being, **in.**

[8] Lindner (1981) points out that *in* has developed a 'special' sense of the TR being in the default location. For a person, we often think of the default location as the home.

[9] Other spatial particles, such as *on* and *at*, can also denote State Senses. We believe that these State Senses derive from the ubiquitous experiential correlation between states and location. However, we also believe there are systematic, subtle differences in the properties of the states denoted by each preposition and thus, in many cases, we can identify motivation for conventionalized uses of particular prepositions with particular states. For instance, an important motivation for

The spatial particle *in* can be employed with certain states which are conceptualized as constraining the TR or posing difficulty in leaving, for example *She looked peaceful in death*; *They're always getting in trouble*; or with situations which can be conceptualized and hence lexicalized as states, *We're in a state of war/emergency/holy matrimony/martial law/anarchy*, etc. The reason for this is that there is a tight correlation between being located in a bounded LM and a particular state which is conferred by virtue of being so located. To clarify, consider the following example:

(7.11)   a. She is in prison
          b. She is a prisoner

The sentence in (7.11a) designates a scene in which the TR, *she*, is located in a particular bounded LM, *prison*. The express purpose of bounded LMs of this kind to restrict the freedom of the inmates. Hence, the state of being a prisoner, described in (7.11b), tightly correlates with being located within the confines of the prison. This tight correlation between being located within a bounded LM and the state experienced motivates a distinct State Sense having become conventionally associated with *in*.

A consequence of the State Sense being instantiated in permanent memory is that *in* can denote relations between TRs and non-physical LMs. This is because

conventional uses of *in* seems to relate to the constraint in extracting oneself from, or placing oneself in, the state, i.e., State Sense uses of *in* often draw on the notion of containment. For instance, English speakers seem to conceptualize an emotional state such as love in such a way that once one is 'in' love, one cannot easily or voluntarily leave that emotional state; similarly, once one is 'out of' love with a particular person, it is difficult to get back 'in' the state of being in love. Similarly, if one is 'in trouble', it is often a state not easily escaped. In contrast, states such as being 'on the take' or 'on the pill' are often seen as being a choice, and hence potentially more easily escaped. This is coherent with the proto-scene for *on*, which does not involve boundaries or constraint on motion. Moreover, State Senses denoted by 'on' often involve some sense of support, which is also coherent with the proto-scene. Analogously, the use of 'at' in a State use such as 'at war' may be due to the oppositional sense associated with 'at', e.g., *He rushed at me*. We suggest that the meanings associated with these examples reflect nuances from a number of senses designated by each spatial particle, which is expected if the semantic network is a semantic continuum. Thus, although we hypothesize that all State Senses are motivated by the correlation between location and state, we also suggest that there are nuances, such as 'boundedness' or 'constraint', associated with uses, such as 'in love', 'in trouble', etc., which relate to the semantic network for the particular spatial particle in question.

However, in some contexts more than one spatial particle might conceivably constitute a 'best fit'. Accordingly, while two particles may be motivated, a language or dialect may choose to conventionalize one while another may conventionalize another. An example of this is the distinction between British and American speakers. One of us is American and the other British. For the speaker of American English it feels 'more natural' to describe the situation in which a female dog is fertile as: *The neighbour's dog is in heat*. For the speaker of British English it feels 'more natural' to describe the same situation as: *The neighbour's dog is on heat*. Indeed, both particles are motivated. A state of 'heat' is relatively speaking short, hence *on*; yet the animal cannot voluntarily escape this state, thus motivating the use of *in*. Hence, while both *in* and *on* are motivated, in this context which one is selected is a matter of conventionalization.

in this sense *in* denotes relations between TRs and states, rather than bounded LMs per se. This follows, as once a particular sense is instantiated in memory it can be employed in contexts of use in the absence of those that originally motivated it.

The Activity Sense In addition to the tight correlation between bounded LMs and states, noted in the foregoing, there is a similarly tight and ubiquitous correlation between a particular activity and the bounded LM in which the activity occurs. For instance, a person who works for a government official (the activity) might conceivably be described in the following way in response to a question as to the TR's profession

(7.12)   A: What's his line of work?
         B: He's in the governor's office [= works for the governor]

This example nicely illustrates the correlation between an activity and the bounded LM at which the activity takes place. Working for the governor takes place in a bounded LM referred to as the governor's office(s). Hence, the location can stand metonymically for the activity.

A consequence of the correlation between activities and bounded LMs is that the notion of an activity can come, through pragmatic strengthening, to be reanalysed as a distinct meaning associated with *in*. Once instantiated in semantic memory, *in* can mediate a relation between a TR and an activity even when the activity designated is no longer overtly associated with a particular bounded LM. Consider some illustrative examples of the Activity Sense:

(7.13)   a. He works in stocks and shares
         b. She's in medicine
         c. They are in [the manufacture of] expensive baby clothes
         d. She's in graduate school[10]

---

[10] At this point it is worth contrasting the principled polysemy approach to the conceptual metaphor approach. In their early study of conceptual metaphors, Lakoff and Johnson (1980: chapter 7) suggested that in an example such as (7.13b), what they termed an ontological metaphor licensed the use of an 'abstract' concept, such as love or medicine, being conceptualized as a container. The present approach suggests that it may be misleading to posit that a native speaker is somehow understanding a concept such as love as a bounded LM which physically contains the TR. Rather, due to a complex semantic network, *in* has associated with it a conventional State Sense, which licenses such uses. This sense, while conventionally associated with *in*, is derived ultimately from a tight correlation in experience between spatial regions, which are conceptualized as being bounded, and states (cf. Grady's 1997a groundbreaking work on experiential correlation). Hence, while states are not straightforwardly conceptualized in terms of containers, as sometimes implied in the conceptual metaphor literature, it is worth emphasizing that the present principled polysemy approach does maintain that the polysemy associated with *in* (and with other spatial particles) is firmly grounded in spatio-physical experiential correlates.

While we hypothesize that once distinct senses are conventionalized, they no longer straightforwardly draw on the experiential correlations that gave rise to them, these same experiential

The Means Sense As we have just noted in the foregoing discussion, locations and activities are strongly correlated in experience. One result of this conceptual association between activities and locations is reflected in the lexical pattern of expressing aspects of activities with the particle *in*. Moreover, it is often the case that a particular activity utilizes one (or more) particular means in order to be accomplished. Owing to the tight correlation in experience between an activity and the means of accomplishing the activity, *in* has developed a distinct Means Sense. This has been possible precisely because *in* had an antecedent Activity Sense associated with it. Consider some examples of the Means Sense.

(7.14)   a. She wrote in ink
          b. He spoke in Italian

In (7.14a) *in* denotes the relation between a particular activity and the means of accomplishing the activity, ink versus pencil, for instance. Similarly, the activity in (7.14b) is accomplished through the medium of Italian rather than Japanese, say.

The correlation between activities and their means of accomplishment has led, then, through pragmatic strengthening to the development of the Means Sense. This provides an elegant illustration of the way in which a spatial particle, through the development of conventionalized senses (e.g., the Activity Sense), and recursive experiences correlating with these derived senses (activities correlate with means of accomplishment), can give rise to further senses (the Means Sense).

In addition, the means used to accomplish an activity can be conceptualized as crucially influencing or constraining the activity. This conceptualization is coherent with the notion of containment present in the proto-scene for *in*. Returning to the example in (7.14a), the activity of writing is constrained by the means used to accomplish the writing, that is, by the writer using ink. For instance, the writing is not easily erased so the writer must take certain additional care in the process.

The Vantage Point is Interior Cluster

Up to this point, the spatial scenes associated with *in* that we have explored have all assumed an 'off-stage' vantage point. However, as we discussed in

correlations, as well as coherent perceptual resemblances, are still an active part of human experience and, hence, remain available for the creation of novel utterances. Moreover, we acknowledge Lakoff and Johnson's (1980) important insight that metaphorical patterns tend to be consistent or coherent throughout the language. The fact that emotional states and atmospheric conditions are both associated with a bounded region and that emotional states are conceptualized (through perceptual resemblance) as weather conditions, as in *They're in a stormy relation* or *She's in a bright, sunny mood,* form a coherent, reinforcing pattern of conceptualization.

chapter 3 in relation to the notion of subjectivity and as we saw with *over* in chapter 4, there are spatial scenes in which the vantage point can be located 'on-stage', that is, within the spatial scene being conceptualized. This has profound implications for how the scene is viewed and, consequently, for senses derived from such a viewing arrangement. In spatial scenes involving a bounded LM, one obvious vantage point is interior to the bounded LM. The interior vantage point gives rise to a number of distinct senses, one of which is detailed in this section: the Perceptual Accessibility Sense.

Following work by discourse analysts such as Schiffrin (1992), we hypothesize that taking the interior perspective can coincide with a shift in deictic centre of the scene (what we are terming the *vantage point*). Taking the interior region as the vantage point concomitantly highlights the perspective of the TR. We discuss two senses, the In Favour Sense and the Arriving Sense, in which the TR within the interior region is the vantage point from which the scene is viewed. Hence, while in the Perceptual Accessibility Sense the vantage point is within the bounded LM but distinct from the TR, in the In Favour and Arriving Senses, the vantage point and TR coincide.

The Perceptual Accessibility Sense A consequence of the experiencer and vantage point being located within a bounded LM is that TR(s) and interior environment contained by the LM are available to the experiencer (and hence vantage point) by virtue of his or her sense-perceptory apparatus. Take vision for instance. Unless we possess X-ray vision à la Superman, for the contents of a bounded LM (such as a closed room) to be visible to us, we must ordinarily be located within the bounded LM. This is a significantly different occurrence from that which takes place when the experiencer is located outside the bounded LM. When the experiencer is located exterior to the bounded LM, the interior region and TR(s) tend not to be accessible. At the same time, when the experiencer is located interior to the bounded LM, the limits of the LM and the limits of perceptual accessibility tend to coincide. For instance, if we are in a room, all we have visual access to is in that room. Again, this reflects a substantially different consequence from being located exterior to the LM. Being located within a bounded LM (which we have defined as consisting of an exterior region, a boundary and an interior region) results in the experiencer having no sense of his or her general perception of the larger scene. This follows, as the LM's boundary serves to delimit the extent of perceptual accessibility. Hence, due to the frequently co-occurring experiences of the construer being located within the bounded LM and the resulting perceptual accessibility of the interior bounded space and the TR to the construer, *in* has developed a Perceptual Accessibility Sense. Consider some examples:

(7.15)   a. I have it in view
          b. I have him in sight

    c. I stayed (with)in earshot of baby Max's cry
    d. Thoreau always stayed in range of his mother's dinner bell
    e. Susan always tries to stay in touch

In the sentences in (7.15), *in* denotes a relation between a TR and sense-perceptory availability with respect to a particular experiencer (the vantage point). Notice that the sensory perception which is available is delimited by the LM, the bounding element. We suggest that this linguistic coding reflects the lived experience of the boundaries of the LM, placing limits on perceptual accessibility when the experiencer is located interior to a bounded region.

It might be objected at this point that some things are literally *in* the visual field, for instance, while others are not. That is, the field of vision has certain natural limits, due to human physiology and the nature of the physical properties of the environment. On this view, vision is naturally bounded, that is, there is a delimited region of space we can see in any given moment, and hence the use of *in* to mediate the visual field represents use of the primary sense for *in*, without requiring a distinct Perceptual Accessibility Sense. From this 'common-sense' perspective it might appear, on first inspection, that it is erroneous to posit a distinct Perceptual Accessibility Sense associated with *in*.

However, while human sensory perception may be limited, a limit does not necessarily entail a three-dimensional bounded LM. For instance, when we look into the sky, although our visual apparatus allows us to see only so much, there is a lot beyond our vision. While we conceptualize that limit as a boundary, the boundary does not veridically exist. We suggest that we conceptualize the limits of our physical perceptions as a three-dimensional container (a bounded LM) because of our experiences of being located inside three-dimensional containers with physical walls (like rooms), which obviously place additional limits on our ability to use our sensory perception organs to their fullest potential. Moreover, this tight experiential correlation is reflected in the linguistic system not only by the particular spatial particles which are used to denote the limits of our perceptual access (in and out), but also by the nouns which are used, for example *field* (e.g., *field of vision, visual field*, etc.), which is often conceptualized as a bounded LM, and *range* (e.g., *range of vision, the visual range, He's out of range*, etc. meaning here something like 'limits'), which is clearly associated with boundaries and bounded LMs.

Further evidence for positing a distinct Perceptual Accessibility Sense comes from the following. If we deny that *in* has a conventional Perceptual Accessibility Sense associated with it, we might wonder why it should be that *in* rather than any other preposition is systematically employed to mediate a relation between a particular TR and perceptual accessibility. After all, sentences such as: ?*He stays on/at/beside/in front of the sound of my voice* are decidedly odd to say the least. In other words, without positing a distinct Perceptual Accessibility Sense associated with *in* there is no way of predicting the fact that *in* systematically mediates an experiencer and perception of sound or touch, for instance, while other prepositions do not.

The In Favour Sense The notion of being *in* has come to be associated with being valued or considered privileged. We hypothesize that the In Favour Sense derives largely from the tight correlation between gaining access or entry to certain kinds of bounded LMs and the desirability of the event or activity within the confines of the bounded LM. For instance, we form lines to gain access to a whole host of venues on a regular basis. We must wait in line to gain access to the cinema to see the latest blockbuster on the first day of release, or for tickets to enter a theme park, a sports stadium, or when waiting for a free table in a packed restaurant. Entry to a whole host of such venues is often by no means guaranteed, precisely because the activities inside are desirable and thus sought after. Hence, to gain access is to be in a favourable or privileged position. Owing to the tight correlation between being within the LM, and hence being in a favourable position, *in* has developed an In Favour Sense.[11]

To make this point consider the following example:

(7.16)   He managed to get in the stadium, even though places were limited

In this example, which relates to the proto-scene, there is an implicature that being *in*, with respect to the bounded LM, the *stadium*, is to be in a favourable position. Through pragmatic strengthening this implicature has come to be reanalysed such that *in* designates the notion of an entity being valued or judged as positive in some way. Consider some examples of this sense:

(7.17)   a. He's in (with the boss)
         b. She's part of the in-crowd

In these examples, *in* clearly denotes relations with other people, which seem closely associated with being In Favour. However, this sense of *in* is not limited to human relations, as evidenced by the following:

(7.18)   a. Turbans are in (this season)!
         b. That's the in-joke this week

In these examples, *in* has the interpretation of 'favourable' or 'privileged'.

---

[11] In addition, items that are valuable are often kept in containers to protect them. Hence, this sense while emphasizing inclusion status of the TR(s) may also draw upon our understanding that containers serve as a means of protecting items from potential externally originating harm, as when currency, jewels, and other valuable items are locked in safes, containers par excellence, which are meant to act as impenetrable barriers in order to protect their contents.

Our understanding of human intentions leads us to infer that a primary motivation for placing items in a safe container is because those items are positively valued. Accordingly, in this sense, *in* designates the notion of an entity or an activity being valued or judged as positive in some way. Through pragmatic strengthening, the implicature of value associated with *in* has given rise to a conventionalized In Favour Sense.

Clearly the use of *in* to designate a favourable or positive meaning element is distinct from the previous senses discussed. As evidenced in the examples in (7.17), this sense is apparent in contexts that no longer relate to the original context of use, that is, with LMs that cannot be construed as bounded. This strongly supports the view that this is a distinct sense instantiated in semantic memory.

The Arrival Sense   In many spatial scenes in which the experiencer is located within a bounded LM, a TR at one point located outside the LM undergoes locomotion such that it comes to be located within the LM, as when a train, for instance, pulls into a train station. From the perspective of an experiencer located interior to the LM, the TR is perceived as moving closer to the interior vantage point. This gives rise to an implicature of arrival. This notion of arrival has become instantiated in semantic memory as a distinct sense, as evidenced by the following:

(7.19)   The train is finally in

In this sentence, not only is the TR, *the train*, within the bounded LM, the train station, but it has arrived, as attested by the following, which represents a close paraphrase:

(7.20)   The train has finally arrived

Moreover, this sense is attested in verb-particle constructions such as the following:

(7.21)   He reeled the fish in

In this example, to *reel* the fish *in* reflects drawing the fish towards the fisherman such that it comes to be proximal to the fisherman. While the fisherman may then place the fish in a bucket, for instance, which is a bounded LM, the use of *in* in *reel in* relates to the notion of coming towards and thus arrival, rather than specifically designating a particular bounded LM. As such, we suggest that examples such as (7.19) and (7.21) relate to a distinct meaning component of arrival associated with *in*. This meaning component is also apparent in sentences such as: *She clocked/ punched in at work.*

The Vantage Point is Exterior Cluster

Another common position from which bounded LMs are viewed is one in which the experiencer (and hence the vantage point) is located exterior to the LM. Spatial scenes of this kind give rise to a number of distinct senses subsumed under what we will term the Vantage Point is Exterior Cluster. Here we will briefly consider what we term the Disappearance Sense.

The Disappearance Sense The nature of many physical entities with an interior is that they are made of opaque substances and thus the boundary of the LM often obstructs the observer's view of the interior and hence the contents. Certainly many of an infant's earliest experiences with bounded LMs – LMs which possess interiors – would be of not being able to see the contents contained by such LMs. Food put into a care-giver's mouth cannot be seen, neither can toes and feet put into socks, toys put into cupboards, people moving to a different room, and so forth. Interestingly, nine-month-old infants perform better on object-hiding tasks when the occluder consists of an upright and hence prototypical container (Freeman, Lloyd and Sinha, 1980; Lloyd, Sinha and Freeman, 1981). Freeman *et al.* suggest that this superior performance with containers as occluders provides evidence that these infants have established a concept of containers as places where things disappear and reappear.

We suggest that due to the tight correlation between LMs with interiors and occlusion, *in* has come to be reanalysed as having a distinct Disappearance Sense, as evidenced by the examples given below:

(7.22) a. The wine quickly soaked in
        b. Millie rubbed in the lotion
        c. The sun has gone in / The sun is in

The reason for thinking that examples such as these evidence a distinct Disappearance Sense relates to our two criteria for determining whether a sense is distinct or not. First, a meaning of disappearance is not evident in any of the other senses associated with *in*. Second, the examples in (7.22) are context independent. That is, they cannot be predicted based on any of the other senses for *in* considered. After all, in (7.22a) the wine is being absorbed by what appears to be a solid element with no discernible internal spaces (at least to the naked eye). Similarly, when we say in (7.22b) that *Millie rubbed in the lotion*, the lotion is not entering the skin, only to be free to leave again. The skin is not being conceived as an entity with interior space. Rather, in all these examples, the correlation between containment and disappearance, from the perspective of a vantage point exterior to the container, is that *in* derives a Disappearance Sense which can come to be used in contexts unrelated to the original context that motivated this sense in the first place.

Moreover, it is worth mentioning at this point that by acknowledging that spatial scenes can be viewed from different vantage points, we have a straightforward explanation for why *in* has senses which are near opposites, the Perceptual Accessibility Sense and the Disappearance Sense.

The Segmentation Cluster

An important aspect of bounded LMs is the notion of a boundary, which in part distinguishes between interior and exterior. In this cluster of senses, the notion of segmentation or boundedness is privileged. A salient aspect of spatial scenes involving bounded LMs is that they serve to partition the environment, providing a physical means of separation and delimitation. Consider the following sentence:

(7.23)   The farmer put the seed in a sealed box for next year

In this sentence, which is consistent with the proto-scene, by virtue of being in a sealed box, the seed is protected from external forces, and effectively separated from other seed. In a sentence such as:

(7.24)   The prisoner was locked in his cell for 23 hours a day

(which is also consistent with the proto-scene) the LM acts as a container serving to restrict the prisoner's, the TR's, movement and, hence, separates the TR from other members of society. Thus, an important and frequent implicature associated with the proto-scene of *in* involves the interpretation that bounded LMs effectively partition and segment that which is inside from that which is outside. We will survey two senses subsumed under this cluster: the Shape As Boundary Sense and the Blockage Sense.

The Shape As Boundary Sense Langacker (1987) noted that the shape of an object is almost certainly part of our mental representation of that object. Since the shape of a bounded LM is necessarily closely related to its boundaries, it is not surprising that *in* has come to designate a relation in which the shape of the LM constitutes both the entity and the boundary. In the Shape As Boundary Sense, the TR constitutes part of a delimited configuration forming a shape. Consider the following example:

(7.25)   Ok, class, put your chairs in a circle

This utterance is not typically interpreted as a command to place the chairs inside a circle drawn on the floor. Rather, its interpretation has to do with arranging the chairs such that they form a circle shape; in other words, the arrangement forms a boundary that delimits a circle. Other examples that evidence this sense include the following:

(7.26)   a. If fire breaks out get in single file before leaving
          b. Can you get in line?

We suggest that since a salient aspect of a bounded LM is its boundary, the use of *in* to relate a TR and a bounded LM thereby highlights a salient aspect of bounded LMs. Through pragmatic strengthening *in* has derived a Shape As Boundary Sense.

The Blockage Sense One consequence of being located within a bounded LM is that the boundary can serve to prevent the TR from moving beyond the LM. This situation is evident in the following sentences which appear to derive from the proto-scene but which have the implication of blocking the movement of the TR out of the LM.

(7.27)   a. Oxygen must be held in a sealed container (to keep it from escaping into the air)

          b. In some ancient cultures, live slaves were sealed in tombs with their dead masters

This notion of blockage or constraint on movement has become conventionally associated with *in*, as evidenced by the following:

(7.28)   a. When I got back to my car, someone had boxed/blocked me in

          b. In the northern territories you can get snowed in for months

In both of these examples, rather than being contained by the LM, an entity's movement is obstructed or blocked in some way. This notion of blockage is denoted by *in*. In (7.28a), the speaker's car is the TR, which is blocked from moving by the placement of another vehicle. In (7.28b), the TR is people who are blocked from moving because of the barrier created by the snow.

    In addition to the foregoing, there also appears to be a second type of experiential correlation which may motivate the Blockage Sense. Here the bounded LM typically facilitates, or is associated with, passage. If the TR is sufficiently large it may fill or obstruct the LM, hence preventing passage. Consider the following examples, which are consistent with the proto-scene.

(7.29)   a. We couldn't move the car because a fallen tree was in the driveway

          b. The portly gentleman got a fish-bone lodged in his throat

As noted, in these examples the LM is conceptualized as a passage, usually a relatively empty space, which is being blocked by the TR. The implicature of blockage apparent here appears to have also contributed to the Blockage Sense associated with *in*. For instance, this notion of blockage is illustrated in the following examples:

(7.30)   a. There's a bad accident in the roadway with traffic backed up to the Wilson Bridge

          b. The rock is in my way

In these sentences there is a Blockage meaning associated with *in*. That is, *in* does not relate to containment but rather to a constraint on movement. This is strongly suggestive that there is a distinct Blockage Sense conventionally associated with *in*.

Reflexivity

The Reflexive Sense In her study of verb-particle constructions (VPCs), Lindner (1981) noticed that some spatial particles have a reflexive meaning element associated with them. *In* is such a spatial particle. After all, in many everyday interactions with bounded LMs, such as crushing a box or a plastic coffee cup, when the sides of the container move inwards, they eventually come to occupy what would have originally been the interior space and the position canonically occupied by the TR. Crucially then, *in* mediates a spatial relation between the same entity at two temporally discontinuous points. Clearly, the boundary of a particular LM cannot simultaneously occupy two different locations at once. Yet, in the Reflexive Sense the same entity is conceptualized as constituting the TR and the covert LM (i.e., the LM is contextually understood rather than being linguistically encoded). As with other spatial Reflexive Senses (e.g., recall the discussion of *over* in chapter 4), this sense represents a sequence of events rather than a single event. Two consequences of the boundary of the LM moving inward are that (i) the LM loses its original shape and (ii) the original interior space no longer exists as interior space. Not surprisingly, the Reflexive Sense is often associated with collapsing and destruction of the LM and the contents. Consider some illustrative examples of the Reflexive Sense associated with *in*:

(7.31)   a. The walls of the sandcastle fell in
          b. The house caved in

In versus *into*

Having considered the spatial particle *in*, we now turn to a brief discussion of the contrast between *in* and *into*. In Old English, *in* could be employed either to mark location within a bounded LM or to express orientation towards the LM. The former was expressed in conjunction with dative case marking, and the latter by virtue of accusative marking.[12] By Middle English these case distinctions had disappeared and the orientation meaning associated with uses of *in* + accusative came to be coded with the compound preposition *into*. This distinction between *in* and *into* continues, as illustrated in the following:

---

[12] When *in* occurred in contexts involving a TR in accusative case and a verb of motion, a reading arose involving a TR that was initially exterior to and oriented towards the LM coming to be located within the LM.

(7.32)   a. He ran in the room [the running is within the confines of the room]
         b. He ran into the room [the TR begins outside and oriented towards
            the room, and runs, such that the TR comes to be located within the
            room]

The synchronic distinction between the English *in* and *into* contrasts with
the modern German *in*. German has not lost its case system, and hence still
employs *in* with locative as well as orientation readings:

(7.33)   a. Wir wanderten in den (DAT) Bergen
            'We wandered around in the mountains'
         b. Wir wanderten in die (ACC) Berge
            'We wandered into the mountains' (Langacker, 1999b: 35)

While the English spatial particle *in* no longer relates to orientation, but simply
location within a bounded LM, sentences such as (7.34) suggest that the spatial
particle *into* does relate to orientation.

(7.34)   The child stood still for several moments, gazing through the window
         into the room full of toys

In (7.34), *into* mediates a spatial relation in which the TR is located on the
exterior of a bounded LM and is oriented towards the LM. Given the tight
experiential correlation between an animate TR being oriented towards a LM
and intention/desire to reach the LM discussed in the previous chapter, *into* has
a functional component of goal associated with it, such that the LM constitutes
the TR's objective, as evidenced by examples such as the following:

(7.35)   The robber peered into the bank, before entering

In this sentence, the bank constitutes the TR's physical goal or objective,
presumably in order to rob it. The proto-scene for *into* is diagrammed in
figure 7.4. In the diagram the arrow signals that the TR is oriented with respect to the bounded LM.

Figure 7.4 Proto-scene for *into*

The semantics of *out*

As noted in chapter 5, the semantics associated with spatial particles form a (largely) systematic contrast set for coding conceived space. Just as *in* relates to the spatial notion of a bounded LM and the functional element of containment, *out* also relates to such attributes. We suggest that the primary meaning associated with *out* designates a spatial relation in which the TR is exterior to a bounded LM. The functional element we have posited for *in* is containment, which is a multifaceted but fairly unified concept, for which English has developed a lexical label. We can easily enumerate the consequences for a TR being exterior to a bounded region – for example its movements are unconstrained, it is visible to the world outside the bounded region, it is unprotected, its location is not assured by the location of the LM, etc. However, English has no ready label for this set of consequences. This lack of a label suggests that we may not conceptualize the state of not being contained as a unified experience. Grady (personal communication) has suggested that this might count as evidence for the spatial particle denoting a cluster of functional elements rather than a single functional element. Nevertheless, in parallel with our analysis for *in*, we will posit a single functional component for *out* and term it non-containment.

Positing that *out* involves the exterior element of a bounded LM and a functional element of non-containment predicts that many of the senses associated with *out* will involve opposing inferences from those arising with *in* and the functional element of containment. However, the relation designated by *out* does not sit in 'simple' opposition with respect to *in*. Even in grammatical terms, *out* – unlike *in* – rarely functions as a preposition but rather is often combined with verbs in verb-particle constructions (e.g., He **took out** the trash/rubbish), or with *of* in the preposition *out of* (e.g., He took the lighter **out of** his pocket; cf. *He took the lighter **out** his pocket). Moreover, a semantics of simple opposition is inadequate to account for the range of senses found with both these two spatial particles. The basic experiences of being contained and not being contained each add unique elements and inferences.

Further, an understanding that *out* is partially defined in terms of the *conceptual base* (in Langacker's, 1987, terms) of containment, explains why *out* should participate in the complex preposition *out of*. As we will see later in this chapter, *of* is the spatial particle that prompts for part-whole and source relations. The spatial relation designated by *out* is one in which the TR is not contained by the bounded LM. However, in our everyday interaction with objects and our environment, it is evident that many TRs that are not contained by LMs at one time were. Thus, when a spatial scene involves both the notion of the TR not being contained and specific reference to the container, two conceptually distinct spatial relations are being evoked. We will argue that the distinction between *out* and *out of* parallels that between *in* and *into*. Just as

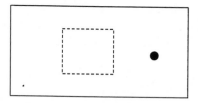

Figure 7.5 Proto-scene for *out*

into designates a functional component distinct from *in*, that is, goal, *out of* designates a functional component distinct from *out*, that is, source.

The proto-scene for 'out'

Consider some examples which evidence the semantic elements of the proto-scene for *out*:

(7.36)   a. He took out the lighter/penknife
          b. They put the rubbish/trash out.
          c. Are the scissors in the drawer? No, they're out on the counter

In the examples in (7.36a) and (7.36b) *out* mediates a spatial relation in which the TR, the lighter/penknife and the rubbish/trash respectively, are exterior to a covert LM, that is, one that is not explicitly coded.[13] Correlated with this spatial relation is the functional aspect of the TR not being contained. A consequence of not being contained is that the TR is unrestricted and hence accessible. For instance, in the example in (7.36a), by virtue of being *out*, the lighter is accessible and hence available for use. Similarly, by virtue of being *out*, household rubbish is accessible for refuse collection. Crucially, the vantage point from which spatial scenes of this kind are viewed involves the construer being off-stage.

We diagram the proto-scene for *out* in figure 7.5. The shaded sphere represents the TR while the dashed square represents the covert bounded LM. The LM is covert in the sense that it is not profiled by *out*, as evidenced by the examples in (7.36). A consequence of this is that *out* seldom functions as a preposition (cf. *out of*, discussed below). The functional element associated with *out* is non-containment.

Beyond the proto-scene

In our full analysis of *out*, we have identified six clusters of senses, which largely parallel those associated with *in*. Owing to space constraints, we will,

---

[13] See the discussion of *out of* in which we argue that the bounded LM is overt.

as with discussion for *in*, provide brief overviews of representative senses, in order to give a sense of how *out* contrasts with *in*, and how it relates to our experience and interaction with bounded LMs. Given the proto-scene provided above, which indicates that this spatial particle does not profile a LM, it follows that *out* is seldom used as a preposition, but is primarily found in verb-particle constructions (VPCs), as an adprep, or in compounds (e.g., *outlaws*).

In this analysis, we have identified patterns of VPCs involving *out* in order to determine senses. However, the interaction between *out* and the verb with which it forms a VPC constitutes a composite construction, with its own degree of conventionality that cannot be divided into a distinct sense associated with *out* plus a verb. Meaning is not compositional in this way (see Lindner, 1981; Morgan, 1997). However, there are patterns in usage which allow us to idealize what, for the purposes of consistency and comparison with *in*, we will assume are distinct senses associated with *out*.

The Location Cluster

As with the Location Cluster of senses associated with *in*, this cluster of senses derives from the locational function provided by a bounded LM. As bounded LMs are themselves frequently conceptualized as locations, by virtue of bearing a specific relationship to the bounded, locational LM within a spatial scene, the TR has also developed a locational interpretation. While there are some parallels in the range of senses subsumed under this cluster, vis-à-vis those associated with the Location Cluster for *in*, such as the Not In Situ Sense for *out*, we will also consider here two senses which do not have parallels in the Location Cluster for *in*, namely the No More Sense and the Completion Sense.

The Not In Situ Sense As we noted above, *in* has developed a distinct sense in which the bounded LM has the default interpretation of 'home' or location where a TR spends extended periods of time. In parallel fashion, *out* is regularly employed in order to mediate a relation in which the TR is not in its default location. The following examples are illustrative:

(7.37)   a. Amy is out sick for the day
         b. The Robinsons ate out last night
         c. The workers are out on strike

The typical interpretation of (7.37a) is that Amy is not present at her normal station (usually a workplace) because she is sick. Normal interpretation of the sentence in (7.37b) is that the Robinsons ate their meal at some location other than their own 'base' location (in this context their own home). Similarly, in (7.37c) the workers are away from their 'normal' location, that is, their place of work. The interpretation of all three sentences involves additional meaning beyond simply that, say, the Robinsons ate in a location such that they were exterior to a covert LM; the LM in question constitutes their 'base' location. Thus, in the Not In Situ Sense, *out* designates that the exterior location is exterior to the 'base' location with respect to which the TR is not in situ.

The No More Sense

By virtue of a TR no longer being located on the interior of a container, there is no more of the TR in a container. In many everyday situations involving bounded LMs, the TR is a consumable entity and our default interactions with many of these consumable entities involve them in a state of containment and hence being located in their containers. If there is no longer any of the TR in the container, there is no more of the TR available. This correlation between a TR being exterior with respect to a bounded LM and the consequence that there is no more of the TR available has given rise to a No More Sense becoming associated with *out*, as evidenced by the following:

(7.38)   A: Have we got any milk left?
         B: No, we're (all) out!

In (7.38) the conventional reading associated with *out* is that there is no more of the TR, here *the milk*.

Notice that the expected TR–LM configuration is no longer apparent in this use; the elements we normally think of as the TR, *the milk*, show up linguistically in the LM position. We hypothesize that this use parallels the State Sense with *in*, for example *We're in the money*, where the money is metonymic for a state holding such that money is available. While the State Sense for *in* relates to a 'moneyful' state, the No More Sense with *out* relates here to a 'milk-less' state. This contrast is apparent with other states:

(7.39)   a. We're in luck/business/sync/love
         b. We're out of luck/business/sync/love

Interestingly, in (7.39b) the use of the No More Sense is only possible if the preposition *out of* is employed. We will discuss the distinction between *out* and *out of* in detail below, and why *out of* is required in such examples.

A further point of interest is that the No More Sense is nearly the mirror-image of an implicature associated with the proto-scene for *out*. For instance, in the examples in (7.36), one consequence of the TR being exterior to the LM (assuming the default 'off-stage' vantage point) involves the TR being available for use. On the face of it, the existence of these contradictory interpretations of *out*, No More and available-for-use, appears rather arbitrary. However, by considering how ways of viewing a scene and implicatures associated with particular experiential correlations become strengthened, we see that the apparent 'conflicts' in meanings are, in fact, well motivated.

The Completion Sense In this sense there is a meaning of completion associated with *out*, as evidenced by the following:

(7.40)   a. This jacket needs to dry out before you wear it again
          b. The ground has now thawed out

In these sentences *out* adds a meaning of completion. Hence, in each of these examples *out* can be paraphrased by the lexeme *completely*. In this sense, *out* designates the end point of a process, drying and thawing respectively.

We suggest that the Completion Sense is motivated by the correlation between an entity or entities leaving a particular bounded LM, and the process of leaving being complete. For instance, in a sentence such as the following:

(7.41)   After unplugging the bath the water drained out

out relates to the proto-scene. That is, the TR, *the water*, comes to be exterior to the bounded LM, *the bath*. A consequence of all the water being *out*, with respect to the bath, is that the process of draining the water is complete. Through pragmatic strengthening we suggest that this implicature of completion associated with such spatial scenes has given rise to a distinct Completion Sense associated with *out*. This is evidenced in the examples in (7.40), which are context-independent uses of the Completion Sense. That is, the LMs in question are not bounded LMs. Hence, the Completion Sense is being used in contexts which deviate from those such as (7.41) which motivated the sense in the first place.

The Vantage Point is Interior Cluster

With the proto-scene for *out* and the extended senses discussed so far, we have assumed the default, 'off-stage' vantage point. However, our experience with bounded LMs often involves the viewer being inside the LM. For instance, an everyday experience is for a person to be located in a building and to be observing, through a doorway or a window, objects and events that are located exterior with respect to the bounded LM. A number of implicatures arising from this particular vantage point have come to be conventionally associated with *out*.

This cluster of senses offers interesting parallels with the senses making up the Vantage Point is Interior Cluster associated with *in*. In both cases, the viewer (or vantage point) is located interior to the bounded LM. The major difference with the spatial scenes denoted by *in* and *out* is the location of the TR. In scenes involving *in*, the TR is located interior to the bounded LM; in scenes involving *out*, the TR is exterior to the LM, even though the vantage point is interior. That is, the experiencer's vantage point on the scene is from the region bounded by the LM. The TR is understood as being outside the boundaries in which the experiencer is located. We will here describe two representative senses: the Exclusion Sense and the Lack of Visibility Sense.

The Exclusion Sense As bounded LMs often prevent physical access to the interior by virtue of their boundaries, a consequence of being exterior is that the TR is excluded from the interior environment. From the perspective of the experiencer, located in the interior regions, the exclusion of the TR is often an intentional act.

(7.42) a. They used a special filter to block out the radio waves
        b. We use mesh screens to keep the insects out
        c. The report left out a number of vital facts

Owing to contexts of use where the interior environment is perceived to be desirable (in part because of the experiential correlation discussed earlier in which access to a particular bounded LM correlates with a favourable or privileged position, and hence its corollary that failing to gain access correlates with an unfavourable position), *out* has developed a distinct Exclusion Sense. In this sense being *out* is construed as non-desirable, as illustrated by the following:

(7.43) The homeless shelter locks out anyone who isn't there by 9pm. This means that some homeless are literally left out in the cold

Key to this example is the notion not only that the TR is exterior to the LM, but that the TR is actively prevented from gaining access to the interior. This suggests that the Exclusion Sense relates to an assessment as to the positive nature of the interior environment vis-à-vis the less desirable, or even negative, exterior environment. As a result of pragmatic strengthening, the Exclusion Sense can be employed in contexts of use which are not purely spatial in nature, as evidenced by the following:

(7.44) a. They voted out the unpopular member
        b. Boots were out of fashion but now they are back in
        c. The runner was out at third base

What is crucial about this sense is not that social groups, for instance as in (7.44a), are being conceptualized as bounded LMs (which is achieved presumably by conceptualizing a social group as a mass entity with boundaries, which thereby contains the set of things which comprises it), but that the notion of being *out* designates an unfavourable situation. It is this notion of exclusion as unfavourable, punitive or disadvantageous which is key for this sense.

This punitive sense is particularly apparent in (7.44c) which denotes a baseball player being excluded from being an active participant in the ongoing play.

The Lack of Visibility Sense One consequence of spatial scenes in which the TR is located exterior to the LM and in which the viewer is located within the bounded LM is that the TR is often not visible (or perceptually accessible, in general). One such commonly occurring experience involves children leaving the house and parents, who are located in the house, no longer being able to see the child, as evidenced by the following:

(7.45)   The moment her son went out, Katie started wondering what he was doing

In our understanding of this sentence, the TR, *her son*, is located exterior to the implicit bounded LM, *the house*. The strong implicature is that *her son* is no longer visible to *Katie*. That this sense of lack of visibility has become conventionally associated with *out* is illustrated in the following:

(7.46)   He switched the light out

A light, when no longer visible, can be described as being *out* even when no bounded LM is involved in the interpretation. After all, the light is not physically located *out*, with respect to a particular bounded LM. We could only understand *out* relating to lack of visibility in this sentence, if there were a conventional Lack of Visibility Sense associated with *out*. Such a sense is further evidenced in the following:

(7.47)   a. During the Blitz, London was blacked out each evening
          b. He crossed/whited out the typo

The Vantage Point is Exterior Cluster

In the previous sense, we suggested that a conventional meaning of Lack of Visibility derived from the vantage point being located interior to the bounded LM. However, in many everyday spatial scenes involving bounded LMs, the scene is construed such that the vantage point is exterior to the LM. This way of viewing a spatial scene has given rise to a number of distinct senses associated with *out*. We will consider two: the Visibility Sense and the Knowing Sense.

The Visibility Sense In spatial scenes in which the vantage point is exterior to the bounded LM, it follows that if the TR is also exterior then the TR is often visible (perceptually accessible in general; see the Perceptual Accessibility Sense for *in*). This common scene gives rise to *out* having developed a Visibility Sense. For instance, in a spatial scene involving a magician, a top hat and a white rabbit, by virtue of pulling the rabbit out from the interior of the hat, the audience is able to view the rabbit. That is, by virtue of the rabbit being *out*, it is also visible. This notion of visibility has become conventionally associated with *out* such that it can be used in contexts where it is by no means clear what the bounded LM might be:

(7.48)   A: I can't find my glasses
         B: They're on the table out in plain view
(7.49)   The sun/moon is out

In examples such as these, there is a conventional interpretation that the glasses, sun or moon are visible.

It is interesting to contrast this sense with the Lack of Visibility Sense in the previous cluster. By virtue of positing that spatial experience is 'cut up' into spatial scenes, which can be viewed from different and distinct perspectives, we have a way of understanding why *out* can be associated with contrary readings, a Lack of Visibility Sense, as in examples such as: *The light is out* [cannot be seen], which contrasts with the Visibility Sense: *The sun is out* [can be seen].

The Knowing Sense   An experiential correlation of being able to see that something is the case, such as seeing that the sun is *out*, is knowing that it is the case, knowing that the sun is *out*. Through pragmatic strengthening, this correlation has given rise to an additional sense associated with *out*, in which *out* relates to knowing that something is the case. Consider some examples:

(7.50)   a. The secret is out [cf. The cat is out of the bag = the secret is revealed]
         b. These days, people get outed for being liberals
         c. We figured out the problem

In these examples, there is nothing that can be physically seen. While we know a secret, a secret cannot be physically seen. Similarly, being declared a liberal is not something that is any way ocular. However, there is a tight and recurring correlation in experience between seeing and knowing, as evidenced by sentences such as: *I see [know] what you mean*. As *out* has an antecedent Visibility Sense, in which there is a conventional meaning of visibility associated with *out*, and as there is an independently motivated experiential correlation between seeing that something is the case and knowing that something is the case, in certain contexts the use of *out* to designate visibility naturally implies knowledge. We suggest that due to the recurrence of such contextualized implicatures, the meaning of knowing has come to be strengthened, such that it represents a conventional sense associated with *out*.

The Segmentation Cluster

Just as with *in*, *out* also has a Segmentation Cluster. As bounded LMs serve to delimit the environment, they accordingly segment the interior of the LM from that which is exterior. Being *out* signals a focus on the exterior space and the objects situated therein. Hence, due to the nature of experience, a number of distinct 'segmentation' senses arise, of which we will consider one which we term the Distribution Sense.

The Distribution Sense In our everyday experience we often separate a TR from a bounded LM in order to distribute the entity. For instance, we take plates from a cupboard and distribute them to guests seated at a table. A teacher takes graded homework assignments from a bag and distributes them to his or her pupils, etc. Hence, the purpose of separation is often distribution. In this sense, *out* designates a relation in which the TR is distributed. Consider some examples:

(7.51)   a. The player dealt out the cards
          b. The teacher handed out the test papers
          c. My father always doles out pocket money to the grandchildren
          d. The chef dishes out the food

As the Distribution Sense has become entrenched in semantic memory, it can be employed in situations not involving a clearly bounded LM, as evidenced by the examples in (7.52):

(7.52)   a. The police seem to enjoy giving out speeding tickets
          b. I'm always having to fork out on my old car

Reflexivity

The Reflexive Sense As with *in*, *out* also features a Reflexive Sense (see Lindner, 1981). In this sense, the LM is also the TR, and the TR comes to be located exterior to the original boundary of the LM. Consider some examples:

(7.53)   a. The syrup spread out
          b. The peacock fanned out its tail
          c. The boy stretched out his hand
          d. The seamstress let out the waist of the skirt

In each of these examples, the LM is identical to the TR. The boundary of the LM is defined by the outer limits of the original position occupied by the LM. For instance, in (7.53a) the boundary of the LM is determined by virtue of the original position of the syrup. As the syrup moves under the force of gravity, its outer limit constitutes its new position. This new position is exterior to the original position. As we have seen with Reflexive Senses associated with other forms such as *over* and *in*, Reflexive Senses are interesting as they represent complex conceptualizations in which the multiple temporally discontinuous locations of a single entity are integrated into a single scene in which the two temporally distinct locations are conceptualized as participating in a synchronic spatial relation.

The semantics for *of*

Having surveyed the different clusters of senses associated with *out*, our next step is to contrast *out* with *out of*. However, before considering *out of*, we will briefly consider the spatial particle *of*. This is necessary as establishing the proto-scene for *of* will allow us to see from where *out of* obtains its functional component of source, which provides a crucial distinction between *out* and *out of*.

Of is particularly interesting as it appears to be one of only a few spatial particles, which, in synchronic terms, seems to have become largely dissociated from its spatial origin. According to the OED, '[T]he primary sense was *away, away from*, a sense now obsolete, except in so far as it is retained under the spelling OFF' (now a distinct spatial particle, but one which originally derived from *of*). 'From its original sense, *of* was naturally used in the expression of the notions of removal, separation, privation, derivation, origin or source, starting point, spring of action, cause, agent, material, and other senses which involve the notion of taking, coming, arising or resulting *from*' (p. 711). In Anglo-Saxon, *of* had already developed senses involving the idea of 'resulting from' as those of derivation, source, agents, and material (*Webster's New International Dictionary, Second Edition Unabridged*). The common notion of *of* denoting a relation between a TR and a source in these early uses may have contributed to its displacement of the genitive case ('which expresses primarily the relationship of source or possession' OED) from Anglo-Saxon, so that by the time of Bede's *History of Britain* in the eighth century, for instance, the genitive case of Old English and its replacement, *of*, were in free variation. In addition, historical sources (e.g., the OED) indicate that *of* was standardly used to translate Latin *ab, de* and *ex*. Owing to the influence of Latin and then French in medieval England, *of* was employed in translation in place of the French *de*, further cementing the displacement of the native genitive case marker.

The earlier spatial sense is no longer widely in evidence. Perhaps the closest sense in which *of* designates a spatial relation involves examples of the following kind, which we assume to be the synchronic primary sense:

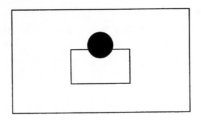

Figure 7.6 Proto-scene for *of*

(7.54)   a. The top of the hill/fence/building
          b. The front of the chair
          c. The side of the road

In these examples, the TR designates a particular spatial region within a larger spatio-physical region. The spatial relation denoted by *of* in examples such as these therefore involves a part-whole designation, with the TR being a specified part of the LM. The designation of the spatial elements of the synchronic primary sense for *of* is diagrammed as our proto-scene in figure 7.6. The spatial part-whole relation designated by *of* is captured by virtue of the TR, the sphere, emerging from the LM, the square. At this point, we want to clarify that, despite the particular TR–LM we have posited for *of*, we are not claiming that all part-whole relationships (nor all uses of *of*) necessarily involve contact between the TR and the LM. In many part-whole relationships, the TR can be physically detached from the LM. For instance, most would agree that an engine is an integral part of a functioning automobile; thus, an engine is part of the larger whole we term an automobile. In certain situations, as for repairs, the engine can be physically removed from the automobile. Even in this physically separated state, the engine is considered part of the automobile.

In terms of the synchronic functional element, we hypothesize that a natural inference the construer would draw upon observing this TR–LM configuration is that the TR and LM are related to each other in some fundamental way that is not accidental. For instance, if we see a cake from which a wedge has been cut and we see a wedge of cake that appears to be of the same composition (e.g., dense, dark chocolate) on the counter next to the larger cake, a natural inference is that the wedge of cake originated from the nearby cake. We typically draw this inference even though we did not see the cake when it was intact or when it was being cut, nor when the piece was removed. Thus, we would not have absolute evidence that there is a non-accidental, non-random relationship between the larger cake and the wedge, but we automatically infer this to be the case and we treat the two objects as if it were the case. So, if we taste the wedge of cake and find it unpleasant, we are not likely to cut a piece from the larger cake to test its taste. This is so because we assume that the wedge of cake and the larger cake will taste the same, as we assume they are intrinsically related.[14] In other words, we suggest that a consequence of the TR–LM relationship denoted by *of* is that humans will typically interpret the TR and LM as being related in some non-accidental, non-random way and will interact with the two entities in particular ways because of this interpretation. We term this functional element as the TR and LM being in an *intrinsic relationship*.

The functional element of intrinsic relationship is an interactive consequence of the part-whole relation. The notion of intrinsic relationship between the TR and LM, that is, that the TR belongs to, or is a property of, the LM as opposed to being accidentally connected, is coherent with a wide range of senses commonly denoted by *of,* such as Locational Source, Material Source, Apposition such as *State of California*, and definitional uses such as *state of war*. This proposal also provides an elegant way of accounting for the possession constructions in which *of* often participates. As already noted, *of* replaced the genitive case of Old English. That this should have been the case is motivated by the semantics of *of* we propose.

Of has a number of distinct senses associated with it. We will briefly deal with two of these as they are relevant for our discussion of *out of*. Interestingly *of* has two distinct 'source' senses associated with it. Although in the proto-scene the TR constitutes a subpart of the LM, and often cannot be physically separated, in many situations entities which originate in a particular location can be removed. Removing an entity from another entity to which it belongs can result in the latter being conceptualized as the 'source' of the removed entity.

For instance, consider grapes growing in a vineyard in southern Italy. Al-though the grapes are physically attached to the Italian soil in which they grow (courtesy of the vines), grapes can be picked, processed and sent abroad in the guise of wine. Consider therefore the following sentence:

(7.55)   This wine is a product of Italy

In this sentence there is not a part-whole relationship between the wine and the LM, *Italy*. However, *of* mediates a source relation, in the sense that Italy is the physical origin of the wine. This sense we term the Locational Source Sense.

---

[14] Our analysis is importantly indebted to Langacker's 1999a discussion of *of,* which crucially involves the notion of 'intrinsic relationship'. Although he does not specifically discuss *of* as denoting both a spatial-configurational relationship and a functional element, we believe our analysis is largely coherent with his. For instance, Langacker provides the following examples which are similar to those in (7.54):
a. The palm of his hand
b. The rim of the canyon
c. The handle of the cup [After Langacker, 1992: 296]
He suggests that in these examples the TR is an intrinsic subpart of the LM.

The second 'source' sense relating to *of* concerns the manufacturing process itself, in which a particular entity is 'transformed' into another. Consider the following sentence:

(7.56)   This carving is made of oak

In this example the LM, *oak*, does not designate a physical location, but rather a material which is used to fashion a product, namely a carving. This sense associated with *of* we term the Material Source Sense.

The semantic notion of 'source' associated with *of* is important for our discussion of the preposition *out of*. This is so as we will argue that the distinction between *out* and *out of* is that the latter explicitly designates a source whereas the former does not.

Out versus out of

We noted above that *out* seldom functions as a preposition. This contrasts with the syntactic behaviour of *out of*. While *out* profiles a TR–LM relation in which the LM is covert, *out of* profiles a TR–LM relation in which the LM is overt. This is illustrated below:

(7.57)   He took the lighter out (cf. *He took the lighter out his pocket*)

The unacceptable use of *out* to code a LM contrasts with the acceptable use of *out of*:

(7.58)   He took the lighter out of his pocket

Many of the senses associated with *out* also apply to *out of*. A key difference, however, is that in such senses *out of* overtly codes the LM. For instance, in the Not In Situ Sense, *out* functions as an adprep :

(7.59)   A: Is it possible to see the doctor this afternoon?
         B: I'm afraid she's out all day

In contrast, *out of* functions as a preposition, specifically requiring an overtly articulated LM which surfaces as a noun:

(7.60)   The doctor is out of the office (cf. *The doctor is out the office today*)

We argue that this difference is a consequence of the status of the LM in the two proto-scenes. In the proto-scene associated with *out of*, the LM is profiled. This follows as it inherits the functional element of 'intrinsically related' from *of*, but the functional element of 'not-contained' from *out*. Hence, the TR is not contained by the LM to which it is intrinsically related, so the LM is the source. By virtue of the notion of source being added by *of,* the spatial particle *out of*

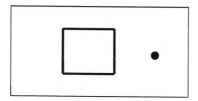

Figure 7.7 Proto-scene for *out of*

explicitly codes a LM, while the LM is covert or de-profiled in the proto-scene associated with *out*.

The view that the functional component associated with *of* is the notion of 'intrinsic relation' makes it an ideal candidate for combining with *out* in order to create the spatial particle *out of*. As we observed at the outset of this chapter, humans interact with bounded LMs in a variety of ways on a daily basis. We saw in our discussion of the spatial particle *into*, that the TR can be oriented with respect to the bounded LM. Alternatively, a TR can have originated within the bounded LM and now be exterior to it. This is the conceptualization coded for by *out of*.

We capture these facts diagrammatically in figures 7.5 (the proto-scene for *out* diagrammed previously) and figure 7.7. In figure 7.5 the LM consisted of a dashed square, reflecting the fact that the LM is covert. In figure 7.7 the LM is outlined in bold, reflecting the notion that the LM is profiled. This semantic distinction is reflected in the syntactic behaviour of the two spatial particles, and further supports our contention that syntax has conceptual significance (recall the discussion in chapter 3). The functional element associated with *out of*, like *out*, relates to the notion of not being contained. An added functional element is that the bounded LM is the source of the TR. Hence, in spatial scenes mediated by *out of*, the TR is conceptualized as having originated in the interior of the LM. It is for this reason, we shall suggest, that the LM is profiled in the proto-scene for *out of*, and hence the semantic distinction with *out*.

Evidence for *out of* having the functional element of 'source' associated with it comes from examples such as the following:

(7.61)   a. Grandfather smuggled grape roots out of southern Italy at the turn of the century
       b. This wood came out of the old growth forest

In (7.61a) the TR, *the grape roots*, derives from a physical location, namely Italy, which counts as the locational source of the TR. Similarly in (7.61b) the LM, *the old growth forest*, is a location from which the TR originates. While this sense is closely related to the Locational Source Sense associated with *of*, the functional element of 'source' associated with *out of* means that examples such as those in (7.61) relate to the proto-scene for *out of*.

A further instance of the proto-scene is evidenced by examples such as the following:

(7.62)   Telecommuting lets people work out of their homes

What makes this example interesting is that it has a conventional reading which might be paraphrased as: 'telecommuting allows people to work at home, i.e., produce their work at home'. In other words, the locational source of the work **is** the home. Accordingly, the question which presents itself is why *out of*, which presumably means 'not at home', here appears to mean 'at home'. The solution relates to the nature of telecommuting. Telecommuting allows professionals to connect with their place of work electronically, typically a modem connection from their computer at home. Consequently, the TR is at work in a virtual sense, while being physically located at home. Hence, the work itself is produced 'at work', on the workplace server, etc., although the source-location is the home. Accordingly, this use of *out of* does in fact cohere with the proto-scene.

Beyond the proto-scene for 'out of'

Although many uses of *out of* parallel those of *out,* in some instances, *out of* provides senses which are not part of the semantic network associated with *out.* We will conclude our discussion of *out* and *out of* by discussing three of these: the Beyond Sense, the Material Source Sense and the Cause Sense.

The Beyond Sense   One consequence of a TR no longer being contained by a bounded LM is that the LM can no longer exert as strong an influence on the TR as when the TR was interior to the LM. As such, the TR is beyond the range in which it can be influenced. This notion of being located beyond, and hence away from the influence of, the LM, constitutes a distinct sense associated with *out of*. Consider the following:

(7.63)   Once the puppy was out of the box, it immediately began chewing Ted's best leather shoes

In interpreting this sentence, which involves the proto-scene for *out of*, the implicature is that the puppy's behaviour was constrained when it was in the box, in a way that it was not once it was exterior to the box. This implicature of the TR being beyond the range in which its actions can be influenced or constrained by the LM has become entrenched as a distinct sense for *out of*, as illustrated in the following:

(7.64) a. The ball landed just out of reach [= beyond reach]
        b. The racing car spun out of control [= beyond control]

Crucially, *out* does not have a Beyond Sense associated with it. By virtue of not profiling the LM, *out* has no means of overtly evoking the LM, and therefore does not prompt for the implicature that the TR has been contained and influenced by the LM.

The Material Source Sense As with *of*, the spatial particle *out of* also has a Material Source Sense. This is evidenced by (7.65a), which is a close paraphrase of (7.66b), involving *of*.

(7.65) a. The chair is made out of wood
        b. The chair is made of wood

It is clear why *of* should have a Material Source Sense. After all, due to the part-whole connection associated with the proto-scene for *of*, the TR and LM are physically connected. In the Material Source Sense, the physical connection is temporally discontinuous. However, it is a physical connection nonetheless. After all, the LM and the TR consist of the same material, even if their characteristics, shape, texture, etc., are different, a consequence of the manufacturing process.

It is less clear from examples such as (7.65a), however, why *out of* should also have developed a Material Source Sense. Clearly the LM does not in any way serve as a veridical container out of which the TR, *the chair*, literally emerges. Nevertheless, there is a plausible motivation for this sense, which relates to the progeneration associated with humans, and indeed with other organisms.

In experiential terms a mother's body produces a baby, derived from part of her own material, an egg, in conjunction with the father's sperm. Not only does the genetic material which gives rise to the baby derive from the mother (as does the baby's natural food supply, etc.), but the baby is physically attached to the mother via the umbilical cord for nine months. Moreover, the mother also contains the baby while the fetus is in utero. Human birth involves a tight correlation between the mother (container-source), the baby (the TR) and the emergence of the baby, that is, the baby becoming non-contained or 'out'. This represents a powerful, intrinsic human experience, which plausibly motivates the Material Source Sense becoming associated with *out of*. Once conventionalized in memory, this sense can be applied to LMs which are not prototypical containers, as in the example in (7.65a).

The Cause Sense We now turn to the final sense that we will deal with for *out of*. This is the Cause Sense. In this sense a particular emotion or attitude, the LM, motivates a particular action, event or outcome. That is, the emotion or attitude 'causes' the outcome. Consider some illustrative examples:

(7.66)   a. John sacrificed himself out of love
          b. Iago tricked Othello out of spite
          c. Eliot spoke out of anger

We suggest that the motivation for this sense is the tight correlation between an event or activity which takes place in a particular bounded LM, and the consequences upon its emergence from the bounded LM. By way of illustration, consider the following example:

(7.67)   The rat that popped out of the cake created a lot of commotion

Clearly in (7.67) there is a definite sense of a physical emergence of a TR from a bounded LM. While this sentence is consistent with the proto-scene the strong implicature is that the emergence of the TR 'causes', that is, motivates the commotion. We can make this relationship more explicit by rephrasing the sentences as (7.69):

(7.68)   The commotion came out of the rat being in the cake

Once the cause implicature has become strengthened, resulting in a distinct sense, it can be employed in contexts of use unrelated to ones which originally motivated it. Such contexts include the sentences in (7.66), and also the following:

(7.69)   The bad feelings came out of ideological conflicts

It is worth pointing out that we do not believe that in examples such as these, native speakers are somehow perceiving states such as 'ideological conflict' as being bounded LMs, which potentially contain the TR or action. Rather, due to the process of pragmatic strengthening, a particular implicature has become associated with *out of*. This results in *out of* being associated with this conventional meaning component, cause. While this cause component is ultimately grounded in embodied experience and the chain of experiential correlations and situated language use from which this sense is ultimately derived, we argue that it would be wrong to claim that this sense is somehow 'metaphoric' if by that it is meant that the meaning of cause is not conventionally associated with the form *out of*. The theory of principled polysemy advocated throughout this book, then, suggests that, due to experiential grounding, meanings come to be routinely instantiated in the semantic network associated with a particular lexical form, without requiring further analysis on the part of the language user. Indeed, it may be for this reason that Rice *et al.* (1999) found that speakers of Dutch and English fail to view temporal senses of spatial particles as being related to their spatial senses (see Evans, 2000: chapter 3, for a review).[15] At the same time, the experiential correlations which originally gave rise to these meanings continue to be an active part of human experience so that novel metaphoric uses, which are coherent with the established patterns of word meaning, continue to be available to speakers of the language.

The semantics for *through*

We turn now to the final spatial particle associated with a bounded LM that we shall consider, *through*.

The proto-scene for 'through'

While the spatial relation designated by *through* relates to the structural elements interior, boundary and exterior, and hence a bounded LM, it comprises additional structural elements which we term entrance point, exit point, and the contiguous locations between the entrance point and exit point. In other words, the proto-scene for *through* is like no other spatial scene we have encountered thus far (save perhaps the Reflexive Senses associated with *over*, *in* and *out*). It designates a spatial relation in which the TR is held to occupy a contiguous series of spatial points with respect to a LM, which has an interior structural element, such that these points are located on the exterior side of the LM co-incident with the entrance point, within the LM and on the exterior side of the LM opposite to the entrance point, that is, the exit point. A consequence of the particular spatial designation associated with *through* is that the functional notion of *path* is evoked.

Path, as we will understand it here, is a functional notion closely associated with motion. However, the notion of path is distinct both from the motion undergone by a TR and from the trajectory followed by the TR. While motion relates to change of location, trajectory relates to the 'shape' of the motion event.[16] Path, while related, is a consequence of an end point or goal being related to a starting point or locational source by virtue of a series of contiguous

---

[15] It is worth observing that not all cause–effect relationships are prompted by *out of*:
   a. The bridge eventually collapsed because of major structural damage
   b. The bridge eventually collapsed from major structural damage
   c. ??The bridge eventually collapsed out of major structural damage
   Out of seems to mediate a relation between a cause and an effect somehow involving animate entities. This follows as the experiential correlation which motivates the Cause Sense relates to the emergence of an event or entity from a bounded LM, which typically requires motility, and hence animacy. As entities such as bridges are inanimate and hence cannot self-locomote, they are anomalous with this sense of *out of*.

[16] The alert reader may have already discerned that we have implicitly distinguished between *trajectory* and *path* throughout this book. This represents a departure from previous analyses (e.g., Herskovits, 1986; Lakoff, 1987; Langacker, 1987; Talmy, 2000; Vandeloise, 1991).

points. That is, the concept of path requires a particular spatial goal, which is achieved by being connected to a spatial source by virtue of a series of contiguous points. As paths correlate with motion they are necessarily linear. However, from this it does not follow that a path must be a straight line. In other words, the source and goal need not be connected by the shortest distance between them. After all, as TRs can follow diverse trajectories (e.g., arc-shaped, zig-zagged, circular, etc.) it is entailed that paths can have a diverse range of 'shapes' associated with them.

As noted, path is a functional element which arises because of the way we interact with and reach goals, given that we begin from a particular starting point or locational source. Accordingly, this concept is distinct from those of trajectory and motion. For instance, in the following sentence:

(7.70)   The tunnel through Vale Mountain was finished in the 1980s

by virtue of a tunnel existing in (7.70), passage from one side of an otherwise impenetrable barrier, the mountain, is facilitated, whether or not the scene involves a TR capable of undergoing motion. It is this notion, conceptually independent of a motile TR and its trajectory, which constitutes the concept of path. As we have observed in chapter 6, previous scholars have often conflated the notions of path and locomotion (and indeed orientation).

Further evidence for the functional notion of path in the absence of motion comes from scenes involving 'traces' of a TR's passage, even when the TR itself is no longer apparent. For instance, a line of trampled grass transecting a field, or a smoke-trail across the sky, are labelled paths, even though the respective TRs, for example, a person and a plane, respectively, are no longer in view. However, a means of passage, such as a tunnel, or a 'trace' of passage is merely associated with the notion of path, rather than constituting the notion. After all, a path is conceptualized even for entities whose 'motion' is unobservable for example, photons travelling from the sun to the earth, invisible to the naked eye, follow a path. Hence, we reiterate that the concept of path concerns a starting point or locational source being related to an end point or goal by virtue of a series of contiguous points intervening between the two extremities.

As *through* characterizes a spatial relation denoting a TR and a bounded LM in which two locations on either side of a LM are related (the entrance point and exit point respectively), the associated functional element is that of path. Hence, like the Reflexive Senses discussed earlier, *through* designates a temporally evolving relation conceived in summary fashion. As such, the path is held to be conceptually distinct from the motion often associated with

---

Our view is that the trajectory is inseparable from a motile TR and represents the course of motion the TR undergoes. Thus, a trajectory is an abstract representation of the process of moving.

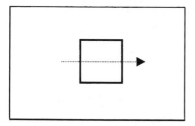

Figure 7.8 Proto-scene for *through*

it. Interestingly, as paths are often associated with motion,[17] motion can be evoked due to background knowledge, even in spatial scenes, which are wholly non-dynamic in nature, as in (7.71) below:

(7.71)   a. The sunlight shone through the glass door
         b. I sensed the cold through the glass door
           (cf. John walked right through the glass door)

In the example in (7.71a), there is no (perceptible) motion associated with the spatial scene, Indeed, motion is typically coded by verbs, which involve events evolving through time. As *through* is a spatial particle and hence atemporal it does not code for motion. However, by virtue of *through* being employed, the notion of a path is salient, which strongly correlates with the idea of the TR physically passing or having passed from one side of the TR to the other. For instance, the sunlight is conceived as physically having passed from one side of the door to the other in (7.71a). In (7.71b) the cold is sensed (and thus experienced) on one side of the door, even though it originated on the other. The use of *through* is strongly suggestive that the coldness is experienced by virtue of a physical transfer from one side of the door to the other.

Thus, the relation described by *through* describes a spatial relation in which a bounded LM is transected by virtue of an entrance point and an exit point. The functional element evoked is that of path. For this reason *through* is often associated with motion. The proto-scene for *through* is diagrammed in figure 7.8. It is worth noting that the proto-scene we posit is consonant with the 'spatial image' of *through* presented by Hilferty (1999).

The view of *through* we have presented allows us to understand the range of contexts in which the proto-scene is employed. As with *in*, we will argue that TR–LM relations mediated by *through*, which involve non-canonical, non-three-dimensional bounded LMs, are licensed by virtue of such LMs being conceptualized as bounded LMs. *Through* frequently occurs with LMs

---

[17] Note that a path does not require motion. For instance, disused tunnels still constitute paths, even though they are no longer in use.

which act as barriers or obstacles to forward motion. Many everyday barriers, such as walls, are experienced as planar surfaces, and thus not as three-dimensional objects. However, when such LMs are breached, as in a sentence such as:

(7.72)   They knocked a hole through the wall

the construal of the wall as consisting of a boundary and interior structure is highlighted; the passageway through the wall exposes its internal structure, analogous to the pothole exposing the internal structure of the street, discussed at the outset of this chapter.

'Through' versus 'across'

In Old English *through* was a nominal form for a trough, pipe or channel for water which typically transected bounded regions such as fields. Thus, a *through* was a passageway or means of facilitating the passage of water which transected bounded areas. The English spatial particle that appears to be semantically closest to *through* is *across*. Like *through*, the origins of *across* lie in a noun, *cross*, that labels an entity whose physical configuration involves transection; in both cases, a salient aspect of the original noun visually resembles a path. The primary distinction between *through* and *across* is that *through* mediates a relation between a TR and a bounded LM while *across* mediates one between a TR and a planar LM. Obviously, the contextual interpretation of the dimensionality of the entity conceptualized as the LM is dependent on the construal assigned by the speaker. The distinction in the use of *across* and *through* is illustrated clearly in the following:

(7.73)   a. Chance, the gardener, walked across the water
          b. Chance, the gardener, walked through the water

In the example in (7.73a) *the water* is construed as a solid surface which can be walked upon by the TR. As this contradicts our normal human experience of the nature of water and human bodies, such an activity has been deemed noteworthy. In (7.73b), the use of *through* provides an interpretation of water as a bounded LM, which involves the TR actually being at least partially submerged within or enclosed by the water.

Beyond the proto-scene

Having considered the proto-scene for *through*, we turn our attention to the wider semantic network. We will present a brief analysis of seven distinct senses associated with *through*. Again, our main point is to reveal how spatial experience, which arises due to tight correlations in experience, gives rise to implicatures that can be reanalysed as distinct meaning components. That is, spatial experience is foundational, giving rise in motivated and systematic ways to rich and complex meanings which come to form part of the conventional meanings associated with words.

The Extended Action Sense As we will see time and again in our discussion of the Extended Senses associated with *through*, the functional element of path is crucial in the development of Extended Senses. Accordingly, it is appropriate to begin this illustration with the Extended Action Sense.

In the spatial scene depicted by a sentence such as *Mary walked through the tunnel*, the TR is understood to travel from one point to another. We argued in our discussion of the proto-scene that the two points are interpreted as the entering location and exiting location of a path that transects the bounded LM. Grady (1997a) and Lakoff and Johnson (1999) have convincingly argued that there is a strong experiential correlation between motion along a path and purposeful activity. This correlation is illustrated in a sentence such as (7.74):

(7.74)   Lance is halfway through the race

In interpreting this sentence, we understand that the TR has travelled half of the planned distance or path and concomitantly that the TR has completed half the planned activity. As a result of this correlation, the starting and exit points can be understood as components of a particular action or activity, the beginning and ending components, which mediate a series of sequentially medial components. Hence, the LM serves to define the sequence of action components which together comprise an extended action or event. This sense is illustrated in the following sentence:

(7.75)   Mary worked through the pages of math exercises

The normal interpretation of this sentence is **not** that there are holes in the pages, which allow Mary somehow to move physically through them, such that she reaches the other side of the pages, as would be predicted by the proto-scene. The interpretation of sentence (7.75) is that an extended action takes place, with a definite sequence. This reading is only possible, we suggest, due to the existence of a distinct Extended Action Sense.

The Temporal Sense An extended action, comprising a number of sequential components, correlates with the passage of time. Owing to this tight and ubiquitous correlation, *through* has developed a Temporal Sense. This correlation involves a temporal relation between an action carried out by the TR, or a state experienced by a TR, and a particular time period for which the action or state continues. Consider some examples:

(7.76)   a. The young man stood through the entire show
         b. The law students were required to sit through a trial

In the scenes described, the LM constitutes a series of events, which are scheduled to take place over an extended period of time. The sequences of events which are labelled *the show*, or *the trial*, each have a clearly defined beginning and end (first event and final event). The TRs, *the young man* and *the law students*, are understood to be involved with the sequence from the first event to the last, that is, for the duration of the temporal event in question. Other examples of this sense include the following:

(7.77)   a. John will be gone from June through August
         b. The professor will be on leave through January

The On-the-other-side-of Sense   An experiential correlate of completing the activity of traversing a LM is that the TR has moved from one side of the LM to the other. The result of the motion is arriving at a particular location. When a person completes the action of walking through a field, it is impossible not to be on the other side of the field from where he or she started:

(7.78)   a. Once she passed through the doorway at the end of the dark hallway, she found herself in a sunny enclosed porch

The normal interpretation of this sentence is that the TR moves along the hallway, the LM, passes beyond the hallway, which is bounded by the doorway, and ends up on the other side of the doorway in an entirely different room.

An unavoidable consequence of traversing a designated LM, then, is that when the motion is complete, the TR is located on the other side of the LM relative to the starting point of the trajectory. The On-the-other-side-of Sense has come to be associated with certain uses of *through* which are not derivable from context. Consider the following sentence:

(7.79)   My office is located just through that door

The normal interpretation of this sentence is that the office is located on the other side of the door, not that the office somehow transects the door. We see no principled way of deriving an On-the-other-side-of Sense from the proto-scene and this sentential context.

Moreover, as with the On-the-other-side-of Sense associated with *over*, the On-the-other-side-of Sense associated with *through* assumes a particular vantage point, that is, roughly the entry point or beginning of the path. To say *My office is through that door* could only be felicitous if the speaker is on the side of the door opposite to the side on which the office is located. Thus, we argue that this distinct sense came to be instantiated in memory as a result of two factors: (1) the pragmatic strengthening of the experiential correlate associated with the experiencer travelling a path that transects a LM that is conceptualized as bounded, such as a field or a forest; and (2) the shift in vantage point from off-stage to the entrance point.

Lakoff (1987) accounted for On-the-other-side-of-type meanings associated with *over* by invoking what he termed an end-point focus transformation. This he described as follows: 'It is a common experience to follow the path of a moving object until it comes to rest, and then, to focus on where it is. This corresponds to the path focus and end-point focus transformation' (p. 442). In many ways our account is consonant with this perspective. However, what our account adds is a more detailed view as to the nature of the experiences which are involved, that is, that this 'transformation' is based in experiential correlations. And second, by invoking the notion of pragmatic strengthening and the conventionalization of implicatures, we demonstrate the subtle and complex character of semantic change and the extension of meaning, providing a fuller account of the phenomena in question.

The Completion Sense We now turn to an examination of the Completion Sense. When *through* occurs in context with a verb of motion, it crucially influences the inferred trajectory by contributing the information that the TR enters and exits the LM. Reaching the far side of the LM is understood as completing a defined segment of action. Recall that we noted in the discussion of *over* in chapter 4 that the end point of any trajectory (which is an abstract representation of the process of moving) is commonly understood as representing the completion of the process. Thus, the spatial location, exit point, associated with *through* has been reconceptualized as completion.

(7.80)   a. Jane is through with the book
          b. I'm through with all these fad diets
          c. The relationship is through

Once reanalysis has taken place, the distinct Completion Sense comes to be associated with the form *through* in the semantic network via pragmatic strengthening.

Notice that the Completion Sense adds information that is distinct from the Extended Action Sense:

(7.81)   a. Adele read through the book (Extended Action)
          b. Adele is through with the book (Completion)

In (7.81a), we have the Extended Action Sense; there is no entailment that Adele is finished with her examination of the book. In (7.81b), the interpretation is that Adele is no longer interacting with the book. Either she has read it completely and is done with it, or she has read as much as she is interested in reading and will not be reading any more. Thus, we are arguing that the meaning component of completion results from reanalysis of the physical location of the TR as standing for an aspect of a process. In such an interpretation, the Completion Sense is not describing a purely spatial relation. As a result, the Completion Sense is adverbial in nature. The Completion Sense differs crucially from the On-the-other-side-of Sense in that the latter focuses on the spatial location of the TR when the process is completed. In contrast, the former focuses on interpreting the end point of the trajectory as the end of the motion or process.

Hilferty's 'metaphoric' senses of 'through'

We now turn to a discussion of the three final senses we will deal with in this chapter. We will label these the Transmission Sense, the Means Sense and the Cause Sense. In his study of 'Through as a means to metaphor', Hilferty (1999) described senses of this kind as metaphoric extensions of the prototypical spatial 'image' of through. While it may be useful to identify more abstract meanings as 'metaphoric', as Hilferty does, we seek to make the point that the distinction between a more 'concrete' and presumably more literal sense associated with through, and a more 'abstract' and hence more figurative sense is a matter of degree rather than being criterial in nature. As we saw above, the extension from the proto-scene to senses such as the Extended Activity and On-the-other-side-of Senses relies on tight correlations in experience. Similarly, we will see below that the Transmission, Means and Cause Senses equally rely on experiential correlations. Hence, the mechanism whereby 'metaphoric' senses are derived is in principle of the same order as all the other kinds of sense extension we have considered for through, and indeed for the other spatial particles throughout this book.

Of course, the point we are making does not deny the insight of Hilferty's analysis. Indeed, the account we present is consonant in many respects, although it emphasizes points not dealt with in Hilferty's account. Nevertheless, labelling certain senses as metaphoric can give the misleading impression that there is an absolute distinction between the way some senses are derived with respect to others.

Finally, it is worth noting that in terms of 'abstract' meaning, it might be argued that the Temporal Sense and the Completion Sense qualify as being metaphoric, although these senses are not ones that Hilferty deals with.

The Transmission Sense A common experience in our everyday lives is to receive an entity from a sender via a bounded LM. For instance, consider the following sentence:

(7.82)   The comatose patient was fed through a tube

In this sentence medical staff supply an unconscious patient with food by in-
serting a tube directly into the patient's blood supply. While this sentence is
consistent with the proto-scene the implicature of transmission can become
strengthened, and, in due course, instantiated as a conventional sense in semantic memory. Evidence that this has occurred comes from sentences such as
those in (7.83), which apply to LMs which are not bounded. However, what
such LMs have in common is that they serve to transmit a particular entity:

(7.83)   a. HIV can be transmitted through sexual intercourse
         b. He received a package through the mail
         c. The medium received a strange premonition through the ether
         d. Max gets his blue eyes through his mother

In these examples a particular entity, the TR (i.e., *HIV, the package, the premo-
nition* and *blue eyes*), is transmitted via a particular medium, the LM (i.e., *sexual
intercourse, the mail, the ether* and *his mother*), from some covert entity. The
covert entity is implied rather than being encoded linguistically, for example a
sexual partner, a sender, a spirit and the maternal genetic stock, respectively.
Clearly, unless there were a conventional Transmission Sense associated with
through, it would be difficult to predict that any of the LMs in question, which
clearly do not match the LM for the primary sense of *through* given in figure 7.8,
can serve as a medium of transmission. That is, once the implicature of transmission associated with *through* has been conventionalized, it can be applied to
entities which are conceptualized as intermediaries, regardless of whether they
constitute bounded LMs.

The Means Sense In many situations paths provide an important
means of reaching a particular goal. For instance, consider the following, which
is consistent with the proto-scene:

(7.84)   To escape I had to choose between hacking through the dense jungle,
         or swimming through the crocodile-infested lake

In this sentence, two means of escape, neither particularly inviting, involve
'creating' a path through a particular bounded LM. To make the connection
between a path and a means of reaching a goal clearer, consider the following:

(7.85)   To return home, he had to find the path through the jungle

The correlation between following a path and reaching a particular goal gives
rise to the implicature of means associated with paths (the path provides a means
of reaching the goal). As the functional element of path is strongly associated
with the semantics of *through*, this implicature is apparent in certain contexts
involving *through*. Via pragmatic strengthening, this implicature has become

conventionalized as a distinct sense, the Means Sense, licensing examples which do not involve bounded LMs. Consider some illustrative examples:

(7.86)   a. The conference was funded through the miscellaneous budget
          b. I get my coffee through an on-line retailer

In these sentences a particular outcome (i.e., conference funding, and obtaining coffee) is facilitated by a particular LM (the miscellaneous budget, and an online retailer). These LMs provide the means whereby the outcome is achieved. Notice that this sense is distinct from the Transmission Sense. For instance, in (7.86b) although the outcome involves coffee being obtained, there is not, unlike the Transmission Sense, a third party, linguistically covert, which supplies the coffee via the on-line retailer. Rather, the on-line retailer is both the supplier and the means of supply. Unless we assume a conventional Means Sense, we would have no way of predicting that *through* can give rise to a Means meaning. In other words, we would not be able to construe the abstract entity, *an on-line retailer*, which only exists in cyberspace, as constituting the means of obtaining coffee.

The Cause Sense   The final sense that we will deal with is the Cause Sense. In this sense *through* mediates a relation between a situation or state, the TR, and a particular process, the LM, which motivates the TR. Consider the following example:

(7.87)   The accused murderer's wife was able to remain loyal through her conviction of his innocence

In this sentence a particular activity, 'remaining loyal', is caused, that is, motivated, by an on-going conviction, manifesting itself in tangible demonstrations, such as, for instance, visiting him in jail. That this sentence evidences a sense distinct from the Means Sense can be tested in the following way. While *through* can be paraphrased by *via* in a Means reading, *through* can be paraphrased by *because of* with a Cause meaning. Consider the following examples:

(7.88)   a. She remained loyal to him because of her conviction of his innocence
          b. ??She remained loyal to him via (her) conviction of his innocence

Similarly, the examples in (7.86) can be paraphrased by *via* but not by *because of*:

(7.89)   a. I get my coffee via an on-line retailer
          b. ??I get my coffee because of an on-line retailer

The fact that (7.88a) is acceptable with *because of*, but not *via*, while (7.89a) is acceptable with *via* but not *because of* is suggestive that the former designates a Cause reading and the latter a Means reading.

Finally, it is worth pointing out a constraint on the Cause Sense of *through* first noticed by Hilferty (1999). Certain LMs cannot be employed using *through*. For instance, Hilferty notes that native speakers of English tend to find sentences of the following kind unacceptable:

(7.90)   *The fish died through pollution (Hilferty, 1999: 359)

This contrasts with sentences of the following type which are acceptable with *through*:

(7.91)   a. The milk went sour through a lack of proper refrigeration
          b. Computer technology has evolved through constant research (ibid.)

This follows, he suggests, because pollution denotes the by-product of a particular contaminating activity, not the activity which directly affected the environment. So states such as holding a conviction in (7.87) or the LMs in (7.91), a lack of proper refrigeration, and constant research respectively, do designate the direct state or process motivating the resulting situation.

Conclusion

In this chapter we have examined in some detail a range of spatial particles associated with bounded LMs. We defined a bounded LM as a LM which possesses an interior and thereby a boundary and an exterior. Canonical bounded LMs are three-dimensional, but two-dimensional planar LMs can be conceptualized as bounded, if they are construed as possessing an interior, with respect to a boundary and an exterior. We have argued that due to the nature of bounded LMs, the way in which humans interact with such landmarks on a daily basis, and the complex ways these interactions are conceptualized, other senses, including non-spatial meaning components such as completion, have arisen. This analysis lends further support to the view that meaning is derived from the nature of embodied experience.

An important observation to have emerged during the course of this chapter is that it may be over-simplistic to assume, as some metaphor theorists have done, that 'abstract' concepts such as vision, love, etc., are conceptualized as bounded LMs which are thereby construed as containing a particular TR. We have suggested that spatial particles such as *in* and *out*, etc., are associated with conventionalized senses that allow relations involving these concepts to be denoted by such lexical items. While the motivation for these distinct senses is grounded in spatio-physical experience and the way in which we interact with spatial scenes, including sets of tight correlations in experience, it does not follow that language users are conceptualizing entities such as love, for instance, as in: *John is in love*, in terms of a bounded LM, that is, a physical container.

8   Conclusion

The focus of this investigation has been to account for the wide array of meanings associated with English spatial particles. In contrast to most previous investigations of spatial particles, we have been particularly concerned with the many *non-spatial* meanings associated with these forms. The hypothesis that English spatial particles are polysemous (as opposed to homosemous or monosemous) and therefore that the many-to-one mappings between meanings and form are largely systematic is central to our analysis. In the course of this exploration, we have developed a model which we term principled polysemy.

The principled polysemy model takes a number of key assumptions about language as foundational. Many of these assumptions are more general in nature and must be recognized by any serious approach to language; others are informed by the perspective of cognitive linguistics. The approach rests fundamentally on the assumption that the primary reason humans use language is to communicate with one another and that this motivation constrains semantic extensions in non-trivial ways. Moreover, when lexical items are uttered (or written), they do not occur in isolation. Rather, they are embedded in longer segments of language, that is, naturally occurring language is always contextualized. Language itself radically underdetermines the rich interpretations regularly assigned to naturally occurring utterances (e.g., Green, 1989; Grice, 1975; Gumperz, 1982). Thus, any approach to language which attempts to account for how humans use language to communicate successfully must recognize that utterances serve as prompts for the elaboration of cognitive structure, which includes the interlocutors' knowledge of the world and their prior experiences with the world, including their prior experience with language.

Each time a lexical item is interpreted in context, its precise interpretation is affected by the context in which the lexical item occurs. (This context includes the inevitable inferences involved in establishing an overall interpretation for the utterance.) Meaning, of a sentence or an individual lexical item, thus arises from how the linguistic unit is used by speakers in the course of communication. When spatial particles are used in the description of recurring situations, the inferences which arise in connection with their contextualized use are also recurrent; these regularly occurring inferences often become associated with the spatial particle through a process which, following Traugott, we label prag-matic strengthening. Thus, language is a continually evolving, organic system, and a single lexical form (a form and its semantic network) will exhibit the co-existing 'layers' of its past and the communicative contexts in which it has regularly occurred.

We have argued that the representation of meaning is fundamentally concep-tual in nature. Rather than referring directly to the 'real world', language refers to what is represented in the human conceptual system. Conceptual structure is a product of how we, as human beings, experience and interact with the spatio-physical world we inhabit, in other words, the way in which spatio-physical entities and configurations are meaningful to us. The spatio-physical world 'out there' provides much of the raw sense-perceptual substrate for the concep-tual system. However, how and what we experience is crucially mediated by the precise nature of our bodies, our unique neuro-anatomical architecture and our purposeful actions in the world.

These assumptions are elaborated in: (1) our representations of the proto-scene, or primary sense, for each spatial particle; (2) our adoption of Langacker's notion that variation in ways of seeing a scene ultimately involves a variety of construals; (3) our adoption of Grady's refinements of the notion of experiential correlation; and (4) the inferencing strategies we posit. (We have found the strategies of best fit, topological extension and knowledge of force dynamics most useful.)

The nature of the proto-scene which we posit is distinct from previous anal-yses (e.g., Brugman and Lakoff, 1988; Herskovits, 1986; Kreitzer, 1997; and Vandeloise, 1991) in that it involves both a highly abstract representation of a conceptual spatial configuration between a TR and a LM (whose metric properties are not represented) and a functional element which is a natural con-sequence of that spatial configuration and human interaction with the world. The functional element reflects the interactive relationship between the TR and LM, and acknowledges the meaningful consequences to us, as human be-ings, of entities occurring in particular spatial relationships. We have argued that the extended, non-spatial meanings for each spatial particle derive from both the conceptual spatial configurations and the functional elements, as these particles occur in context. For instance, we have hypothesized that the proto-scene prompted for by the particle *in* involves a spatial configuration between a bounded LM and a TR located in the interior region. This conceptual spatial configuration interacts in important ways with the vantage point from which the scene is viewed (whether the vantage point is off-stage or on-stage, and if it is on-stage, the specific vantage point taken). Different non-spatial senses arise in *in*'s semantic network depending on whether the vantage point is interior to the LM (as in: *Hiking boots are **in** this season*) or exterior to the LM (as in: *The stars have gone **in** for the evening*). We have further argued that the functional element arising from the spatial configuration involving a TR located in the interior region of a bounded LM is containment. One of the consequences of containment is that the container locates the TR. Owing to this tight correlation in experience, a Location Sense has come to be associated with *in*, as evidenced by examples such as: *It is raining in some parts*, where the LM, *some parts*, is neutral with respect to the notion of boundedness.

The notion of experiential correlation (Grady, 1997a, 1999a; Lakoff and Johnson, 1980), which emphasizes that two dissimilar events or conditions are recurrently observed in the world and become strongly associated in memory, has proved an invaluable mechanism for explaining the derivation of many non-spatial meaning extensions. For instance, we argued in chapter 4 that the non-spatial Completion Sense associated with *over*, as in: *The film is over*, results from the tight correlation between certain locations and the end point in a process. As being *over* (in the sense of on the other side of) correlates with a particular trajectory being finished or complete, a distinct Completion Sense has been derived.

A two-fold methodological challenge exists for any model of polysemy. The methodology should provide an articulated system for: (1) determining which among the many senses should be taken as primary (in our particular case, which should be identified as the proto-scene), and (2) distinguishing between senses which are instantiated in memory and those which are constructed on-line for the purposes of local interpretation of a lexical item as it occurs in context. A key contribution that the present work makes is the articulation of such a methodology.

In proposing this methodology, we emphasize that we are not suggesting a set of criterial features that can be uniformly applied to all spatial particles. For instance, we have found that in determining the proto-scene, the earliest attested use was often a valuable criterion. However, in certain cases, such as *before*, earliest attested use was not a useful criterion because the earliest records in Sanskrit and Old English reveal both a sequential and a locative sense.

In articulating a methodology in conjunction with a set of inferencing strategies and principles of construal, our goal has been to develop a replicable, motivated account of spatial particles and their extended uses. In developing a motivated account, we acknowledge that the contexts and communicative motivations behind some usages may no longer be accessible to native speakers of the language.

Motivated systematicity

Applying this methodology and framework has resulted in the confirmation of motivated systematicity in the extended, non-spatial senses associated with spatial particles. We have found a good deal of evidence for the position that, for the most part, senses that derived from a proto-scene are extended in constrained, systematic ways. Some of the specific revelations follow.

Contrast sets, such as *in* and *out*, have traditionally been represented as opposites or antonyms. However, careful examination of the many non-spatial senses prompted by these particles clearly shows that they do not sit in simple opposition. The present analysis demonstrates that members of contrast sets develop meanings unique to the particular spatial configuration coded by the individual particle, the functional element that arises from the configuration, and human interactions with entities in that configuration. For example, *over* and *under* have often been represented as antonyms; however, *over* has developed a wide range of meanings that are not mirrored by *under*. We have argued that this is so because in many cases the LM referenced is the earth's surface and humans' interactions with entities that are higher than the earth's surface are far more extensive than their interactions with entities that are below the earth's surface.

One semantic pattern that led traditional analysts to conclude that the semantics of spatial particles is largely arbitrary is that many particles that appear to be near antonyms in terms of their TR–LM configurations have near synonymous uses.[1] For instance, in terms of spatial configuration, *over* and *under* are near antonyms, but both have developed a Control Sense. We have argued that these extensions are often motivated on the basis of the two particles having similar functional elements, in this case, the TR and LM being within each other's spheres of influence. A second example is the Visibility Sense associated with both *in* and *out*, as in: *Finally, our destination is **in** sight* and *When the full moon is **out**, the night sky is full of light.* In these examples, we argue that the senses arise from somewhat different paths – *in sight* arises from the functional element of containment in conjunction with an interior vantage point (if the construer is contained in the same area as other entities, those entities are often visible to the construer), while *out* arises from the functional element of non-containment and an external vantage point (if the construer is located exterior to a container and the TR is also located exterior to the container, the TR is often visible to the construer).

Another seemingly arbitrary pattern is that individual particles have senses that are near antonyms. For instance, in a sentence such as: *Lou put the appetizers **out** for the guests, out* has an interpretation of the TR, *the appetizers*, being available. However, in the context: *Do we have any more appetizers? No, we're all **out**,* the particle prompts for the interpretation that the TR is not available. Similarly, *out* has a Not Visible sense as in: *The light is **out**,* as well

---

[1] It is important to acknowledge that scholars working within a cognitive linguistic framework (e.g., Lindner, 1981; Lindstromberg, 1998; Vandeloise, 1991) have recognized this phenomenon.

as the Visibility Sense just discussed. We have argued that, far from being arbitrary, these non-spatial meanings are motivated and systematic given a complex proto-scene and basic patterns of construal, such as varying ways of viewing a scene.

Yet another pattern involves particles whose spatial configurations are distinct but which exhibit similar meanings. We hypothesized that this phenomenon occurs by virtue of the particles appearing in similar spatial scenes. For instance, *over, through* and *up* all have Completion Senses, even though the spatial configurations prompted for by each are quite distinct. These Completion Senses are demonstrated in the following: *The game is over, Liz is through with the book, Your time is up.* We have argued that for each of these particles, the Completion Sense arises from a spatial scene that involves a TR completing an action or activity, or a specific segment of an action or activity. In the case of *over*, we argued that an inevitable consequence (which is inferred, rather than coded) of many TRs being in a vertically elevated position is that the TR must eventually return to earth. So, in the sentence: *The cat jumped over the wall* the inevitable inference is that the cat came back down to earth. In a sentence such as: *Joan filled up the watering can,* the activity of putting water in the can is completed when the level of water rises (i.e., is in an up position) to the capacity of the container. Finally, in a sentence such as: *The train has just passed through the Chunnel,* the TR is understood to have completed the action of moving from one side of the English Channel to the other and, hence, completed that segment of its movement. Thus, all three particles occur in contexts which prompt for a spatial scene in which an activity or segment of an activity has been completed. Through pragmatic strengthening, the concept of completion has been added to the semantic network of each particle. This is an elegant demonstration of the importance of a spatial scene as a conceptual unit and its role in systematic meaning extension.

Our analysis has also uncovered the phenomenon that particles which share certain configurational properties develop similar, extended meanings. *To, for* and *after* all involve oriented TRs which are directed towards the LM. They have all developed goal senses.

Finally, we have provided evidence which suggests that orientation, path and motion are distinct concepts. This has allowed us to distinguish spatial particles which code for orientation but not path (e.g., *The clock tower faces to the east*), and spatial particles which do code for path (e.g., *The tunnel through Vale Mountain was completed in the 1980s*). We have also argued that spatial particles do not code for motion; rather, information concerning motion arises primarily from the verb (and in some instances from general background knowledge). In previous accounts, these three concepts have often been conflated, which has led to confusion in analyses.

Potential applications for second language learning and teaching

Learners and teachers of English as a second language have long recognized spatial particles as one of the most difficult aspects of the language to master. We believe that part of the difficulty non-native speakers have experienced with English spatial particles stems from the lack of descriptive adequacy of the models which have formed the basis for the presentations in EFL/ESL texts and grammars. There has been a tendency to adopt a partial homonymy position, primarily listing various meanings associated with a preposition, while offering sketchy explanations concerning the relationship between the spatial meaning and the non-spatial extensions. Exceptions to this trend include Celce-Murcia and Larsen-Freeman (1999), who rely on Dirven's (1993) cognitive analysis, and Lindstromberg (1998), who adopts a general cognitive approach with particular reliance on metaphor theory. While we feel Lindstromberg's work offers an exceptionally insightful presentation of prepositions, it suffers from the weaknesses of the previous analyses of conceptual metaphor theory and polysemy networks critiqued throughout this book. For instance, many of the explanations of non-spatial senses remain quite vague and are simply asserted to be metaphoric. We are hopeful that the principled polysemy approach, with its proto-scenes, which include a functional element, and its adoption of experiential correlation and perceptual resemblance, will provide a more clearly articulated framework on which to build a systematic, accessible account of English spatial particles for EFL/ESL teachers and learners. As applied linguists who have long been involved in issues of second language learning, our experience tells us this would be the case. However, classroom applications of the approach need to be carefully tested before we can say with confidence that adopting the principled polysemy model provides a substantially improved approach to L2 learning of spatial particles.

A second potential source of difficulty in L2 acquisition of English spatial particles involves cross-linguistic differences in how spatial relations and the functional relations which arise from these configurations are coded. Cross-linguistic variation includes differences in the type of grammatical form that conveys the spatial-relational information; for example, Korean and Japanese use a combination of special nouns and verbs, while many other languages use case marking (e.g., Finnish, Lithuanian). In addition to variation in form, languages vary in how they segment spatial scenes. Choi and Bowerman's (1992) work has shown that Korean makes distinctions in the scenes involving three-dimensional LMs and TRs located in the interior region based on degree of contact between the LM and TR, a distinction which is ignored in English. Similarly, Dutch particles which code for a support relation distinguish between the LM being vertical versus the LM being horizontal. We would expect these differences to potentially affect the patterns of extension to non-spatial senses.

We hypothesize that a functional element is a universal part of all linguistic subsystems which code spatial configurations, but this hypothesis is completely unexplored. The only other language whose spatial relational markers have been analysed from such a perspective is French, in the work of Vandeloise (1991) which has so strongly influenced our thinking. From Vandeloise's work, we can see that French spatial particles, although quite similar to English, also vary in a number of subtle ways; such variation could contribute to difficulties in second language acquisition. Since we have hypothesized that, in many cases, extended, non-spatial meanings crucially reference the functional element, we would expect the extended, non-spatial meanings of spatial particles from different languages whose functional elements vary from those of English to develop a somewhat different set of extended senses. Again these differences could result in L2 learners experiencing difficulty in sorting out the meanings of the particles in the target language.

It is our belief that the principled polysemy model, with its articulated methodology, offers an appropriately flexible, yet specified framework from which to investigate the spatial-relational systems of languages with substantially different typology. The creation of comparable analyses across a number of unrelated languages would be of great value to language teachers and language learners.

Limitations

In spite of the relatively thorough treatment of a relatively narrow topic offered by the present work, there is a good deal of descriptive work on English spatial particles within the model we have outlined which remains to be done. One of the most intriguing areas that we have left largely unaddressed involves the temporal senses of spatial particles. We did offer an explanation of a temporal use of *over*, as in: *Over the years, Washington has grown into a large metropolitan area.* We argued that this particular temporal sense derived from the A-B-C trajectory and the ubiquitous experience of movement from one location to another inevitably involving the passage of time. However, many spatial particles have temporal senses associated with them, and not all are derived via this particular process.

Another largely untouched area is the examination of the more highly grammaticalized uses of particles, such as *to* when it functions as an infinitival marker or the many grammatical senses associated with *of*. Wierzbicka (1988) has argued that the uses of *to* and *for* in complementation are ultimately motivated by their spatial origins. This analysis suggests therefore that even in their highly grammaticalized uses, these particles retain vestiges of their spatio-configurational basis (see Langacker, 1992). We believe that analyses of spatial particles as grammatical markers could be deepened and extended through application of the methods and insights provided by the principled polysemy approach.

The data sources for our current investigation included numerous dictionaries, grammars and histories of English, as well as our native speaker intuitions. In our example sentences, we strove for naturalistic sentences. Nevertheless, we acknowledge that a significant limitation on our analysis is its reliance on sentence-level, often self-generated data. The analyses upon which this book is based included a full development of the polysemy network for fifteen spatial particles, along the lines of the analysis presented for *over*. Space and rhetorical reasons kept us from presenting a complete analysis for the remaining fourteen particles. However, without discourse-level data from a broad-based corpus, we cannot say with confidence that we have accounted for all the senses of the English spatial particles we have investigated. We believe that such an analysis would largely confirm our model, but it would not be surprising if a corpus-based investigation also revealed additional uses and even seemingly anomalous uses which would challenge our model in various ways. Coriston-Oliver (2001), using a corpus-based analysis, discovered that the spatial use of *by* accounted for only 10 percent of its uses. This led her to hypothesize that, in the synchronic grammar, the spatial-physical sense may not be the most appropriate primary sense. The patterns she discovered and her conclusion raise important questions concerning the fit between the criteria we have developed to determine the proto-scene and distribution of uses of particular particles. Such hypotheses are not likely to arise and, hence, be examined, in the absence of a corpus-based investigation. Thus, an important next step, necessary to test and refine the model, is the use of corpus data and an examination of how these particles are used in discourse. Such an investigation would also shed light on the issue of how the spatial particles behave in constructions, particularly phrasal verbs, but also recurring collocations and larger syntactic constructions.

Experimental investigations, along the lines of those of Sandra and Rice (1995) and Garrod *et al.* (1999), offer another valuable approach to appraising the validity of the proto-scenes and polysemy networks posited here. The work of these psycholinguists has begun to establish replicable methodology for comparing the claims of competing models of spatial particles. Moreover, the model developed in the present volume is sufficiently precise to be tested experimentally. Tyler *et al.* (2001) report on the preliminary results of an experiment designed to compare the appropriateness of Lakoff's (1987) fine-grained, metric representations of the LM in various uses of *over* and the proto-scene posited here with native speakers' categorizations of the use of *over*. Subjects were asked to categorize sentences such as the following on the basis of how *over* was used in the sentence: *The plane flew over the mountain peak* versus *The helicopter flew over the desert*. Lakoff's model would predict that subjects would distinguish between the two sentences based on the differences in verticality of the LM. In contrast, the principled polysemy approach, which posits that both these sentences represent examples of the proto-scene, predicts that subjects would not distinguish between the two sentences. Tyler *et al.* (2001) found that the groupings of sentences created by their subjects closely matched the predictions of the principled polysemy approach and offered little support for the fine-grained analysis posited by Lakoff (1987). Certainly, one experiment is not sufficient to prove the superiority of a particular model in terms of how well it matches native speakers' mental representations. A cluster of experiments which offer convergent evidence, some of which involve on-line processing, is needed. The more significant point is that the principled polysemy approach provides a sufficiently developed framework to make specific, testable predictions.

In sum, we believe that the principled polysemy model represents a serious advance in the study of meaning, the way meanings are systematically extended and the nature of semantic polysemy networks. It is our hope that the framework will provide a springboard for a range of studies from corpus- and discourse-based investigations, to language acquisition studies, to psycholinguistic experiments. The findings from these endeavours will no doubt reveal gaps in our thinking which will, in turn, lead to the creation of even more insightful analyses. We look forward to these discoveries.

References

Baillargeon, R. 1993. The object concept revisited: new directions in the investigation of infants' physical knowledge. In *Visual Perception and Cognition in Infancy*, ed. by C. Granrud, 265–315. Hillsdale, NJ: Lawrence Erlbaum.

——— 1995. *A Model of Physical Reasoning in Infancy*. Advances in Infancy Research, volume IX, ed. by C. Rovee-Collier and L. Lipsitt, 305–71. Norwood, NJ: Ablex.

Baillargeon, R., A. Needham, and J. DeVos. 1991. Location memory in 8-month-old infants in a non-search AB task: further evidence. *Cognitive Development*, 4: 345–67.

Barnhart, Robert. 1988. *Barnhart Concise Dictionary of Etymology: The Origins of American English Words*. New York: HarperCollins.

Bertenthal, B. 1993. Infants' perception of biomechanical motions: intrinsic image and knowledge-based constraints. In *Visual Perception and Cognition in Infancy*, ed. by C. Granrud, 175–214. Hillsdale, NJ: Lawrence Erlbaum.

Bietel, Dinara, Raymond Gibbs, and Paul Sanders. 1997. The embodied approach to the polysemy of the spatial preposition *on*. In *Polysemy in Cognitive Linguistics: Selected Papers from the Fifth International Cognitive Linguistics Conference*, ed. by H. Cuyckens and B. Zawada, 241–60. Amsterdam: John Benjamins.

Bloomfield, Leonard. 1933. *Language*. New York: Holt, Rinehart and Winston.

Bolinger, Dwight. 1971. *The Phrasal Verb in English*. Cambridge, MA: Harvard University Press.

Bowerman, Melissa. 1996. Learning how to structure space for language: a crosslinguistic perspective. In *Language and Space*, ed. by P. Bloom, M. Peterson, L. Nadel, and M. Garrett, 385–436. Cambridge, MA: MIT Press.

Bransford, J., and M. K. Johnson. 1973. Consideration of some problems in comprehension. In *Visual Information Processing*, ed. by W. G. Chase, 39–61. New York: Academic Press.

Brisard, Frank. 1997. The English tense-system as an epistemic category: the case of futurity. In *Lexical and Syntactical Constructions and the Construction of Meaning*, ed. by M. Verspoor, K. D. Lee, and E. Sweetser, 271–86. Amsterdam: John Benjamins.

Brugman, Claudia. 1981. The story of *over*. MA thesis, Dept. of Linguistics, UC Berkeley. Published, 1988, as *The Story of Over: Polysemy, Semantics and the Structure of the Lexicon*. New York: Garland Press.

Brugman, Claudia, and George Lakoff. 1988. Cognitive topology and lexical networks. In *Lexical Ambiguity Resolution*, ed. by S. Small, G. Cottrell and M. Tannenhaus, 477–507. San Mateo, CA: Morgan Kaufman.

Bybee, Joan, Revere Perkins, and William Pagliuca. 1994. *The Evolution of Grammar: Tense, Aspect and Modality in the Languages of the World*. Chicago: University of Chicago Press.

Celce-Murcia, Marianne, and Diane Larsen-Freeman. 1999. *The Grammar Book: An ESL/EFL Teacher's Course*. Rowley, MA: Heinle and Heinle.

Choi, Sylvia, and Melissa Bowerman. 1992. Learning to express motion events in English and Korean: the influence of language-specific lexicalization patterns. *Cognition*, 41: 83–121.

Chomsky, Noam. 1957. *Syntactic Structures*. The Hague: Mouton.

1995. *The Minimalist Program*. Cambridge, MA: MIT Press.

Clark, Eve. 1973. Nonlinguistic strategies in the acquisition of word meanings. *Cognition*, 2: 161–82.

Clark, Herbert, H. 1973. Space, time, semantics and the child. In *Cognitive Development and the Acquisition of Language*, ed. by T. E. Moore, 27–64. New York: Academic Press.

Coriston-Oliver, Monica. 2001. Central meanings of polysemous prepositions: challenging the assumptions. Paper given at International Cognitive Linguistics Conference, Santa Barbara, CA.

Croft, William. 1998. Linguistic evidence and mental representations. *Cognitive Linguistics*, 9 (2): 151–74.

Cruse, Alan. 1986. *Lexical Semantics*. Cambridge: Cambridge University Press.

Cuyckens, Hubert, Dominiek Sandra, and Sally Rice. 1997. Towards an empirical lexical semantics. In *Human Contact Through Language and Linguistics*, ed. by B. Smieja and M. Tasch, 35–54. Berlin: Peter Lang.

Deane, Paul. 1992. *Grammar in Mind and Brain: Explorations in Cognitive Syntax*. Berlin: Mouton de Gruyter.

Dennett, Daniel. 1991. *Consciousness Explained*. Boston: Little Brown.

Dewell, Robert. 1994. *Over* again: image-schema transformations in semantic analysis. *Cognitive Linguistics*, 5 (4): 351–80.

Dirven, René. 1993. Dividing up physical and mental space into conceptual categories by means of English prepositions. In *The Semantics of Prepositions: From Mental Processing to Natural Language*, ed. by C. Zelinsky-Wibbelt, 73–97. Berlin: Mouton de Gruyter.

Eimas, P., and P. Quinn. 1994. Studies on the formation of perceptually based basic-level categories in young infants. *Child Development*, 65: 903–17.

Evans, Vyvyan. 2000. The structure of time: language, meaning and temporal cognition. PhD thesis, Dept. of Linguistics, Georgetown University.

Fauconnier, Gilles. 1994. *Mental Spaces*. Cambridge: Cambridge University Press.

1997. *Mappings in Thought and Language*. Cambridge: Cambridge University Press.

Fauconnier, Gilles, and Mark Turner. 1998. Conceptual integration networks. *Cognitive Science*, 22 (2): 133–87.

2002. *The Way We Think: Conceptual Blending and the Mind's Hidden Complexities*. New York: Basic Books.

Fillmore, Charles. 1971. Towards a theory of deixis. The PCCLLU Papers, 3 (4): 219–41. Dept. of Linguistics, University of Hawaii.

Fillmore, Charles, Paul Kay, and Mary Catherine O'Connor. 1988. Regularity and idiomaticity in grammatical constructions: the case of *let alone*. *Language*, 64 (3): 501–38.

Fleischman, Suzanne. 1999. Discourse markers across languages: implications of a case study for historico-comparative and sociolinguistics. Paper presented at Dept. of Linguistics, Georgetown University, November 1999.

Frank, Marcella. 1972. *Modern English: A Practical Reference Guide*. Englewood Cliffs, NJ: Prentice Hall.

Freeman, N., S. Lloyd, and C. Sinha. 1980. Infant search tasks reveal early concepts of containment and canonical usage of objects. *Cognition*, 8: 243–62.

Frisson, S., Dominiek Sandra, Frank Brisard, and Hubert Cuyckens. 1996. From one meaning to the next: the effects of polysemous relationships in lexical learning. In *The Construal of Space in Language and Thought*, ed. by M. Putz and René Dirven, 613–47. Berlin: Mouton de Gruyter.

Garrod, Simon, Gillian Ferrier, and Siobhan Campbell. 1999. In and on: investigating the functional geometry of spatial prepositions. *Cognition*, 72: 167–89.

Gibbs, Raymond, and Teenie Matlock. 1997. Psycholinguistic perspectives on polysemy. In *Polysemy in Cognitive Linguistics: Selected Papers from the Fifth International Cognitive Linguistics Conference*, ed. by H. Cuyckens and B. Zawada, 213–39. Amsterdam: John Benjamins.

Gleitman, Leila. 2000. Remarks on language acquisition in the first 2 years. Paper given at the University of Maryland Child Language Acquisition Symposium, College Park, MD, March 2000.

Goldberg, Adele. 1995. *Constructions: A Construction Grammar Approach to Argument Structure*. Chicago: University of Chicago Press.

Grady, Joseph. 1997a. Foundations of meaning: primary metaphors and primary scenes. PhD dissertation, Dept. of Linguistics, UC Berkeley.

1997b. THEORIES ARE BUILDING revisited. *Cognitive Linguistics*, 4 (4): 267–90.

1999a. A typology of motivation for conceptual metaphor: correlation versus resemblance. In *Metaphor in Cognitive Linguistics*, ed. by R. Gibbs and G. Steen, 79–100. Philadelphia: John Benjamins.

1999b. Cross-linguistic regularities. Paper presented at the Annual Meeting of the LSA, January 1999, Los Angeles.

In preparation. Foundations of meaning (ms.). Cultural Logic, Washington, DC.

Green, Georgia. 1989. *Pragmatics and Natural Language Understanding*. Hillsdale, NJ: Lawrence Erlbaum.

Grice, Paul. 1975. Logic and conversation. In *Syntax and Semantics*, vol. III, *Speech Acts*, ed. by P. Cole and J. Morgan, 41–58. New York: Academic Press.

1978. Further notes on logic and conversation. In *Syntax and Semantics*, vol. IX, *Pragmatics*, ed. by P. Cole, 113–28. New York: Academic Press.

Gumperz, John. 1982. *Discourse Strategies*. Cambridge: Cambridge University Press.

Haiman, John. 1980. Dictionaries and encyclopedias. *Lingua*, 50: 326–57.

Harley, Trevor. 1995. *The Psychology of Language*. Hove: Psychology Press

Hawkins, Bruce. 1988. The category MEDIUM. In *Topics in Cognitive Grammar*, ed. by B. Rudzka-Ostyn, 231–70. Amsterdam: John Benjamins.

Heine, Bernd. 1997. *Cognitive Foundations of Grammar*. Oxford: Oxford University Press.

Heine, Bernd, Ulrike Claudi, and Friederike Hünnemeyer. 1991. *Grammaticalization: A Conceptual Framework*. Chicago: University of Chicago Press.

Herskovits, Annette. 1986. *Language and Spatial Cognition: An Interdisciplinary Study of the Prepositions in English*. Cambridge: Cambridge University Press.

1988. Spatial expressions and the plasticity of meaning. In *Topics in Cognitive Grammar*, ed. by B. Rudzka-Ostyn, 271–98. Amsterdam: John Benjamins.

Hilferty, Joseph. 1999. *Through* as a means to metaphor. In *Issues in Cognitive Linguistics*, ed. by L. de Stadler and C. Eyrich, 347–66. Berlin: Mouton de Gruyter.

Hill, Clifford Alden. 1978. Linguistic representation of spatial and temporal orientation. In *Proceedings of the Fourth Annual Meeting of the Berkeley Linguistics Society*, 524–38. Berkeley: UC Berkeley Press.

Hopper, Paul, and Elizabeth Closs Traugott. 1993. *Grammaticalization*. Cambridge: Cambridge University Press.

Hottenroth, Priska-Monika. 1993. Prepositions and object concepts: a contribution to cognitive semantics. In *The Semantics of Prepositions*, ed. by C. Zelinsky-Wibbelt, 179–219. Berlin: Mouton de Gruyter.

Jackendoff, Ray. 1983. *Semantics and Cognition*. Cambridge, MA: MIT Press.

1987. *Consciousness and the Computational Mind*. Cambridge, MA: MIT Press.

1990. *Semantic Structures*. Cambridge, MA: MIT Press.

1992. *Languages of the Mind*. Cambridge, MA: MIT Press.

1997. *The Architecture of the Language Faculty*. Cambridge, MA: MIT Press.

Johnson, Mark. 1987. *The Body in the Mind*. Chicago: University of Chicago Press.

Johnson, Christopher. 1999. Metaphor vs. conflation in the acquisition of polysemy: the case of *see*. In *Cultural, Typological and Psychological Perspectives in Cognitive Linguistics*, ed. by M. Hiraga, C. Sinha and S. Wilcox, 155–69. Amsterdam: John Benjamins.

Jones, S., and L. Smith. 1993. The place of perception in children's concepts. *Cognitive Development*, 8: 113–39.

Kay, Paul, and Charles Fillmore. 1999. Grammatical constructions and linguistic generalizations: the what's X doing Y? construction. *Language*, 75 (1): 1–33.

Kreitzer, Anatol. 1997. Multiple levels of schematization: a study in the conceptualization of space. *Cognitive Linguistics*, 8 (4): 291–325.

Lakoff, George. 1987. *Women, Fire and Dangerous Things: What Categories Reveal about the Mind*. Chicago: University of Chicago Press.

1993. *The Contemporary Theory of Metaphor. Metaphor and Thought* (second edition), ed. by A. Ortony. Cambridge: Cambridge University Press.

Lakoff, George, and Mark Johnson. 1980. *Metaphors We Live By*. Chicago: University of Chicago Press.

1999. *Philosophy in the Flesh: The Embodied Mind and its Challenge to Western Thought*. New York: Basic Books.

Lakoff, George, and Mark Turner. 1989. *More than Cool Reason: A Field Guide to Poetic Metaphor*. Chicago: University of Chicago Press.

Langacker, Ronald. 1987. *Foundations of Cognitive Grammar*, vol. I. Stanford, CA: Stanford University Press.

1991a. *Concept, Image and Symbol*. Berlin: Mouton de Gruyter.

1991b. *Foundations of Cognitive Grammar*, vol. II. Stanford, CA: Stanford University Press.

1992. Prepositions as grammaticalizing elements. *Leuvense Bijdragen*, 81: 287–309.

1999a. *Grammar and Conceptualization*. Berlin: Mouton de Gruyter.

1999b. Assessing the cognitive linguistic enterprise. In *Cognitive Linguistics: Foundations, Scope and Methodology*, ed. by Theo Janssen and Gisela Redeker, 13–59. Berlin: Mouton de Gruyter.

Lanman, Charles Rockwell. 1884. *A Sanskrit Reader*. Cambridge, MA: Harvard University Press.

Legerstee, M. 1992. A review of the animate–inanimate distinction in infancy: implications for models of social and cognitive knowing. *Early Development and Parenting*, 1: 59–67.

Leslie, A. 1984. Infant perception of a manual pick-up event. *British Journal of Developmental Psychology*, 2: 19–32.

Levin, Beth. 1993. *Towards a Lexical Organization of English Verbs*. Chicago: University of Chicago Press.

Levinson, Stephen. 1983. *Pragmatics*. Cambridge: Cambridge University Press.

Lindner, Susan. 1981. A lexico-semantic analysis of English verb particle constructions with *out* and *up*. PhD thesis, Dept. of Linguistics, UC San Diego.

Lindstromberg, Seth. 1998. *English Prepositions Explained*. Amsterdam: John Benjamins.

Lloyd, S., C. Sinha, and N. Freeman. 1981. Spatial reference systems and the canonicality effect in infant search. *Journal of Experimental Child Psychology*, 32: 1–10.

Mandler, Jean. 1988. How to build a baby: on the development of an accessible representational system. *Cognitive Development*, 3: 113–36.

  1992. How to build a baby: II. Conceptual primitives. *Psychological Review*, 99: 587–604.

  1996. Preverbal representation and language. In *Language and Space*, ed. by P. Bloom, M. Peterson, L. Nadel and M. Garrett, 365–84. Cambridge, MA: MIT Press.

Miller, George, and Phillip Johnson-Laird. 1976. *Language and Perception*. Cambridge: Cambridge University Press.

Morgan, Pamela. 1997. Figuring out *figure out*: metaphor and the semantics of the English verb-particle construction. *Cognitive Linguistics*, 8 (4): 327–57.

O'Dowd, Elizabeth. 1998. *Prepositions and Particles in English: A Discourse-functional Account*. New York: Oxford University Press.

Panther, Klaus-Uwe, and Günter Radden. 1999. *Metonymy in Language and Thought*. Amsterdam: John Benjamins.

Pfleider, Jean, and Michael Preston. 1981. *A Complete Concordance to the Chester Mystery Plays*. New York: Garland.

Piaget, Jean. 1951. *Play, Dreams and Imitation in Childhood*. London: Kegan Paul, Trench and Trübner.

Pustejovsky, James. 1998. *The Generative Lexicon*. Cambridge, MA: MIT Press.

Putnam, Hilary, 1981. *Reason, Truth and History*. Cambridge: Cambridge University Press.

Quinn, P., and P. Eimas. 1997. Perceptual organization and categorization in young infants. In *Advances in Infancy Research*, vol. XI, ed. by C. Rovee-Collier and L. Lipsitt, 1–36. Norwood, NJ: Ablex.

Quinn, P., P. Eimas, and S. Rosenkrantz. 1993. Evidence for representations of perceptual similar categories by 3-month-old infants. *Perception*, 22: 463–75.

Quirk, Randolph, Sidney Greenbaum, Geoffrey Leech, and Jan Svartvik. 1972. *A Grammar of Contemporary English*. Harlow, England: Longman.

  1985. *A Comprehensive Grammar of the English Language*. Harlow, England: Longman.

Reddy, Michael. 1979. The conduit metaphor: a case of frame conflict in our language about language. In *Metaphor and Thought*, ed. by A. Ortony, 284–324. Cambridge: Cambridge University Press.

Rice, Sally. 1993. Far afield in lexical fields: the English prepositions. *ESCOL'92* (ed. by M. Bernstein), 206–17.

Rice, Sally, Dominiek Sandra, and Mia Vanrespaille. 1999. Prepositional semantics and the fragile link between space and time. In *Cultural, Psychological and Typological Issues in Cognitive Linguistics: Selected Papers of the Bi-annual ICLA Meeting in Albuquerque, July 1995*, ed. by M. Hiraga, C. Sinha and S. Wilcox, 108–27. Philadelphia: John Benjamins.

Rosch, Eleanor. 1975. Cognitive representations of semantic categories. *Journal of Experimental Psychology: General*, 104: 192–233.

    1978. Principles of categorization. In *Cognition and Categorization*, ed. by E. Rosch and B. Lloyd, 27–48. Hillsdale, NJ: Lawrence Erlbaum.

Ruhl, Charles. 1989. *On Monosemy: A Study in Linguistic Semantics*. Albany: State University of New York.

Rummelhart, David. 1975. Notes on a schema for stories. In *Representations and Understanding*, ed. by D. Bobrow and A. Collins, 211–36. New York: Academic Press.

Sandra, Dominiek. 1998. What linguists can and can't tell us about the mind: a reply to Croft. *Cognitive Linguistics*, 9 (4): 361–78.

Sandra, Dominiek, and Sally Rice. 1995. Network analyses of prepositional meaning: mirroring whose mind – the linguist's or the language user's? *Cognitive Linguistics*, 6 (1): 89–130.

Saussure, Ferdinand De. [1915] 1983. *Course in General Linguistics*. Trans. and annot. by Roy Harris. London: Duckworth.

Schiffrin, Deborah. 1992. Anaphoric then: aspectual, textual and epistemic meaning. *Linguistics*, 30: 753–92.

Sinha, Chris, and Kristine Jensen De López. 2000. Language, culture and the embodiment of spatial cognition. *Cognitive Linguistics*, 11 (1/2): 17–42.

Slobin, Dan. 1991. Learning to think for speaking. *Pragmatics* 1, 7–25.

Spelke, E. 1988. Where perceiving ends and thinking begins: the apprehension of objects in infancy. In *Perceptual Development in Infancy*, ed. by A. Yonas, 197–234. Hillsdale, NJ: Lawrence Erlbaum.

Sperber, Dan, and Deirdre Wilson. 1986. *Relevance: Communication and Cognition*. Oxford: Blackwell.

Svorou, Soteria. 1994. *The Grammar of Space*. Amsterdam: John Benjamins.

Sweetser, Eve. 1990. *From Etymology to Pragmatics: Metaphorical and Cultural Aspects of Semantic Structure*. Cambridge: Cambridge University Press.

    1997. Role and individual interpretations of change predicates. In *Language and Conceptualization*, ed. by J. Nuyts and E. Pederson, 116–36. Cambridge: Cambridge University Press.

Talmy, Leonard. 1983. How language structures space. *Spatial Orientation: Theory, Research and Application*, ed. by H. Pick and L. Acredolo, 225–82. New York: Plenum.

    1985. Lexicalization patterns: semantic structure in lexical forms. In *Language Typology and Syntactic Descriptions*, vol. III, ed. by T. Shopen, 57–149. Cambridge: Cambridge University Press.

1988a. Force dynamics in language and cognition. *Cognitive Science*, 12: 49–100.

1988b. The relation of grammar to cognition. In *Topics in Cognitive Linguistics*, ed. by B. Rudzka-Ostyn, 165–205. Amsterdam: John Benjamins.

1996. Fictive motion in language and 'ception'. In *Language and Space*, ed. by P. Bloom, M. Peterson, L. Nadel and M. Garrett, 211–76. Cambridge, MA: MIT Press.

2000. *Toward a Cognitive Semantics* (2 vols.). Cambridge, MA: MIT Press.

Taylor, John. 1989. *Linguistic Categorization*. Oxford: Oxford University Press.

Traugott, Elizabeth Closs. 1975. Spatial expressions of tense and temporal sequencing. *Semiotica*, 15 (3): 207–30.

1978. On the expression of spatio-temporal relations in language. In *Universals of Human Language*, ed. by J. Greenberg, 369–400. Stanford: Stanford University Press.

1989. On the rise of epistemic meanings in English: an example of subjectification in semantic change. *Language*, 65 (1): 31–55.

Turner, Mark. 1987. *Death is the Mother of Beauty: Mind, Metaphor, Criticism*. Chicago: University of Chicago Press.

1991. *Reading Minds*. Princeton: Princeton University Press.

1996. *The Literary Mind*. New York: Oxford University Press.

Tyler, Andrea, and Vyvyan Evans. 1999. Applying cognitive linguistics to language teaching: the prepositions of verticality. Paper presented at the Annual Association of Applied Linguistics, Stamford, Connecticut, March 1999.

2001a. The relation between experience, conceptual structure and meaning: non-temporal uses of tense and language teaching. In *Applied Cognitive Linguistics: Theory, Acquisition and Language Pedagogy*, ed. by M. Pütz, S. Niemeier and R. Dirven, 63–105. Berlin: Mouton de Gruyter.

2001b. Reconsidering prepositional polysemy networks: the case of *over*. *Language*, 77 (4): 724–65.

Tyler, Andrea, Akiko Fuji, Seon Jeon, Dainora Kupcinskas, Olga Liamkina, David Macgregor, Kristin Mulrooney, and Mari Takada. 2001. Competing models of *over*: an experimental investigation. Paper presented at Washington CogLink Symposium. Georgetown University, Washington, DC. October 2001.

Ungerer, Friedrich, and Hans Jürg Schmid. 1996. *An Introduction to Cognitive Linguistics*. London: Longman.

Vandeloise, Claude. 1990. Representation, prototypes and centrality. In *Meanings and Prototypes: Studies in Linguistic Categorization*, ed. by S. Tsohatzidis, 403–37. London: Routledge.

1991. *Spatial Prepositions: A Case Study in French*. Chicago: University of Chicago Press.

1994. Methodology and analyses of the preposition *in*. *Cognitive Linguistics*, 5 (2): 157–84.

Varela, Francisco, Evan Thompson, and Eleanor Rosch. 1991. *The Embodied Mind: Cognitive Science and Human Experience*. Cambridge, MA: MIT Press.

Wierzbicka, Anna. 1988. *The Semantics of Grammar*. Amsterdam: John Benjamins.

1990. 'Prototypes save': on the uses and abuses of the notion of 'prototype' in linguistics and related fields. In *Meanings and Prototypes: Studies in Linguistic Categorization*, ed. by S. Tsohatzidis, 347–67. London: Routledge.

1993. Why do we say in April, on Thursday, at 10 o'clock? In search of an explanation. *Studies in Language*, 17 (2): 437–54.

1996. *Semantics: Primes and Universals*. New York: Oxford University Press.

Wilson, Paul, and Richard Anderson. 1986. What they don't know will hurt them: the role of prior knowledge in comprehension. In *Reading Comprehension: From Research to Practice*, ed. by J. Orasunu, 31–48. Hillsdale, NJ: Lawrence Erlbaum.

Ziegler, Debra. 1997. Retention in ontogenetic and diachronic grammaticalization. *Cognitive Linguistics*, 8 (3): 207–41.

Index